T0350603

CRITICAL THINKING²

A FORCE MULTIPLIER

Jerry J. Marty, MD MBA

CRITICAL THINKING² — A FORCE MULTIPLIER

This publication is designed to provide accurate and authoritative information about the subject matter covered. However, it is sold with the understanding that neither the author nor the publisher renders accounting, financial, investment, legal, managerial, medical, or other professional services, consultation, or advice. While the publisher and author have used their best efforts to prepare this book, they make no representations or warranties concerning its contents' accuracy, contemporaneousness, or completeness. They expressly disclaim any implied warranties of merchantability or fitness for a particular purpose. No warranty is implied or may be created or extended by sales representatives, written sales, advertising, promotional, or marketing materials. Any perceived advice or strategies contained herein may not be suitable or apply to your general or specific situation. You should consult with a professional when and where appropriate. Neither the publisher nor the author shall be liable for any particular loss, loss of profit, any untoward effect, or any other commercial or civil damages, including but not limited to special, incidental, consequential, personal, or other damages.

Book Cover and Illustrations by Author
Edition One [2024]

Print ISBN: 979-8-35093-895-1
eBook ISBN: 979-8-35093-896-8

DEDICATION

I want to acknowledge and thank my wife,
Angelina Iacono Marty, for her wisdom, advice, and
inordinate patience in seeing this work through its finalization.

This work is also dedicated to our son, John Raphael Marty, who,
after obtaining his Master of Business Administration (MBA)
degree, has recently found a niche in Artificial Intelligence (AI).

EPIGRAPH

"Critical Thinking^2 Lies at the Interface of
Problem Analysis and Decision-Making"

"Doors are Passageways—Find the Next and Open Them"

"The Ability to Problem Solve, and Course Correct,
Makes for Forward Progress"

JERRY J. MARTY, MD, MBA

I trust there are Life lessons and Management insights, as well as
a smattering of helpful information within this Book that will assist in
Critical Thinking^2, Problem Analysis, and Decision-Making.

CONTENTS

INTRODUCTION

APHORISMS CAN TEACH MUCH ABOUT LIFE, IN GENERAL, AND Management. The header Aphorisms throughout have relevance to the individual specific Book Chapters.

The Author provides a précis of the definition, principles, and challenges related to:

Critical Thinking[2] — A Force Multiplier

In Management, one faces many challenges, especially uncertainty, lack of information, unpredictability, and ambiguity. Problems that need systematic analysis will invariably arise.

The Title and Subtitle of this book are apt descriptors of its contents. Still, its metaphoric soul is the introduction to Problem Identification, Problem Analysis, the use of reasoning and Logic, and the employment of Methodological Tools of Discernment. Confirmation and Cognitive Biases, Heuristic Thinking, Logical Fallacies, and dissemble—all represent obstacles to avoid on the way to the goal of Problem Analysis and Decision-Making. Business and Management models predominate in everyday Life. Additional illustrative examples are provided from the vantage point and perspective of the Author's unique medical background. Many medical examples, as well as examples of the Pathological Diagnoses of Cancer, are woven into the fabric of the Book.

The fundamental proposition of this Book is that Critical Thinking[2] lies at the interface of Problem Analysis and Decision-Making. Stepwise methodical Problem Analysis leads to decisive Decision-Making. The Author defines what constitutes Critical Thinking[2] and provides an overview of Critical Thinking[2]—A Force Multiplier in Management, Problem Analysis, and Decision-Making. Incisive comments about Competence versus Incompetence and the Dunning-Kruger effect ("If you don't know what you don't know," and the "Confidence Gap") are made in Chapter One, along with an in-depth discussion of intellectual curiosity, deliberation, and Decision-Making. Many of the more common Methodologies and Techniques utilized in Problem Analysis, in particular, the Delphi Technique, Strengths, Weaknesses, Opportunities, and Threats (SWOT), the Cause and Effect (Fishbone or Ishikawa) diagram, Root Cause Analysis (RCA), Weighted Decision Matrix (WDM), Cost-Benefit Analysis, Breakeven Analysis (BEA), Probability Analysis, Sensitivity Analysis, Pareto Analysis, Analytic Hierarchy Process (AHP), Statistical modeling (especially use of Linear Regression), Bayesian Analysis, Machine Learning (ML), and Artificial Intelligence (AI), are described early, in Chapter Two—Tools that get you from A to Z. An Introduction and Overview to Statistics, especially the discussion of Sample Size, Sample Bias, Statistical Significance, Linear Regression, the "Null" Hypothesis, the T-test, and F-test, and more, are discussed in Chapter Three. The distinction between "Truths" and "Facts," …ending with an explanation of the contrasting Correspondence and Performance Theories of "Truth," is delved into in Chapter Four. Throughout the remainder of the Book, Information, Data, and Facts are emphasized, as distinguished from "Truth," but also Misinformation, Disinformation, Gaslighting, and other relevant related topics. The Decision-Making process is clearly an endpoint, and numerous examples of how one reaches this endpoint are found within the Ten Book Chapters.

Leadership and what constitutes effective Management are discussed as supplementary subject matter in the Epilogue.

The Appendix section has terse Time Management and Organization advice and tips on best using the 1440 minutes you have allocated each day.

This is a Primer on Business and Management, a great introduction to furthering your career and studies, both undergraduate and postgraduate, perhaps even towards a Master of Business Administration (MBA) degree. The wisdom contained within its pages can be utilized to supplement your Life-Long Learning, optimize strategy in the Boardroom, or be a resource reference for Leaders, Business Managers, and Entrepreneurs, as well as those aspiring to reach those lofty heights.

CHAPTER 1

"NOTHING IS SO INSIGNIFICANT THAT IT DOESN'T WARRANT A LENGTHY, SPIRITED DISCUSSION"

THE CHAPTER HEADER (APHORISM) STATEMENT CONVEYS

Intellectual curiosity and exemplifies the need for deliberation. The discourse that follows can eventuate in effective Decision-Making within a problem-solving scenario.

Critical Thinking^2 is a skill that involves analyzing, evaluating, and reasoning about information, facts, and truths in a logical, rational, and objective way. It can assist in identifying and solving problems and making informed, effective decisions. Critical Thinking^2 also helps you understand and critique different sources of information, facts, and truths.

According to the Oxford Dictionaries, Critical Thinking is "the objective analysis and evaluation of an issue to form a judgment." This (generic) Critical Thinking definition includes some of the following examples:

- Comparing the Arguments of two opposing (debating) sides on a controversial topic.

- Identifying the strengths and weaknesses of a research study or an article.

- Testing a Hypothesis against relevant evidence or criteria.

- Recognizing your own Biases and assumptions when encountering new (unvetted) information.

There are steps to improve your basic Critical Thinking skills. These are cogently expressed here, a process that involves turbocharging the basic Critical Thinking process to transform it into (enhanced) ***Critical Thinking² skills:***

- *Developing a keen Intellectual curiosity and penchant for problem-solving.*

- *Asking open-ended questions that challenge your own or others' assumptions is a decidedly Socratic approach to inquiry.*

- *Possessing an interdisciplinary perspective, seeking diverse perspectives and sources of credible, verifiable information.*

- *Evaluating the veracity, relevance, and accuracy of the information you encounter with comprehensive exploration and analysis.*

- *A degree of deliberation that "sorts facts from fiction."*

- *Applying Logic, avoiding Bias, Confirmation and Cognitive Bias, Heuristics, "Group Think," and Logical Fallacies while employing deliberation and reasoning to support your Arguments or Claims or conclusions using the Toulmin method of Argumentation.*

- *Recognizing erroneous, irrelevant information, falsehoods, Misinformation, Disinformation, and Gaslighting.*

- *Possessing deep deductive and inferential analytical abilities.*

- *Reflect inwardly on your thinking processes, learn from "what is correct or accurate," and learn from your mistakes, then accept feedback, sometimes negative.*

- *Avoiding the trap of the Dunning-Kruger effect.*

STARTING THE JOURNEY...

1.1 INTELLECTUAL CURIOSITY — WHERE THE PROCESS BEGINS

- *Intellectual curiosity:* The underpinning of Critical Thinking[2] is Intellectual curiosity, extending beyond the boundaries of what is conventionally considered to be being just inquisitive and reaching beyond the four corners of a defined problem. Problem-solving pursuits are rooted in a fundamental drive to explore and understand. Investigators can exercise curiosity and uncover new insights by engaging in rigorous Socratic discussions. **The Socratic tenets embody the leverage and advantage of *inquiry over information* and *discussion over debate*.** Deliberation may disclose unexpected interconnections, reveal hidden, nuanced patterns, or challenge existing assumptions and Biases, contributing to advancing knowledge in various fields.

- *Interdisciplinary perspectives*: Many research advancements arise from converging ideas and applying novel approaches across different disciplines. Treating all topics as worthy of discussion creates opportunities for interdisciplinary exploration. If a subject appears inconsequential within a specific field, it may still hold relevance in other areas. Engaging in spirited and, at times, lengthy discussions allows for the sufficient exchange of ideas from various perspectives and disciplines, fostering eventual interdisciplinary collaboration and enriching the debate and discourse.

- *Comprehensive exploration and analysis*: In most fields, comprehensive investigation and analysis initiates the process for a thorough understanding and Critical Thinking[2]. By subjecting subjects to rigorous discussion, debate, dialectic, and deliberation, investigators can delve into the more subtle intricacies of the matter. A comprehensive evaluation of all topical aspects, obvious or not, will ensue. Complete and comprehensive exploration guards against oversight considers various viewpoints, minority and majority-held, sometimes contradictory, and promotes intellectual rigor in investigative endeavors. Inquiry can also lead to unexpected discoveries, shedding light on overlooked phenomena and relationships or refining existing theories. Pursuing knowledge should not adhere to preconceived notions of importance; instead, it must thrive on fresh ideas, curiosity, exploration, insights, and the pursuit of truth. Intellectual growth and innovation often emerge from Critical Thinking[2], including from the most unexpected sources, opening doors to yet newer avenues of exploration—"Doors are Passageways—Find the Next and Open Them"

1.2 FACTS AND WHY THEY MATTER

"Ninety *percent of what is said may be erroneous, and irrelevant or both"* … *"while five to ten percent is relevant but may nonetheless, still be erroneous"* … *Therefore, whatever small fraction is correct is accordingly relevant."*

The first part of the statement …"90% of what is said may be erroneous," …has been attributed to Theodore Levitt (1925-2006), an American economist, marketing luminary, and professor at the Harvard Business School. However, this quote's exact origin remains unclear since several variations of this idea or sentiment are attributed to various individuals throughout history. Levitt was widely recognized as one of the most influential figures in marketing and is often called the "father of modern marketing." Throughout his career, he significantly contributed to Marketing Theory and Practice, transforming how Businesses approach and understand their customers. "*Marketing Myopia*," published in 1960, was one of Levitt's most famous and influential conceptual constructs, first appearing in the *Harvard Business Review* (HBR). He argued that Businesses should focus on meeting customer needs and long-term goals over short-term growth, Return On Investment (ROI), and solely prioritizing intrinsic Business needs. The short-term goal eschewed by Levitt was selling products for short-term profit. He emphasized the importance of adopting a customer-centric approach and understanding the broader conditions that products fulfill. This concept became foundational for an evolving, modern marketing Theory.

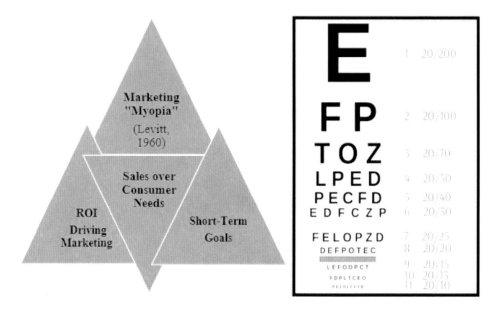

Levitt's legacy for promulgating the latter made him renowned in this area of study. The McKinsey Award for the best HBR article in 1960 was properly given to him for this last cited seminal contribution to the marketing field. Levitt would be awarded three more McKinsey awards, no small achievement. Besides this, Levitt also expounded on the concept of Business globalization and advocated for the idea of worldwide product standardization, that is, "re-engineering," before the concept became commonplace and incorporated in the workplace. He argued that companies could achieve economies of scale and reduce costs by producing uniform, standardized products for the global market. This latter novel notion (at that time) has been a subject of debate that has since shaped discussions on international Business marketing strategies.

Theodore Levitt was, indeed, an iconoclastic contemporary critic of the norm. The Critical Thinker questions "Facts," "Truths," and Information, seeking evidence and corroborative verification before acceptance. Information or declarative statements by individuals, Organizations and Enterprises, and even governments may be inaccurate or false. Intellectual skepticism and pursuing knowledge based on sound confirmatory evidence and reasoning are always *de rigueur*.

1.3 CRITICAL THINKING[2] AND "SORTING FACTS FROM FICTION"

Critical Thinking[2] is vital in assessing the accuracy and relevance of facts, truths, and information in today's information-rich environment.

Five cornerstones of Critical Thinking[2] contribute to advancing knowledge in most fields. Objectively analyzing and evaluating information, ideas, Arguments or Claims, and situations logically and systematically is necessary to be a Critical Thinker. Employing rational and analytical thinking skills to assess information's credibility, integrity, reliability, and relevance is vital to forming well-reasoned judgments to make informed decisions. Critical Thinking[2] goes well beyond simply accepting or rejecting ideas; it involves actively questioning, listening, examining, dissecting, and challenging assumptions, eliminating Biases, and excluding Logical Fallacies.

1.3.1 CRITICAL THINKING[2] — RATIONALE

1. *Observation:* Critical Thinking[2] first involves observation, then introspection, followed by self-awareness. It requires being open to examining one's own Biases, assumptions, and preconceived notions. Reflexive thinking helps to overcome personal Biases

and Heuristics. The process encourages intellectual honesty and humility, allowing for more objective and rational analysis.

2. *Analysis:* Critical Thinking^2 involves breaking down complex ideas or issues into constituent parts to understand their underlying Logic components and interrelationships. It entails examining evidence, identifying patterns, and detecting potential Biases or inconsistencies. Critical Thinking^2 requires assessing the quality, credibility, and relevance of information, Arguments, or Claims. It involves considering the source, context, and evidence supporting a particular conclusion or viewpoint and evaluating the strength of the supporting evidence's reasoning, Logic, and validity.

3. *Inference*: Critical Thinking^2 involves drawing logical, inferential conclusions based on the available information and corroborative, supporting evidence. It requires recognizing logical connections, making reasonable deductive assumptions, and considering alternative explanations or interpretations.

4. *Communication*: The role of communication in Critical Thinking^2 is vital. Effective communication helps convey ideas, analyze information, and exchange thoughts. Expressing perspectives, questioning assumptions, and engaging in constructive debates lead to informed Decision-Making. Clear and open communication fosters interpersonal collaboration, evaluating multiple, diverse, and sometimes divergent viewpoints and exploring potential solutions to complex problems, ultimately strengthening the Critical Thinking^2 analytical process.

5. *Problem-solving*: Critical Thinking^2 is inseparably linked to problem-solving skills. It involves identifying problems or challenges, analyzing viable potential solutions, and selecting the most

effective or logical course of action. Critical Thinkers are adept at evaluating different approaches and perspectives, considering the possible consequences of each choice made or not made.

1.3.2 CRITICAL THINKING[2] — IMPORTANCE IN LIFE, IN GENERAL, AND MANAGEMENT

- *Avoiding erroneous information, Misinformation, Disinformation, and falsehoods*: In an age dominated by a figurative and literal web of social media with instant information access and sharing, the information can spread rapidly (viral worldwide internet dissemination). Discernment and Critical Thinking[2] enable individuals to question and authenticate the accuracy of the information before accepting it as "accurate." One can corroborate and substantiate evidence by actively evaluating sources (presumably multiple) concurrently or (shortly) after checking facts. Individuals, Organizations and Enterprises can avoid being misled by false, inaccurate, erroneous, or misleading information.

- *Fact-Checking the "Fact-Checkers:"* Are there downstream effects related to the purported existence of just six Media companies controlling approximately 90% of the U.S. Media ecosystem (television, radio, print, digital platforms, internet, social media, and related)?

  Who controls what?—Examining the pinnacle of the food chain— "*The Big Six*"

  1. Comcast (CMCSA)—Comcast (NBCUniversal): A telecommunications Corporation that owns NBCUniversal, which includes NBC Network, MSNBC, CNBC, Universal Pictures, and numerous cable channels.

2. Disney (DIS)—The Walt Disney Company: A global entertainment company that owns major TV networks like ABC, Disney Channel, ESPN, and various studios including Marvel, Pixar, and Lucasfilm. Disney also controls Hulu and a sizable portion of the streaming service ESPN+.

3. AT&T (T)—AT&T (WarnerMedia): Through its acquisition of Time Warner, AT&T owns WarnerMedia, which includes HBO, CNN, TBS, TNT, Warner Bros. Pictures, and DC Entertainment.

4. Paramount Global (PARA)—Paramount Global, formerly known as ViacomCBS Inc. (rebranded, February 2022), is a major media agglomeration that operates in various segments of the entertainment industry, including television broadcasting, cable networks, film production, digital streaming services and networks such as CBS, Showtime, MTV, Nickelodeon, BET, Comedy Central, and The CW (through a joint venture), Paramount Pictures, Streaming Services (Paramount+, a subscription-based streaming platform), and other Ventures (in production, distribution, and licensing of content globally), extending its reach far beyond traditional media platforms.

5. SONY (SONY)—Sony Corporation, a Japanese multinational conglomerate, has a significant presence in various sectors, including Sony Pictures and Music Entertainment, consumer electronics, gaming (PlayStation), and financial services. In terms of media control, Sony's influence primarily stems from its core business, with its considerable influence on digital entertainment and interactive media.

6. FOX (FOX)—Fox Corporation: Owning the Fox Broadcasting Company, Fox News Channel, Fox Sports, and local TV stations, this company has a substantial presence in the media landscape.

"The Big Six"—Net Worth and Control: The total estimated net worth of these above entities, or a combination of those mentioned above and the largest subsidiary major Corporations (mainly including the conglomeration of Disney, AT&T, Paramount Global, SONY, and News Corporation (includes FOX, WSJ, NYP, etc.)) is valued at $430 Billion. More remarkable is that an estimated 232 Media executives control the reins!

Undoubtedly, share price, market share, audience reach, and reaction will dictate Corporate and Enterprise behavior. The latter influences the dissemination of news, entertainment content, and advertising. The market capitalization of "The Big Six" and its influence inform us of their disproportionate leverage and great economic dominance over the Media sphere. Understanding Media revenue streams, advertising, and subscriber influence, not to mention market penetration, is crucial to understanding their far-reaching effects, often beyond what is reflected by their financial statements. Does amalgamation affect the plurality and the objectivity of information disseminated to the public? It begs the questions surrounding editorial independence, agenda-setting, and management of information. What of representation of various viewpoints, prejudiced or not? Concerns about Media Bias, information manipulation, lack of diversity, and balanced perspectives influencing public opinion arise (Nalbandian, M., May 2022, and Levy, A. The Motley Fool. November 2023).

Source: The Motley Fool   **The Big 6**   More charts: genuineimpact.substack.com

- *Making informed decisions*: Whether it is with personal decisions, professional choices made, or political judgments, having accurate and relevant information is crucial. Discernment and Critical Thinking[2] allow individuals to evaluate different viewpoints and perspectives, even diametrically opposed positions, consider corroborating evidence, and weigh the merits of various available options. By using these skills, individuals can make better-informed decisions based on credible, validated, and reliable information.

- *Identifying Bias and manipulation*: Information sources often have their own intrinsic Biases and agendas, and some may intentionally manipulate facts or selectively present (or not present) information to influence opinions. Discernment and Critical Thinking[2] empower individuals to recognize Bias, spot Logical Fallacies, Group Think, and uncover the potential manipulation of Facts and tactics. This assists in maintaining a more balanced and objective viewpoint or position when evaluating information.

- *Engaging in constructive discussions*: Critical Thinking[2] skills enable individuals to engage in meaningful and respectful discussions and debates based on accurate information. By evaluating the actual relevance and credibility of information, one can contribute thoughtfully to conversations and discussions, ask informed questions, and challenge unsupported Claims or Arguments. This results in a more productive and constructive dialogue.

- *Nurturing intellectual growth*: Discernment and Critical Thinking[2] are foundational intellectual development and Lifelong learning skills. By questioning assumptions, analyzing evidence, and seeking different perspectives, individuals, Organizations and Enterprises can deepen their understanding of complex issues and develop proportionate, weighed opinions. These skills also help one adapt to new information and incentivize Intellectual curiosity.

- *Strengthening societies*: In democratic societies, the ability to discern correct and relevant information is crucial for an informed citizenry. It enables individuals to participate in public discourse, debate, evaluate policy proposals, and hold political leaders accountable. An informed electorate and citizenry contribute to the overall health of societies. A culture of open dialogue is thereby fostered. These skills are indispensable in today's information-driven, Internet-of-Things (IoT) world. Empowered individuals can navigate the vast sea of information, separate fact from fiction, and make informed decisions that shape their lives and society. By applying these Critical Thinking[2] skills, individuals become more engaged, knowledgeable, and responsible societal participants.

1.4 MAJOR TYPES OF COGNITIVE BIAS

- *Cognitive (Psychological) Bias*: A systematic cognitive process caused by the human tendency to simplify information processing through a filter of personal experience and preferences. The filter is a Psychological "coping" mechanism enabling the brain to prioritize and process vast amounts of information expeditiously and efficiently. Cognitive Bias is the broad category for Confirmation Bias (the most common type, vide infra), Hindsight Bias, Anchoring Bias (judgment influenced and adjusted by initial information, known as an "anchor"), Misinformation Bias, Actor-Observer Bias, False Consensus effect, Halo effect, Self-Serving Bias, Availability Heuristic (reliance on readily available information or recent experiences, assigning credibility especially if shared and vetted, rather than considering comprehensive analytical data), Optimism Bias (Decision-makers may overestimate their analytical abilities or expect different outcomes, leading to excessively optimistic outcome judgments), Status Quo Bias, Apophenia (perceiving patterns in random occurrences), Framing Bias, and many more...

- *Confirmation Bias*: Individuals, as well as Organizational and Enterprise decision-makers, invariably seek information that confirms their pre-existing and current beliefs (Biased or neutral), overlooking contradictory, conflicting, or erroneous evidence, which could potentially lead to a flawed decision. This is an example of the broader rubric category of Cognitive Bias. There are two main attributes to the Cognitive mechanisms at play: "Challenge Avoidance," which is finding out that one is wrong. The other is "Reinforcement Seeking," which is the desire to confirm that one is correct.

1.4.1 THE DUNNING-KRUGER EFFECT AND COMPETENCE – INCOMPETENCE

The particular instance of Cognitive Bias, where a person is unaware of how badly they grasp a subject, not understanding that they are failing at grasping the significance or meaning of a subject or problem, should be highlighted at this juncture. These individuals exhibit the *"Dunning-Kruger effect"* and demonstrate hubris in assuming they are doing as well as "average" or even "above average" in their Competence. They exhibit (over)confidence in their knowledge (or lack thereof) compared to others at higher stages of Competence. Obviously, no information can be repeated too often: "If you don't know what you don't know ..."

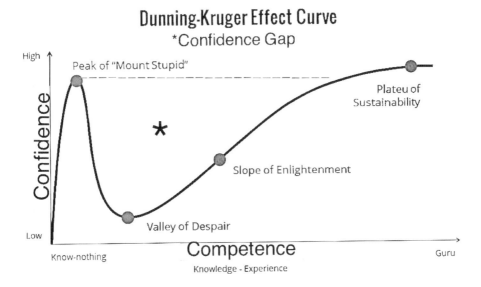

Notably, the axis of Competence-Incompetence is often neglected; competency is assuredly vital in Problem Analysis, particularly in navigating the process and its efficiency going forward from identification of the Root Cause(s) to the actual Problem Analysis using a methodological approach, evaluating the solution proposal, its implementation, and post-Decision-Making monitoring. This category of Cognitive Bias derangement is best understood when realizing there are four stages or steps between Incompetence and Competence:

Stage I: Unconscious Incompetence: You are ignorant of what you do not know.

Stage II: Conscious Incompetence: You know what you do not know but have yet to take any steps to learn more or remedy the knowledge gap.

Stage III: Conscious Competence: You are actively learning and acquiring knowledge about a subject.

Stage IV: Unconscious Competence: You have mastered a subject to the point where you may forget or take how much you truly know for granted.

1.5 PROBLEM IDENTIFICATION, CLASSIFICATION, AND PRIORITIZATION

The evaluation of the significance and impact of a problem needs discernment. Overall goals, aims, and resources need to be considered in the process.

Categorizing and prioritizing problems based on their potential impact, urgency, and alignment with Organizational and Enterprise priorities are obligatory. Even for apparently insignificant or less impactful issues, it is essential to identify their root causes. Understanding the underlying factors can help prevent similar issues from arising in the future or uncover interconnections to more extensive, even more significant problems. A formal Root Cause Analysis (RCA) is just one of many systematic approaches available that can be used to find the underlying causes or factors contributing to a problem. It involves going well beyond the superficial, surface-level evaluation of symptoms and digging much more profoundly to uncover the root causes that, once addressed, can cure and effectively prevent the problem from recurring. Discussing issues can challenge the arbitrary distinction between significant and insignificant. By recognizing the inherent subjectivity of significance, the analyst acknowledges that value is often context-dependent and can vary among individuals, Organizations and Enterprises across various disciplines. Inclusiveness engenders discussion of a diverse range of perspectives for consideration. All topics are valuable subjects of inquiry, reinforcing a culture of intellectual growth and interdisciplinary collaboration and promoting curiosity. The Delphi Technique, Strengths, Weaknesses, Opportunities, and Threats (SWOT) Analysis, the Cause and Effect (Fishbone or Ishikawa) diagram, Root Cause Analysis (RCA), Weighted Decision Matrix (WDM), Breakeven Analysis (BEA), Probability Analysis, Sensitivity Analysis, Pareto Analysis, Analytical Hierarchy Process (AHP), Statistical Modeling (especially Linear Regression), Bayesian Analysis, Machine Learning (ML), Artificial Intelligence (AI), as well as other methods and techniques, help resolve many problems, leading to eventual Decision-Making and solution implementation that is context-appropriate and targeted.

1.6 WHEN FACTS ARE CORRECT BUT IRRELEVANT

A fact can be both correct and irrelevant. In the context of information or knowledge, a fact refers to something objectively accurate or verifiable. However, the relevance of a fact depends on its significance or applicability to a particular situation or specific context. An example that follows is illustrative. Fact: The population of a particular town is ten thousand. In some cases, this fact may be highly relevant. For instance, if the discussion pertains to urban planning, infrastructure resource allocation, or township political representation. The population figure becomes crucial for Decision-Making in the latter contexts. However, in other contexts, the fact may be irrelevant. Namely, suppose the topic of conversation shifts to discussing global economic trends or medical or scientific advancements. In that case, the specific population of the town can be deemed unrelated, irrelevant information that does not contribute to the understanding or resolution of the current problem and its discussion. Therefore, while the fact or information may be correct, its relevance depends on the discussed context or subject. Technically accurate facts can be considered irrelevant in certain situations if they do not directly pertain to the central matter or provide meaningful insights into the subject under consideration.

The following are even more examples provided to clarify the above scenario. One could say that stating a correct and irrelevant fact may be construed as "communicating without communicating." The public, mainstream media, and politicians often use the phrase in the vernacular. In particular, situations arise when facts can be considered correct but irrelevant, meaning they are accurate statements but may not have direct relevance, bearing, or significance in specific contexts. The political sphere is dominated daily by how a Fact can be accurate and objectively true, but its meaning depends on the particular context or subject of discussion.

The Fact or Information is correct, but its relevance depends on the specific context or subject being discussed. Additional examples follow:

1. Candidate A mentions that Candidate B had a failed Business venture in the 1990s during a presidential debate. While this fact may be true, it is likely irrelevant to the currently debated policy issues and the candidates' abilities to address them. The discussion should instead focus on the candidate's proposed policies, Leadership qualities and experience relative to the office sought, and vision.

2. In a Congressional debate about climate change, a candidate raises their opponent's financial investments in a pharmaceutical company. Although this may be factually correct, it is probably irrelevant to the more extensive discussion about the need for

climate action, renewable energy sources, and impactful environmental policies.

3. During a debate on healthcare reform, a candidate highlights their opponent's marital history and recent divorce. While this fact may be true with supportive Court records, it is irrelevant to the discussion about the merits and drawbacks of various proposed healthcare reforms, the accessibility of healthcare, and the affordability of medical services.

Do any of the situations above sound familiar?

1.7 MISDIRECTION PHENOMENON

By understanding the principles of misdirection, we can become more aware of how our attention can be manipulated and develop a more discerning critical mindset when interpreting information or evaluating situations. Misdirection is a Psychological technique that diverts someone's attention or focus from what is happening or about to occur. It is commonly associated with magic tricks and illusions, where the performer intentionally beguiles the audience's attention, drawing attention to one area or action while manipulating or concealing another. Misdirection exploits the limitations of human perception and attention span. Our brains have a limited capacity to process all the information in our environment simultaneously, so we tend to focus on specific cues or stimuli ("the shiny object"). Magicians and illusionists take advantage of the above by (re)directing our attention toward an irrelevant or less important aspect of their performance while simultaneously conducting the actual (magic) trick or deception.

1.7.1 MISDIRECTION PHENOMENON — "THE MAGICIAN'S SLEIGHT OF HAND"

- *Physical Gestures and movements:* Magicians use deliberate hand movements, body language, and theatrical gestures to (re)direct the audience's attention to specific performance areas. By emphasizing certain activities or actions, they manipulate where the audience looks, ensuring that their focus is away from the secret manipulations happening elsewhere on or off-stage.

- *Verbal distraction*: Magicians employ speech patterns, such as halting speech, storytelling, jokes, and witty banter, to engage the audience's auditory senses and occupy their conscious minds. This verbal distraction helps to divert attention away from critical movements, actions, or props involved in the trick.

- *Visual cues and props*: Magicians create focus points that draw the audience's gaze by employing visually captivating or attention-grabbing objects. They skillfully use props, bright colors, or elaborate costumes to capture the audience's attention and keep focus away from the secret movements, actions, or mechanisms involved in executing the illusion.

- *Timing and rhythm*: Misdirection relies on the magician's ability to control the pace and rhythm of their performance. Sudden pauses, rapid actions, or deliberate time delays disrupt the audience's temporal perception, making it harder for them to track the actual timing cadence or sequence of events.

- *Psychological manipulation*: Misdirection plays on the audience's expectations, assumptions, and preconceived notions. Magicians take advantage of our Cognitive Biases, such as Confirmation Bias and selective attention, to (re)direct our focus where they want it.

They exploit our natural human tendencies to fill in information gaps or to seek patterns, leading us astray from the actual workings of the trick.

Misdirection is not just limited to magic performances. It can also be seen in various aspects of Life, such as advertising, mainstream and non-mainstream media reports, and even everyday conversations. It highlights the malleability and limitations of human perception, cognition, and thought processes. It reminds us that *"what we perceive is not always an accurate depiction of reality."*

1.8 LOGICAL FALLACIES — "THE UNIQUE ASSOCIATED CIRCUMSTANCES"

Deceptive, falsely premised Arguments or Claims that do not support the offered conclusion characterize Logical Fallacies. These may be either:

- *Formal* (Arguments that have invalid structure, form, or context errors) or,

- *Informal* (Arguments that are irrelevant or based on incorrect premises).

15 Common Logical Fallacies:

1. *The Straw Man fallacy*: Misrepresentation or over-simplification of an Argument to allow for a more straightforward refutation or to lessen a debate attack instead of addressing the actual primary Argument.

2. *Bandwagon fallacy*: A popular, generally accepted Argument or Claim does not necessarily support an Argument nor validate the same. The population chosen to confirm the Argument is often suspect, ill-defined, or anonymous (unspecified). Contrary evidence may be marginalized, omitted, or suppressed to defocus the issue.

3. *The Appeal to Authority fallacy*: A single or limited domain Authority may be invoked, which may or may not have relevance, especially if the Authority's expertise is outside the scope of the Argument. One expert does not necessarily make an irrefutable, supportive case for an Argument.

4. *The False Dilemma fallacy*: Complex issues with dramatically and inherently opposed Arguments arguing for and against only two mutually exclusive outcomes will be rejected in this scenario. A spectrum of possibilities is thereby denied. Compromise is neither a choice nor any opportunity to re-frame the Argument.

5. *The Hasty Generalization fallacy*: Drawing expansive conclusions based on inadequate or insufficient evidence defines this fallacy. Jumping to conclusions about the validity of a proposition with only partially supporting proof is yet another feature.

6. *The Slothful Induction fallacy*: The inverse of the Hasty Generalization fallacy, attributing outcomes to chance or coincidence or unrelated reason, is suggested when, instead, sufficient

logical evidence strongly supports a particular conclusion as "true," but acknowledgment does not follow its presentation.

7. *The Correlation/Causation fallacy*: The superficial appearance of the correlation between two events or facts does not necessarily show that one position irrefutably caused the second.

8. *The Anecdotal fallacy*: Personal experience or anecdote is substituted for fact or logical evidence to substantiate a conclusion.

9. *The Texas Sharpshooter fallacy:* This is the proverbial "cherry-picking" of data clusters based on a predetermined conclusion. Patterns and correlations are used to support objectives, ignore contradictory evidence, or suggest the data clusters as not Statistically significant.

10. *The Middle Ground fallacy*: A compromise between two extreme, conflicting points of view is assumed as always "true." The Argument ignores the possibility that one or both extreme positions could be ultimately "true" or "false," thereby rendering any compromise between the two Arguments invalid.

11. *The Burden of Proof fallacy*: If a person claims that X is "true," they must supply supportive evidence of the assertion. It is, contrariwise, invalid to claim that X is "true" until someone can disprove the same. It is similarly invalid to claim X is "true" because it is impossible to prove X is "false." In this case, no evidence supporting a position does not mean it is automatically "true."

12. *The Personal Incredulity fallacy*: If one has difficulty understanding how or why something is "true," this alone does not automatically give weight to a "falsehood" in the Argument. A personal or collective understanding is insufficient to render a proffered Claim invalid.

13. *The No True Scotsman fallacy*: This fallacy is often used to protect assertions that rely on universal generalizations. The deflection of counterexamples occurs by changing the position or conditions of the original Claim to exclude the counterexample. Specifically, a counterexample to an original Claim is amended to exclude the counterexample.

14. *The Ad Hominem fallacy*:. An Ad Hominem fallacy is invoked when an individual is attacked personally rather than using a Logic-based Argument or Claim to refute an Argument. Physical appearance, personality traits, or other irrelevant characteristics are used to criticize the other individual's point of view or Argument. Attacks can also be made against groups, institutions, or similar entities, not just individuals.

15. *The Tu Quoque* (Latin for "you also") fallacy: An invalid attempt to discredit an opponent by answering with criticism but never presenting a counterargument to the original disputed Claim or position.

Take note—A fallacy-riddled Claim does not invalidate the premise of an Argument; it just means that the Argument does not confirm the premise, this being a situation where the arguer or debater has poorly constructed or non-incisive Arguments, notwithstanding that the Argument may still be valid.

1.9 THE DECISION-MAKING PROCESS AND STAGES

- *Problem identification*: Decision-Making begins with recognizing a problem or an opportunity that requires action. Problem identification, in particular, involves defining the issue or problem, setting objectives, and clearly understanding the context and system constraints.

- *Problem Analysis*: In this early stage, Problem Analysis gathers information and data relevant to the problem, seeking to understand its root cause(s) and potential implications.

- *Generating alternatives*: Once the problem is identified, as well as analyzed, Decision-Making generates potential solution(s) and alternative(s) to address the issue, seeking a solution.

- *Evaluation and solution Selection*: The proposed solution alternatives are then evaluated based on predetermined criteria, whether derived from a Delphi iterative technique, Strengths, Weaknesses, Opportunities, and Threats (SWOT) analysis, Cause and Effect (Fishbone or Ishikawa) diagram, Root Cause Analysis (RCA) Weighted Decision Matrix, Breakeven Analysis (BEA), Probability Analysis, Sensitivity Analysis, Pareto Analysis, Analytical Hierarchy Process (AHP), Statistical Modeling, (especially Linear Regression analysis, Bayesian Analysis, or other methodology and technique(s). Many other optional methods allow for the appropriate optimization of Business resources (in particular, analyst expertise and labor allocation, time requirements, equipment, such as computer hardware and software resources, and finances), market strategy, risk Management, and more, which are found in various Management and Business publications.

- Upon arriving at the Decision-Making juncture, the distillate of the Problem Analysis will point to the proposed, likely correct solution. Implementation is then weighed and scored as to its feasibility, risks, rewards, and potential outcomes.

- *Implementation and monitoring*: The selected solution is implemented, even if the Problem Analysis is incomplete or partially complete and the suggested solution is sub-optimal. Effectiveness is monitored to assess whether the selected, high-probability-of-success solution achieves the desired or intended result(s).

- Classical Economic Theory posits that individuals, as well as Organizations and Enterprises, make rational choices to maximize utility and profit, given the circumstance and premise of possessing complete information. However, *"Bounded Rationality"* constraints often limit the Decision-Making ability to access all relevant information, leading to deviations from entirely rational Decision-Making. Incomplete, partial, and erroneous information are certain pitfalls. Nobel laureate in Economics Herbert Simon (1916-2001) proposed the above concept of "Bounded Rationality," recognizing that Decision-Making has cognitive limitations and information constraints. Simon's Theory laid the groundwork for understanding how individuals make "satisficing" decisions, that is, choosing a satisfactory option rather than pursuing the optimization necessary to yield a "best choice" decision.

CHAPTER 2

"THERE ARE MANY WAYS TO GET THERE, BUT YOU NEED TO START THE JOURNEY WITH ONE STEP"

EACH METHODOLOGY OR TECHNIQUE FURTHER DISCUSSED IN this Chapter demonstrates unique applications, advantages, and pitfalls, with their selection principally constrained by the availability of analyst expertise, cost, timetable, urgency, and problem context.

2.1 The Delphi Technique
2.1.1 The Delphi Technique – Iterative Discover
2.1.2 The Delphi Technique – Consensus of Opinions
2.2 Strengths, Weaknesses, Opportunities, and Threats (SWOT) Analysis
2.3 Cause and Effect (Fishbone or Ishikawa) Diagram
2.4 Root Cause Analysis (RCA)
2.4.1 Root Cause Analysis (RCA) – Output and Consequences
2.5 Weighted Decision Matrix
2.5.1 Weighted Decision Matrix – Example
2.6 Cost-Benefit Analysis
2.6.1 Cost-Benefit Analysis – Example 1 (Medical)

2.1 THE DELPHI TECHNIQUE

It is worth noting that the Delphi technique can have variations and adaptations depending on the specific context and purpose. The steps described below represent a general overview of the typical Delphi technique for Problem Analysis. The Delphi technique is a process used to debate or commonly analyze a problem by systematically gathering input and feedback from a panel of domain experts or stakeholders. It is designed to reach a consensus or "convergence of opinions" on a specific subject. The panel of experts or stakeholders is carefully selected based on their knowledge, specific domain expertise, and relevance to the discussed topic. The panel can include individuals from diverse backgrounds, representing various perspectives, experiences, and abilities. The facilitator or organizer of the Delphi technique develops an initial questionnaire or series of questions related to the point of view or problem being investigated or argued. These questions are designed to elicit informed responses and insights from the panelists.

Round ONE involves submitting the questionnaire or questions to the expert panelists. Each participant independently replies with their responses and Arguments from their vantage point of view. These responses are kept anonymous from other panelist members to encourage open and unbiased feedback and discussion. The facilitator then collects and analyzes the responses, looking for areas of agreement, disagreement, and emerging themes and trends. The results are compiled, collated, and shared as feedback with the panelists without revealing their identities. The panelists are encouraged to review the feedback, consider alternative perspectives, and refine their Arguments based on the additional collective input provided.

Round TWO of the iterative steps of the process involves sharing the compiled feedback and analysis with the expert panelists. They are then allowed to reconsider their initial responses, considering the feedback from Round ONE and the collective input.

Round THREE …

DELPHI Technique

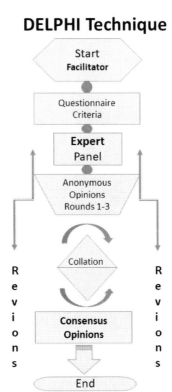

2.1.1 THE DELPHI TECHNIQUE — ITERATIVE DISCOVER

Iterative discovery (also known as iterative Problem Analysis or iterative problem-solving) is at the crux of the technique and process. It refers to an approach where the process of analyzing a problem and finding a solution is conducted in multiple iterations or cycles.

The iterative discovery process involves breaking down the problem into smaller (sub)components, analyzing each part, and then revisiting and refining the analysis based on new insights gained from each iteration (cycle).

- *Problem identification*: The first step is clearly defining and understanding the problem. This involves gathering information, defining the scope of the problem, and naming the key objectives that will, in the end, improve efficiency, decrease production costs, and spare labor resources while yielding higher customer satisfaction scores.

- *Iterative analysis*: The iterative analysis step focuses on examining and evaluating data or information to gain insights, show any overt or nuanced patterns, or uncover trends. It involves repetitive data collection, analysis, interpretation, and refinement cycles to iteratively tamp down even further the understanding or achieving of specific objectives. The iterative analysis process uses various analytical methods and techniques depending on the particular problem category. These may include but are not limited to Statistical analysis, data mining, data visualization, Hypothesis testing, or exploratory data analysis. The choice of methods depends on the problem and type of situation, available data, and the goals of the investigation. This iterative feedback and revision process continues as a loop cycle until a finalized consensus or convergence of opinions appears through the multiple, successive rounds of feedback and revision of opinions. The Delphi technique aims to narrow differences and promote consensus among the panelists. The facilitator typically provides summaries of areas of agreement and disagreement to guide the expert panelists toward a collective understanding, previewing the termination of the process.

The results are compiled, summarized, and reported once a consensus or convergence of opinions is conclusively reached.

2.1.2 THE DELPHI TECHNIQUE – CONSENSUS OF OPINIONS

- *Clear assessment*: When the problem is straightforward, and its impact or consequences are minimal, it becomes easier for people to evaluate and assess its significance. The clarity of understanding helps in aligning perspectives and forming a collective opinion.

- *Objective evaluation*: In situations where the problem lacks complexity or ambiguity, individuals can objectively evaluate and analyze the problem. They can assess relevant factors and corroborative evidence, leading to a convergence of opinions when participants arrive at similar or near-similar conclusions.

- *Consistent information*: If the available information about the problem is consistent and unambiguous, it facilitates a shared understanding among those expert panelists involved in the analysis. When everyone has access to the same data or evidence, opinions are more likely to converge toward consensus.

- *Prioritize and classify*: A requirement exists to evaluate the significance of the problem relative to your specific overall goals, aims, and resources. Issues need to be categorized based on their potential impact, the urgency of the situation, and alignment with Organizational and Enterprise priorities.

  1. "*Low stakes*" are problems with minimal impact or consequences that tend to generate less emotional reaction or sense of a personal stake in the issue. In such cases, participants may be more open to objectively considering the problem's significance and reaching a consensus.

  2. *Limited alternatives*: When there are few or no workable alternatives to address the problem, it becomes easier for individuals to recognize the problem's significance. With a lack of workable solutions or options, convergence toward consensus becomes more likely to be achieved. It is important to note that the perception of problem significance can vary among individuals, and what may be considered insignificant by one person or group may be seen as significant by another. However, in cases where the problem

is objectively assessed and its impact is universally recognized as negligible, the convergence of opinions toward a finality or conclusion is more likely to occur and occur with fewer iterative cycles or rounds. All the preceding becomes decidedly more fractious, contentious, and difficult when the problem is difficult or complex.

- *Final analysis and report*: The facilitator analyzes the responses and discussions from the iterative rounds and summarizes the findings. The final report includes the areas of agreement, differing opinions (usually a minority position), non-conforming viewpoints, and any emerging consensus on the problem or decision. It can serve as a valuable resource for Decision-Making or as a basis for further ongoing investigation and analysis.

The Delphi technique is recognized for its usefulness in facilitating robust and unbiased discussions, mainly when complex or controversial issues are to be unraveled. By systematically gathering input, encouraging anonymity, and promoting iterative feedback, the Delphi technique allows for exploring diverse viewpoints, identifying areas of agreement, and resolving disagreements. The technique provides a structured approach to arguing a point of view by incorporating the collective wisdom and expertise of a panel of domain experts or stakeholders. Secondly, even discussing seemingly insignificant topics can also serve as a means of reinforcing inclusivity and valuing diverse perspectives voiced. Treating all subjects equally reinforces respect for each other's interests, opinions, and cultural viewpoints. Today, cultural sensitivity, as an attribute, is particularly valued within a global multiethnic and multicultural economy. Engaging in rigorous discussions allows for exploring and wringing (out) these diverse perspectives, leading to a meaningful and more inclusive dialogue. The discussion of circumscribed topics can sometimes have far-reaching consequences or serve as gateways to more significant issues. History has shown us that trivial events or decisions can significantly impact society. The opposite, more importantly, is true: important decisions have an expected even more significant impact on society. Engaging in these discussions allows us to analyze the potential ripple effects of small to substantial matters to ensure we consider their broader implications. Breakthrough ideas can emerge from unconventional or unexpected sources, a discovery leading to groundbreaking innovative approaches to existing problems. The Delphi technique goes beyond the rudimentary Nominal Group technique (NGT), relying on a moderator to record spontaneously contributed and gathered ideas via an unsophisticated, uncoordinated brainstorming session. In contrast, The Delphi technique is more robust and iterative. The Delphi technique is used for more consequential Decision-Making. It requires more time, domain experts, anonymity, and multiple rounds (using detailed questionnaires) with secondary and tertiary questionnaires generated by the preceding questionnaire(s). Ideas generated are rank-ordered for prioritization.

2.2 STRENGTHS, WEAKNESSES, OPPORTUNITIES, AND THREATS (SWOT) ANALYSIS

Problem Analysis process tools used are numerous, but one that stands out is the Strengths, Weaknesses, Opportunities, and Threats (SWOT) analysis method. This is a widely used tool, especially in strategic planning. SWOT analysis assesses an Organization's and Enterprise's Strengths, Weaknesses, Opportunities, and Threats, providing a comprehensive overview of the internal and external factors influencing Decision-Making.

The SWOT analysis strategic planning tool evaluates an Organization's and Enterprise's internal strengths and weaknesses, along with parallel identifying significant external opportunities and threats. This holistic tool allows for a criterion-based comparative analysis across an industry and sector. Sometimes, SWOT analysis is local-regional, which directly addresses a market. Understanding the competitive environment with this structured assessment tool aids in Decision-Making. Its robustness lies in its uncomplicated ease of use, flexibility, adaptability to different Business settings, and broad applicability. Notwithstanding, SWOT has limitations such as potential and actual Biases with subjectivity, reflecting the inherent Bias of the individuals who collect the data and participate in the brainstorming session, constraints arising from the structured questionnaire, questions chosen, and oversimplification. The bypassing of subtle details or non-objective qualities that may be missed are additional liabilities.

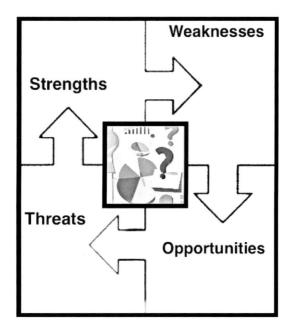

Strengths	My Company	Competitor 1	Competitor 2
What are your business advantages?			
What are your core competencies?			
Where are you making the most money?			
What are you doing well?			
Weaknesses			
What areas are you avoiding?			
Where do you lack resources?			
What are you doing poorly?			
Where are you losing money?			
What needs improvement?			
Opportunities			
Any beneficial trends?			
Niches that competitors are missing?			
New technologies?			
New needs of customers?			
Threats			
Obstacles to overcome?			
Aggressive competitors?			
Successful competitors?			
Negative economic conditions?			
Government regulation?			
Changing business climate?			
Vulnerabilities?			

2.3 CAUSE AND EFFECT (FISHBONE OR ISHIKAWA) DIAGRAM

This leads to another major methodological process that straddles Problem Analysis and Decision-Making. The graphical representation of the output results of this method helps assess the potential consequences of different decision choices and their probability likelihoods, aiding Decision-Making in understanding the best, optimal, or acceptable likely course of action. Root Cause Analysis (RCA) may be used to preface this method, probing precipitating causes and their downstream consequential or derivative effects, all underlying factors causing the problem(s) under investigation. The goal is to eradicate the problem and prevent any recurrence. The Cause and Effect (fishbone or Ishikawa) diagram evaluates short and long-term concerns that are addressed as to causality, enabling definitive problem-solving. This deliberative, thoughtful, intermediate resource-intensive method is unsuitable for urgent or emergent scenarios. The (Medical) example shown in this section was a Root Cause Analysis (RCA) and the identification of contributing factors to the problem of Excess Laboratory (Lab) Testing Occurring in a Hospital System setting. The analysis was prompted by the fact that there is overutilization of lab testing, so much so that an estimated 20 percent of tests are deemed unnecessary in healthcare. Waste and increased costs result in impacting the health care system. Notably, approximately 70 percent of downstream decisions, particularly treatment decisions, are predicated on lab test results. False Positive (FP) and False Negative (FN) results can lead to untoward patient consequences, and there are other consequences.

Ishikawa

Cause and Effect Diagram

Description

This template illustrates a Cause and Effect Diagram, also called a Fishbone or Ishikawa Diagram. A detailed discussion of Cause and Effect Diagrams can be found at www.ASQ.org

Instructions

- Enter the Problem Statement in box provided.

- Brainstorm the major categories of the problem. Generic headings are provided.

- Write the categories of causes as branches from the main arrow.

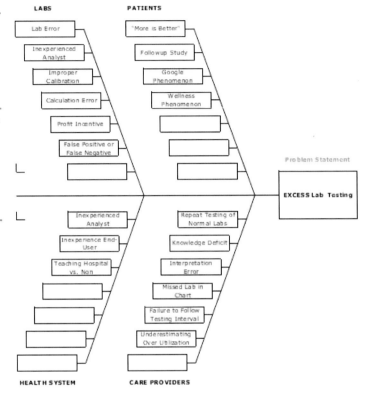

LABS

- Lab Error
- Inexperienced Analyst
- Improper Calibration
- Calculation Error
- Profit Incentive
- False Positive or False Negative

PATIENTS

- "More is Better"
- Followup Study
- Google Phenomenon
- Wellness Phenomenon

Problem Statement

EXCESS Lab Testing

HEALTH SYSTEM

- Inexperienced Analyst
- Inexperience End-User
- Teaching Hospital vs. Non

CARE PROVIDERS

- Repeat Testing of Normal Labs
- Knowledge Deficit
- Interpretation Error
- Missed Lab in Chart
- Failure to Follow Testing Interval
- Underestimating Over Utilization

2.4 ROOT CAUSE ANALYSIS (RCA)

Root Cause Analysis RCA) and the identification of contributing factors:

Steps involved in conducting a robust Root Cause Analysis:

- *Define the problem:* Clearly articulate the problem you want to analyze. Be specific about the issue, its impact, and any related symptoms or consequences.

- *"Decomposing"*: Once the problem is found, it is often helpful to break it down into smaller, more manageable components or sub-problems. This allows for a more focused analysis and understanding of each part individually and its contribution to the whole.

- *Gather data*: Collect relevant data and all possible information related to the problem. This may include incident reports, process documentation, performance metrics, six-sigma data, customer feedback, and all other available sources of data and information.

- *Identify contributing factors*: Brainstorm and list all the factors that may have contributed to the problem. Consider environmental, Organizational and Enterprise, technical, informatics, operational process-related, logistic, and human-related factors. Use techniques such as the *"5 Whys"* (a rudimentary but pragmatic iterative interrogative approach) for identifying the problem. Alternatively, Cause-and-Effect diagrams (e.g., Fishbone or Ishikawa diagrams), as previously discussed, can be used to identify potential causes contributing to the undesirable problem (output) and any other investigative techniques and methodologies.

- *Analyze and prioritize causes*: Evaluate each potential cause based on its likelihood, impact, and relevance to the problem. Use data analysis techniques, such as Statistical or trend analysis, to show correlations or patterns supporting or refuting the probable causes.

- *Verify root causes*: Confirm the potential root causes by conducting further investigations or tests, which may involve conducting experiments, scenario simulations, interviews, or seeing the problem in action. Photography and especially videography may be quite helpful in this latter regard. Ensure that the identified root causes are backed by sufficient corroborating evidence.

- *Determine root causes*: Once the potential cause(s) have been verified, determine the actual, bona fide root causes. These are the underlying factors that, if addressed, would prevent the problem from occurring or recurring. Not surprisingly, there may be multiple root causes contributing to the problem.

- *Develop corrective actions*: Generate specific and actionable corrective actions to address each root cause. These actions should be designed to eliminate or mitigate the identified factors contributing to the problem. Consider a range of solutions, such as process improvements, corrective measures, education and training programs, policy and procedural changes, informatics solutions, or technological equipment upgrades.

- *Implement and monitor*: Implement the corrective action(s) and then monitor their effectiveness over time. Track the progress, gather feedback, and measure the impact of the implemented changes. If necessary, adjust or tweak the actions to prevent recurring problems. Assessing sustainability should be a goal.

Remember that a robust root cause analysis requires an objective and systematic approach. It involves engaging stakeholders, using data-driven insights, and considering multiple perspectives to comprehensively understand the problem's underlying causes. By addressing the root causes, Organizations and Enterprises can achieve effective solutions to their problems.

2.4.1 ROOT CAUSE ANALYSIS (RCA) – OUTPUT AND CONSEQUENCES

- *Evaluate potential consequences*: Assess the potential consequences of unresolved problems. Consider the short-term and long-term effects, internally and externally within your Organization and Enterprise, on customers, stakeholders, and other relevant affected parties. Then, seek input by engaging with stakeholders, shareholders, employees, owners, or subject matter technical experts to gather different unique perspectives. Their insights and experiences may shed further light on the significance or potential implications of the problem, as well as possible viable solutions.

- *Conduct a Cost-Benefit analysis* to evaluate the resources and efforts needed to address the problem versus the potential benefits or savings that could otherwise be gained.

- *Use data and metrics:* Use data and metrics to measure the impact of a problem, even if it initially appears insignificant. Quantifying the issue can help provide a clearer picture of its actual significance and support Decision-Making.

By applying these steps, you can better understand problems and make informed decisions based on their actual or potential impact.

ROOT CAUSE ANALYSIS

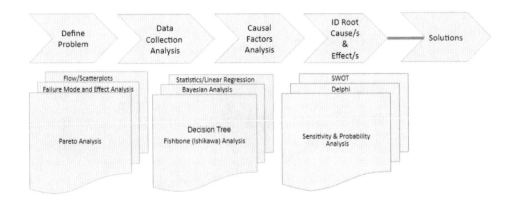

2.5 WEIGHTED DECISION MATRIX

The Weighted Decision Matrix creates a decision matrix that includes the relevant criteria for evaluating the potential solutions. Assign arbitrary weights to each criterion based on its relative importance. Evaluate each solution against each criterion and calculate a weighted score. The solution with the highest overall score is prioritized.

Generating a Weighted Decision Matrix:

- *Identify criteria*: Determine the relevant criteria for evaluating potential solutions. These criteria should be specific, measurable, and related to the problem or decision. For example, if you are assessing the feasibility of installing different software application solutions, criteria could, for instance, include cost, functionality, user-friendliness, interoperability, scalability, and customer support.

- *Assign weights:* Assign arbitrary weights to each criterion to reflect their relative importance or priority. The weights should be assigned based on the significance of each criterion in achieving the desired outcome or solving the identified problem. You can use a scale of one to five (or one to ten), where one represents low importance and ten represents high importance, ensuring that the weights sum up to 100 percent.

- *Rate solutions:* Evaluate each potential solution against each criterion and assign ratings or scores. Use a consistent rating scale, such as one to five or one to ten, where higher values indicate better performance or suitability of the solution. Rate each proposed solution independently for each criterion.

- *Calculate weighted scores*: Multiply the rating of each solution for each selected criterion by the corresponding arbitrary weight assigned to that criterion. This calculation provides the weighted score for each criterion. Repeat this calculation for all criteria and solutions.

- *Sum weighted scores and total weighted score:* Sum up the weighted scores across all criteria for each solution. The calculated total weighted score represents each proposed solution's overall performance or suitability.

- *Analyze and rank solutions:* Compare the total weighted scores of the solutions. Higher total weighted scores indicate more favorable expected solutions. Rank order the solutions in descending order based on their total weighted scores to prioritize.

2.5.1 WEIGHTED DECISION MATRIX EXAMPLE

Let us consider an example where you are evaluating for employment three different potential advertising agencies based on three criteria:

a. Cost, b. Experience, and c. Creativity

The weights assigned to each criterion are:

Cost (40 percent), b. Experience (30 percent) and c. Creativity (30 percent).

Then, rate each advertising agency on a scale of one to five, in this example, for each criterion, with five being the highest rating.

Step 1. Criteria Weights (assigned):
a. Cost: 40 percent (0.4)
b. Experience: 30 percent (0.3)
c. Creativity: 30 percent (0.3)

Step 2. Proposed Solutions (Advertising Agencies):
1. Agency X
2. Agency Y
3. Agency Z

Step 3. Ratings (one to five, with five being the highest):
a. Based on Cost: Agency X (3), Agency Y (4), and Agency Z (2)
b. Based on Experience: Agency X (4), Agency Y (5), and Agency Z (3)
c. Based on Creativity: Agency X (4), Agency Y (3), Agency Z (5)

Step 4. Weighted Scores:
a. Cost: Agency X (1.2), Agency Y (1.6), and Agency Z (0.8)
b. Experience: Agency X (1.2), Agency Y (1.5), and Agency Z (0.9)
c. Creativity: Agency X (1.2), Agency Y (0.9), and Agency Z (1.5)

Step 5. Total Weighted Scores:
> Agency X: 3.6
> Agency Y: 4.0
> Agency Z: 3.0

Step 6. Ranking (Descending Order of Total Weighted Scores):
> 1. Agency Y (4.0)
> 2. Agency X (3,6)
> 3. Agency Z (3.2)

Step 7. Arrive at a conclusion—In this example, based on the (Total) Weighted Decision Matrix, Agency Y receives the highest total weighted score (4.0) and is ranked as the most suitable solution. Agency X is ranked second (3.6), trailed by Agency Z (3.2).

This ranking helps prioritize the Advertising agencies based on their performance across the specified criteria of Cost (a), Experience (b), and Creativity (c).

2.6 COST – BENEFIT ANALYSIS

Quantify the costs and benefits associated with each potential solution. Then, assign monetary values or scores to various aspects such as fiscal impact, resource utilization, or time saved. Calculate the net benefit or Cost-Benefit ratio for each solution. Higher net benefits or favorable Cost-Benefit ratios indicate more promising proposed solutions.

Cost-Benefit Analysis Example:
To conduct a Cost-Benefit analysis, one evaluates the costs associated with a decision or proposed solution and compares them to the expected benefits or advantages.

Step-by-step guide on how to perform a Cost-Benefit analysis:

- *Identify costs:* Identify and list all the costs associated with implementing a particular solution or decision. These costs may include the following:

  1. *Direct costs* (e.g., equipment, supplies and materials, labor).

  2. *Indirect costs* (e.g., training, maintenance, preventive maintenance, informatics, and any ongoing or future operational costs that may arise).

- *Quantify costs:* Assign monetary values to each cost item. This can involve estimating costs based on market prices, historical data, expert opinions, or research. Try to be as accurate and comprehensive as possible in capturing all relevant expenses.

2.6.1 COST-BENEFIT ANALYSIS — EXAMPLE 1 (MEDICAL)

An example in the Medical field is the determination of Hospital-based Laboratory profitability. This starts with a stepwise approach that first entails understanding the Centers for Medicare and Medicaid Services reimbursement (CMS), other payment resources, and constraints. Next, proceed to determine a Return On Investment (ROI).

Initiating the Cost-Benefit Analysis process:

- *Needs assessment,* considering quality, efficiency, safety, attention to the market, and competitive advantage.

- *Estimating initial capital* (equipment) and operational (labor, supplies, etc.) expense outlay or assessing both.

- *Estimating future revenues and expenses*, including "back-end" operations, such as the Laboratory Information System (LIS), waste removal, and billing services.

- *Risk analysis*, including reimbursement and third-party payer contracting, payer mix, and utilization patterns.

An optional step taken, in this example, was the consideration of outsourcing the entire laboratory operation to an outside reference lab since a significant decrease in personnel supply costs, as well as supply costs, would predictably accrue and result in "Value" creation:

	Labor Costs	Supply Costs	Equipment Costs	Value Creation *
Total Hospital Lab X Costs	60%	35%	5%	0%
Reference Total Lab Outsourcing	50%	20%	3%	27%

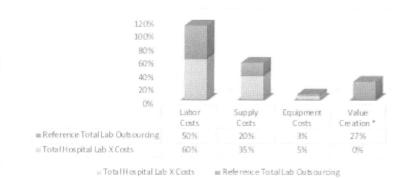

Hospital Lab X vs. Total Lab Outsourcing Option

	Labor Costs	Supply Costs	Equipment Costs	Value Creation *
Total Hospital Lab X Costs	60%	35%	5%	0%
Reference Total Lab Outsourcing	50%	20%	3%	27%

2.6.2 COST-BENEFIT ANALYSIS –
OUTPUT AND COST-BENEFIT RATIO

- *Identify Benefits:* Identify and list all the potential benefits that can be gained from implementing the proposed solution or decision. Benefits include cost savings, increased revenue, improved operational efficiencies, enhanced quality, safety, and other positive outcomes.

- *Quantify benefits:* Assign monetary values or scores to each benefit item. This can be challenging for some intangible benefits, but estimating their value as accurately as possible is essential. Consider factors such as projected revenue and incremental expenses (not always "moving" in parallel), labor and union wage negotiations, time savings, and customer satisfaction improvements.

- *Calculate net benefit:* Calculate the net benefit by subtracting the total costs from the total benefits. The net benefit represents the overall financial gain or loss derived from the proposed solution or decision. A positive net benefit indicates that the benefits outweigh the costs, while a negative net benefit suggests the opposite.

- *Evaluate Cost-Benefit ratio:*
  Calculate the Cost-Benefit ratio by dividing the Total Benefits (TB) by the Total Costs (TC) = TB/TC = The "efficiency" of the investment

TB/TC ratio greater than One (1) indicates that the benefits outweigh the costs, while a ratio less than One (1) suggests that the costs outweigh the benefits.

Remember to consider qualitative factors: While the primary focus of Cost-Benefit analysis is on monetary Return on Investment (ROI), it is essential to consider qualitative factors that may influence a final decision.

These factors could include environmental impacts, social considerations, intangible benefits (like employee morale), brand reputation, and other non-monetary aspects that can significantly influence the overall value of the proposed or potential solution.

2.6.3 COST – BENEFIT ANALYSIS – EXAMPLE 2 (BUSINESS)

Let us consider the example of a company considering installing and implementing a new office computer hardware-software system. One can calculate a simplified breakdown of the costs and benefits associated with the decision:

Costs:
- Software License: $10,000

- Hardware Upgrades: $5,000

- Training Expenses: $2,000

- Maintenance and Support: $3,000 per year

Benefits:
- Time Savings: Estimated to save 10 hours per week, valued at $25 per hour.

- Improved Efficiency: Estimated to reduce errors and rework, saving $8,000 annually.

- Increased Revenue: Estimated to generate $20,000 incremental revenue per year.

Net Benefit Calculation:
Total Costs = $10,000 + $5,000 + $2,000 + ($3,000 * Number of Years) = $20,000 (year one)

Total Benefits = (10 hours/week * 52 weeks * $25/hour) + $8,000 + $20,000

Net Benefit = Total Benefits - Total Costs

In summary, the **Cost-Benefit ratio calculation = Total Benefits (TB) / Total Costs (TC):**

By calculating the net Benefit and Cost-Benefit ratio based on specific figures and estimates, one can assess whether the financial gains outweigh the costs of implementing the new computer hardware-software system. This analysis helps make and justify an informed decision by considering the proposed solution's financial implications and potential Return On Investment (ROI).

2.7 BREAKEVEN ANALYSIS (BEA)

There are "aha moments" and discoveries to be made when correlating Total Costs (TC, Sum of Variable, Semi-Variable, and Fixed Costs) using a Breakeven Analysis (BEA). The analysis is particularly mission-critical for the following reasons:

1. *Assessing the viability of remaining in Business* using the calculation of Fixed and Variable Costs as well as contribution margin and profitability requirements.

2. *Analyzing Expenses* [Total Costs = Fixed Costs plus Variable Costs].

3. *Setting a unit price per product to be profitable.*

4. *The launching of new products and services or both.*

Cost analysis is performed to determine where one exceeds the Breakeven point.

Breakeven Analysis (BEA) calculations, including a graphic representation:

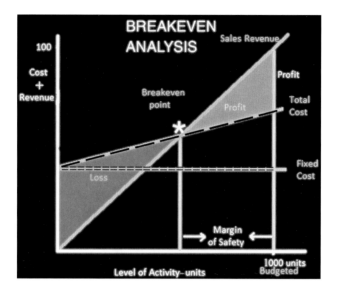

The Breakeven point occurs when the Total Cost (TC) for a product or service equals Total Revenue (TR) received for the product or service:
TC = TR

The Equation for the Breakeven (BE) point in the Breakeven analysis:
Volume at Breakeven point (X, Variable in units) equals Fixed Cost + Profit divided by Selling Price per Unit minus Variable Cost (VC) per Unit

Or, stated differently, we can say:
Breakeven point = Fixed Cost (FC) / Contribution Margin (CM) per Unit

The Operational assumptions are that when:
Total Revenue > Total Costs = Profit, and the inverse, or alternatively when:
Total Revenue < Total Cost = Loss

Explanation of the BEA calculation:
The Breakeven analysis (BEA) is a valuable tool to calculate what a change in Total Fixed Cost (and Variable Costs or both), Volume, or Revenue

may have on the financial Management of a Business, mainly when the Business introduces a new Product or Service. At this point, cost and income are equal, and neither profit nor loss exists. Notably, the breakeven equation can additionally be used to determine what pricing must be charged to a customer-client when the Volume of a Product or Service is known or inflexible. Upon further scrutiny, as Volume increases, Total Cost rises. However, Product or Service per unit cost will decrease (concept of "Economies of Scale") because the Total Fixed Cost is spread out or diluted over a much larger number of the output (Products or Services), but only *until* reaching a specific Volume limit or maximum, where additional Fixed Cost will be required or incurred (such as the requirement for additional Capital, namely, equipment to meet production needs, and labor requirements or both).

2.8 PROBABILITY ANALYSIS

Use Probability Analysis techniques such as a Monte Carlo simulation if you have probabilistic data or estimates. This method helps assess each proposed solution's likelihood and potential outcomes, allowing for probabilistic prioritization based on expected values or probabilities.

Probability Analysis involves assessing the likelihood and potential outcomes of different scenarios or events:

Step-by-step guide on how to perform a Probability Analysis:

- *Identify the scenarios*: Identify the scenarios or events you want to analyze. These could be potential outcomes or future events related to the problem or decision you have under consideration.

- *Assign probabilities:* Assign probabilities to each scenario, representing the likelihood or chance of it occurring. Probabilities can be expressed as percentages, decimals, or fractions. However, ensure that the assigned probabilities sum up to 100 percent or the value of one (1).

- *Determine outcomes*: For each scenario, determine its potential associated outcomes. These outcomes could be positive or negative consequences, financial gains or losses, or other relevant outcomes.

- *Quantify outcomes:* Assign values or scores to each outcome. These values can represent monetary gains or losses, qualitative impacts, or any other measurement that captures the consequences of the outcomes. Use consistent units for measure across the analysis.

- *Calculate expected value:* Calculate the expected value for each scenario by multiplying the probability of the scenario by the value of each associated outcome. Sum up the products to arrive at the expected value for that scenario. This methodology yields the average or expected outcome of that given scenario.

- *Analyze expected values:* Compare the expected values of the different scenarios. Higher expected values indicate more favorable outcomes. Analyze the expected values to determine which scenarios are more likely to yield positive results or align with your Corporate and Enterprise goals and objectives.

- *Sensitivity analysis:* Perform Sensitivity Analysis by varying the probabilities or values assigned to the various scenarios. Assess the impact of changes in probabilities or outcomes on the expected values.

This analysis helps identify scenarios that are more sensitive to changes and those that are ultimately more robust or reliable.

Probability Analysis Example:

Let us consider an example of a Business deciding whether to launch a new product.

Probability Analysis calculation:

Scenarios:

1. High Market Demand (Probability: 30 percent)
2. Moderate Market Demand (Probability: 50 percent)
3. Low Market Demand (Probability: 20 percent)

Outcomes:

High Market Demand: Expected revenue of $200,000
Moderate Market Demand: Expected revenue of $100,000
Low Market Demand: Expected revenue of $50,000

Expected Value Calculation = (Probability * Outcome Value)

Calculated for each designated scenario:

Scenario 1 (High Market Demand): (0.30 * $200,000) = $60,000
Scenario 2 (Moderate Market Demand): (0.50 * $100,000) = $50,000
Scenario 3 (Low Market Demand): (0.20 * $50,000) = $10,000

Summary after Analyzing Expected Values:

Scenario 1: Expected Value of $60,000
Scenario 2: Expected Value of $50,000
Scenario 3: Expected Value of $10,000

In this example, one can assess the potential financial outcomes of launching a new product by analyzing the expected values of the different market demand scenarios. The scenario with the highest expected value (Scenario 1, $60,000) suggests a higher likelihood of generating greater revenue. This Probability Analysis helps evaluate the potential outcomes and make informed decisions based on the likelihood of different scenarios.

2.9 SENSITIVITY ANALYSIS

Sensitivity Analysis is used to determine the impact of varying Variables, parameters, or assumptions on the performance or feasibility of each proposed solution. By exploring different scenarios and assessing their effects, you can identify more robust and less sensitive solutions to changes in the Variables. Sensitivity Analysis involves assessing the impact of varying inputs or assumptions on the outcomes or results of a decision or model. It helps identify the Variables that influence the outcomes most and determines the robustness of the analysis.

Step-by-step guide on how to perform a Sensitivity Analysis:

- *Identify key Variables*: Identify the Variables or inputs that significantly influence the outcomes of the decision or model. You want to analyze these parameters regarding their impact on the results.

- *Define a range:* Determine the range of values or levels for each key Variable you want to evaluate. This can involve selecting a lower and upper range value or establishing a reasonable range based on historical data, domain expert opinions, or other relevant information:

- *Determine increment steps*: Decide on the incremental procedures for changing the values within the defined range. This step helps systematically evaluate the impact of different values rather than all possible combinations.

- *Analyze the outcomes:* For each combination of Variable values, analyze the outcomes or results of the decision or model. Determine how changing the values of the key Variables affects the outcomes of interest. This analysis can involve recalculating the results or running simulations based on the modified inputs.

- *Evaluate sensitivity*: Evaluate the sensitivity of the outcomes to changes in the key Variables. Identify which Variables have the most significant impact on the results. This evaluation can be done by observing the magnitude of differences and their direction in the outcomes as the Variable values change.

- *Interpret findings*: Interpret the findings of the Sensitivity Analysis and draw conclusions. Determine the robustness of the decision or model based on the identified key Variables and their impact. Assess whether the results are sensitive to changes in certain Variables or if they remain stable and unaltered.

- *Consider risk and uncertainty*: Sensitivity Analysis helps assess the risks and uncertainties associated with the decision or model. It provides insights into the potential range of outcomes based on different assumptions or inputs. Consider the implications of these findings when making decisions or drawing conclusions.

2.9.1 SENSITIVITY ANALYSIS — EXAMPLE

Let us consider an example using a financial Business model to analyze the profitability of a new product launch.

The key Variables identified for the Sensitivity analysis are:

1. The selling price.

2. The Cost of Goods Sold (COGS).

A simplified breakdown of *Key Variables*:

1. The *Selling price* ranges from $10 to $20 per unit (in $1 increments)

2. The *Cost of Goods Sold (COGS)*: Range of $5 to $10 per unit (in $1 increments)

Outcomes:

The Profit is calculated based on the following:

1. The Selling Price and,

2. The Cost of Goods Sold (COGS).

Analysis of Outcomes:

- For each combination of Selling Price and COGS values, calculate the Profit.

- Interpret the findings.

- Assess the sensitivity of the profit to changes in the selling price and COGS.

- Identify the values of selling price and COGS that yield the highest and lowest profits.

- Consider risk and uncertainty:

- Based on the Sensitivity Analysis, determine the range of potential profits and assess the risks associated with the pricing and cost assumptions.

In the above Sensitivity Analysis, profit outcomes under varying combinations of selling price and COGS values are determined, and one can assess the sensitivity of profitability to changes in these Variables. This analysis helps to understand the impact of pricing and cost assumptions on the profitability of the new product launch. It allows for *identifying the target price and cost levels that significantly affect the outcomes*, allowing for informed decisions and evaluating the robustness of the financial Business model.

2.10 PARETO ANALYSIS

This analysis method employs the Pareto principle (the 80/20 rule) to prioritize potential solutions. Identify the most significant factors or causes contributing to the problem and focus on solutions that address those essential factors.

This analytical method maximizes the impact sought by targeting the "vital few factors" with the most influence. Pareto Analysis helps identify and prioritize the most significant factors or causes contributing to a problem or desired outcome. It helps focus efforts on those "vital few factors" with the most and often disproportionate impact.

Step-by-step guide on how to perform a Pareto Analysis:

- *Define the problem:* Clearly define the problem or outcome you want to analyze. Ensure that the problem is specific and measurable.

- *Identify and list factors:* Identify and list all the factors or causes contributing to the problem or outcome. These factors can be identified through brainstorming, Statistical data analysis, process mapping, or consulting with domain experts.

- *Collect data:* Gather data or information related to each factor. This would include quantitative data, such as counts or measurements, or qualitative data, such as observations or expert opinions. Ensure that the data is accurate, dependable, and representative.

- *Quantify the impact:* Assess the impact of each factor on the problem or outcome. This can be done by quantifying each factor's frequency, occurrence, or influence. Use consistent units or scales of measurement in the analysis.

- *Sort and rank*: Sort the factors in descending order based on their impact, from highest to lowest. Rank-order them accordingly, with the factor having the highest impact being placed at the top of the list.

- *Calculate cumulative impact*: Calculate the cumulative impact for each factor. This is the sum of the effects of all factors above it in the ranked list. It helps visualize the incremental contribution of each factor to the problem or outcome.

- *Plot the Pareto chart:* Create a Pareto chart, which is a *bar chart graphic that displays the factors in descending order of their impact.* The vertical axis represents the impact (frequency, occurrence, or influence), and the horizontal axis represents the factors. Additionally, superimpose a line graph showing the cumulative effects.

- *Analyze the chart:* Analyze the Pareto chart to identify the "vital few factors" contributing to most of the problem or outcome. The top 20 percent of factors typically contribute to around 80 percent of the impact. Then, focus on these critical factors for further analysis and action.

Unit	Total Boarders	Cumulative Total	Cumulative %
Telemetry	3623	3623	25%
Observation	3193	6816	47%
Tower 5	1934	8750	60%
Tower 1	1742	10492	72%
IMC	1400	11892	82%
Tower 6	926	12818	88%
ICU	546	13364	92%
2T	476	13840	95%
3CB	466	14306	98%
Oncology	273	14579	100%

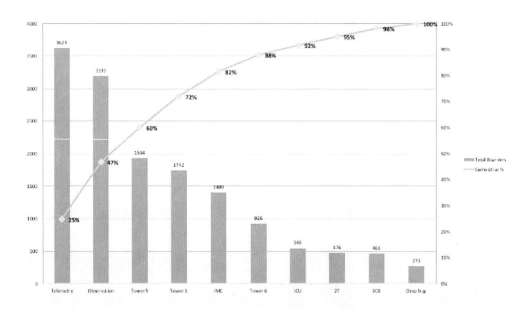

2.10.1 PARETO ANALYSIS — EXAMPLE (BUSINESS)

Let us consider an example of a manufacturing company experiencing product defects.

Here is a simplified breakdown of a Pareto Analysis:

Factors (Causes of defects):
    1. Equipment malfunction
    2. Human error
    3. Material defects
    4. Process variability
    5. Supplier issues
    6. Environmental conditions

Step-by-step guide on how to perform a Pareto Analysis:

- *Data collection*—Collect data on the occurrence or frequency of defects associated with each factor.

- *Quantify impact* and assign a numerical value or count to each factor based on the defects' occurrence or influence.

- *Ranking*—Rank the factors in descending order based on their impact upon the occurrence of the defects.

- *Calculate cumulative impact*—Calculate the cumulative impact for each factor by summing up the effects of all factors above it.

- *Plot Pareto chart*—Create a Pareto chart with factors on the horizontal axis and frequency or impact on the vertical axis. Include a superimposed line graph showing the cumulative effects.

- *Analyze the Chart*—Analyze the Pareto chart to identify the "vital few factors" contributing to most defects. Focus on addressing these critical factors to reduce defects effectively. The Pareto chart will visually represent the factors contributing to the defects, helping the company prioritize its efforts and resources by addressing the "vital few factors" that significantly impact defect occurrence.

2.10.2 PARETO ANALYSIS — EXAMPLE (MEDICAL)

Another example, this real-world one in the healthcare arena, was performed at a major medical center to discern the impact of short-term "Boarders" on resources. A Boarder is a patient designated for admission, usually through the Emergency Department, who does not yet have an available (inpatient) bed. Boarder (holding) status is known to be associated with delayed inpatient care and sub-optimal outcomes. The patient may be placed in a hallway, awaiting an inpatient bed on the floor. The Joint Commission (JC) has identified the phenomenon as a patient safety risk. Therefore, it is wasteful, a genuine patient safety concern, resource intensive, and impacts workflow. In this actual example, Telemetry (cardiac observation with monitoring) comprised a disproportionate 25 percent (3623) of the cumulative total of 14,459 patients during this study period, while Oncology, at the other extreme, had the fewest, with only 273 "Boarders." The graphic presentation of the data, including the other key inpatient units (Observation; Tower 5; Tower 1; Intermediate Care; Tower 6; Intensive Care Unit; 2T; and 3CB), and their relative as well as absolute relationships to one another would not have been disclosed without the use of this powerful analytical tool and graphic output display.

2.11 ANALYTIC HIERARCHY PROCESS (AHP)

AHP is a multi-criteria Decision-Making process that helps prioritize solutions based on a hierarchy of criteria and their relative importance. By pairwise comparisons and assignment of numerical values to the criteria, one can calculate weighted scores for each solution and rank order them accordingly.

Step-by-step guide on how to perform the Analytic Hierarchy Process:
Define the Decision Hierarchy: Identify the proposed solution to a problem and break it down into a hierarchical structure.

The hierarchy consists of the following:
    1. Main objective
    2. Criteria
    3. Sub-criteria
    4. Alternatives

Ensure that the hierarchy is well-structured and represents the Problem Analysis and Decision-Making model:

- *Determine the criteria*: Identify the relevant criteria for evaluating the alternatives. These criteria should be mutually exclusive and collectively exhaustive, covering all aspects of the problem. For example, if you are considering a purchase from a selected array of automobile models, criteria could include cost, safety, design, fuel efficiency, reliability, depreciation, and resale value.

- *Establish a scale*: Establish a numerical scale for pairwise comparisons between criteria or alternatives. The scale can range from one to nine, where one indicates equal importance or preference and nine indicates extreme importance or priority. Intermediate values represent intermediate importance or preference.

- *Perform pairwise comparisons*: Compare each criterion to every other criterion in *relative* importance. Use the established scale to assign values indicating the preference of one criterion over another. Repeat this process to compare alternatives against each criterion. Comparisons should be made based on your judgment or the opinions of relevant experts in the field.

- *Create a comparison matrix*: Create a matrix that captures the pairwise comparison values. Each row of the matrix represents a criterion or alternative, and the values reflect the importance or preference relative to other criteria or alternatives. Ensure that the matrix is consistent by checking for logical inconsistencies or contradictions.

- *Calculate weights and priorities*: Calculate the weights and priorities for each criterion and alternative using mathematical calculations. The AHP algorithm involves eigenvector calculations to derive the weights from the comparison matrix. Of note, weights represent the relative importance or priority of each criterion or alternative. By definition, in the eigenvector calculations, every vector (list of numbers) has a direction when plotted on an XY Chart. Eigenvectors represent those vectors when a linear transformation (such as multiplying it by … scalar) is performed on them. Their vector direction does not change.

- *Check for consistency*: Check the consistency of the pairwise comparisons by calculating the consistency ratio. The consistency ratio assesses the degree to which the pairwise comparisons are logical and consistent, which should be less than or equal to 0.1 as a value. If the consistency ratio exceeds a predefined threshold (e.g., 0.1), you may need to revisit and revise the pairwise comparisons.

- *Perform Sensitivity analysis*: Conduct Sensitivity analysis to assess the impact of varying the pairwise comparison values. Evaluate how changes in the judgments affect the final priority rankings. This analysis helps in understanding the robustness of the results and identifying critical comparisons that significantly influence the rankings.

2.11.1 ANALYTIC HIERARCHY PROCESS (AHP) — EXAMPLE 1

Let us consider an example of selecting a vacation destination based on the criteria of cost, weather, and cultural attractions.

A simplified breakdown of the AHP:
Objective: Select the Best Vacation Destination

Criteria:
1. Cost

2. Weather

3. Cultural Attractions

Alternatives:
- Destination A

- Destination B

- Destination C

Pairwise Comparisons:
- Cost vs. Weather: Cost is assigned a value of 5 (moderate importance) compared to Weather.

- Cost vs. Cultural Attractions: Cost is assigned a value of 3 (slightly less importance) compared to Cultural attractions.

- Weather vs. Cultural Attractions: Weather is assigned a value of 7 (high importance) compared to Cultural attractions.

Comparison Matrix (Criteria):
| Cost | Weather | Cultural Attractions |
Cost | 1 | 5 | 3 |
Weather | 1/5 | 1 | 7 |
Cultural Attractions | 1/3 | 1/7 | 1 |

Calculate Weights and Priorities:
Calculate the weights and priorities using mathematical calculations based on the comparison matrix. This involves deriving the priority eigenvectors and calculating the consistency ratio.

Perform Sensitivity Analysis:
Conduct Sensitivity Analysis by varying the pairwise comparison values. Assess how changes in the judgments impact the priority rankings and evaluate the consistency of the results.

In the above example, the AHP analysis will provide priority rankings for the vacation destinations based on the criteria of Cost, Weather, and Cultural attractions.

The priorities derived from the AHP can guide the Decision-Making process by indicating the most suitable vacation destination based on the relative importance of the criteria.

2.11.2 ANALYTIC HIERARCHY PROCESS (AHP) — EXAMPLE 2 (HYPOTHETICAL)

Let us consider a hypothetical example of a pairwise type comparison study and prioritization, using a tabular output representation of the analysis based on Interview criteria for three individuals seeking employment: Candidates A, B, and C. Each individual is compared against themselves and the other two candidates.

A simplified hypothetical tabular breakdown of an AHP pairwise comparison follows:

	A	B	C	Priority Candidacy Rank	
Interview Candidates					
A	1	0.25	4	0.217	2
B	4	1	9	0.717	1
C	0.25	0.111	1	0.066	3

The Sum of Priorities = 1.00

Inconsistencies = 0.035

In Summary: Candidates in descending Rank Order regarding suitability for Employment are:

B, then A, followed last, by Candidate C (least suitable).

2.12 STATISTICAL MODELING

Statistical modeling utilizes Statistical techniques, such as Linear Regression analysis or predictive modeling, to assess the relationships between Variables and predict the outcomes of each proposed solution. These models can provide insights into each proposed solution's potential effectiveness or impact, aiding prioritization.

More details regarding Statistics and Linear Regression are found and expanded upon in Chapter Three.

Statistical modeling involves Statistical techniques to analyze data, identify patterns or relationships, and make predictions or inferences.

Step-by-step guide on how to perform basic Statistical modeling—Example:

- *Define the research question*: Clearly define the research question or objective you want to address through Statistical modeling. Formulate a specific and testable Hypothesis that you aim to investigate, then accept or reject.

- *Gather and prepare data:* Collect relevant data appropriate for the research question. Scrub and preprocess the data by reconciling missing values, outliers, and formatting issues. Ensure the sample data is representative and reliable for the analysis.

- *Choose the Statistical technique:* Select the appropriate Statistical technique based on the nature of the data and the research question. Standard Statistical modeling techniques include but are not limited to Linear Regression analysis, time series analysis, factor analysis, clustering, and Hypothesis testing.

- *Model selection and specification:* Determine the specific model that best fits your research question and data characteristics. Consider factors such as the type of Variables, distributional assumptions, and potential interactions or nonlinear (non-parametric) relationships.

- *Fit the model:* Estimate the parameters of the selected Statistical model using the available data. This involves using Statistical and predictive software or programming languages to perform the necessary calculations. Fit the model to the data and obtain the parameter estimates.

- *Assess model fit:* Evaluate the model's goodness-of-fit to assess how well it captures the patterns or relationships in the data. Standard techniques for determining model fit include evaluating residuals, calculating measures of fit (e.g., *R-squared* Coefficient of Determination (R^2) and Pearson Correlation Coefficient (r) using Linear Regression models), or conducting Statistical tests.

- *Interpret model results:* Interpret the estimated parameters and Statistical significance (p-value) of the Variables or predictors. Assess the magnitude, direction, and Statistical significance of the relationships between Variables. Consider the practical, real-world implications of the findings concerning the research question.

- *Validate and test the model*: Validate the Statistical model on independent or out-of-sample data. Assess whether the model's performance holds up when applied to new data. Cross-validation techniques or holdout samples can be used for validation.

- *Draw conclusions and make inferences*: Draw conclusions and inferences based on the Statistical modeling results regarding the research question or objective. Consider the limitations, assumptions, and potential implications of the findings. Discuss the practical implications or recommendations based on the results.

- *Critique the Statistical analysis*: Describe exceptions, limits, Confounding Factors, and related.

2.12.1 STATISTICAL MODELING – FORMULATING A RESEARCH QUESTION (BUSINESS)

Statistical Modeling Example (Business) with key questions to ask:

- *Research Question*: Does (Advertising) expenditure significantly impact sales revenue?

- *Data collection*: Gather data on advertising expenditure (independent X Variable) and sales revenue (dependent Y Variable) for a set of products or time periods. Ensure that the data is accurate, complete, and covers a sufficient time range.

- *Statistical technique*: In this case, Linear Regression analysis is utilized to model the relationship between advertising expenditure and sales revenue. It allows one to quantify the relationship between the two Variables and assess the Statistical significance (p-value).

- *Model selection*: Specify a Linear Regression model where sales revenue is the dependent (Y-axis, "The Effect") Variable, and advertising expenditure is the independent (X-axis, The Cause") Variable.

- Consider potential additional Variables or predictors, if applicable.

- *Fit the model*: Use Linear Regression analysis to estimate the model parameters using the available data (The slope or steepness of the line (m) and Y-intercept are determined, where: $Y = mX + b$ (algebraic straight-line equation, where $b = Y$ when $x = 0$).

Fit the model to the data and obtain the estimates.

- Assess model fit: Evaluate the model "goodness-of-fit" of the Linear Regression model using measures such as R-squared (Coefficient of Determination or residual analysis. Assess whether the model adequately captures the relationship between advertising expenditure and sales revenue.

- *Interpret model results:* Interpret the estimated coefficients (slope (m) and Y-intercept) and their Statistical significance p-value). Assess the magnitude and direction of the relationship between advertising expenditure and sales revenue.

- *Validate and test the model*: Validate the Linear Regression model by evaluating it on new data or holdout samples. Assess if the model's performance remains consistent and reliable when applied to independent data.

- *Draw conclusions*: Based on the Statistical modeling results, draw conclusions regarding the impact of advertising expenditure on sales revenue. Discuss the practical implications of the findings and any recommendations for future advertising strategies and spending.

- *Critique the Statistical analysis*: Describe exceptions, limits, Confounding Factors, and related.

In this example, Statistical modeling using Linear Regression analysis would help quantify the relationship between advertising expenditure and sales revenue, allowing for quantifiable, evidence-based Decision-Making in a marketing–advertising Business strategy.

2.13 BAYESIAN ANALYSIS

Bayesian Statistics is a branch of Statistics that provides a framework for updating and revising beliefs or probabilities about uncertain events or hypotheses based on new evidence or data. *After considering further information, it combines prior knowledge or beliefs with observed data to obtain posterior probabilities, representing the updated beliefs.* Statistical inference incorporates prior knowledge (prior probability) or beliefs into the analysis. A framework for probabilistic reasoning and Decision-Making under uncertain conditions is the premise and rationale for its use. Bayesian Statistics finds applications in diverse areas such as Machine Learning, Artificial Intelligence (AI), medical diagnostics, and risk analysis. Bayesian Statistics is named after the Reverend Thomas Bayes, an eighteenth-century mathematician who developed the foundational principles of this analytical approach. The critical concept in Bayesian Statistics is the namesake Bayes' theorem, which mathematically describes how to update prior probabilities based on new evidence.

The theorem is stated as follows:

$P(A|B) = (P(B|A) * P(A)) / P(B)$

In this equation, P(A) and P(B) are the prior probabilities of events A and B, respectively. P(A|B) is the posterior probability of event A, given that event B has occurred, and P(B|A) is the probability of observing event B, given that event A has occurred. Bayes' theorem allows for calculating the posterior probability by combining the prior probability with the likelihood of the observed data.

Bayesian Analysis (using a "Two by Two Table") exemplifies the relationship between Type-I (False Positive (FP)) as well as Type-II (False Negative (FN)) Error types and the calculations to Reject or not to Reject the "Null" Hypothesis.

2.13.1 BAYESIAN ANALYSIS — "NULL" HYPOTHESIS (DEFINITION)

The Hypothesis is that there is <u>no</u> significant difference between the specified samples or populations, any observed difference being due to sampling, chance alone, or experimental error. The term itself relates to the finding of no relationship; therefore, the usage of the "Null" preceding the word Hypothesis. Succinctly, the "Null" Hypothesis is used to assess the credibility of a Hypothesis by interrogating sample data. It is deemed "true" until proven "wrong" at a specified Statistical probability value (p-value) based on the experimental data.

The "Null" Hypothesis ("any difference or significance observed is due to merely chance") … On the basis that it is always assumed, by Statistical convention, that the Hypothesis posited is wrong and the "Null Hypothesis" (that the observed phenomena simply occurred by chance or coincidence) …Statistical analysis will determine whether to reject the "Null" Hypothesis and accept the Alternative (original, speculated) Hypothesis that there is a significant difference between the groups or samples tested.

2.13.2 BAYESIAN ANALYSIS —TYPE-II
(FN) AND TYPE-I (FP) ERRORS

Type-II (FN) and Type-I (FP) Errors and the relationship to incorrectly reject-ing (the former) or incorrectly not rejecting (the latter) the "Null" Hypothesis:

When an observer makes a Type-I (False Positive, FP) error in evaluating a sample against its parent population, they mistakenly think that a Statistical difference exists when, in truth, there is no Statistical difference (or, to put it another way, the "Null" Hypothesis should not be rejected but was mistakenly rejected). In Medicine, for instance, imagine that a pregnancy test has produced a "positive" result (indicating that the woman taking the pregnancy test is pregnant). If the woman is not pregnant, then we conclude the test produced a "false positive" result. In distinction, when an observer makes a Type-II (False Negative, FN) error, the error of failing to reject the "Null" Hypothesis occurs (when the Alternative Hypothesis is the actual state of nature). In the Type-II (FN) error or scenario, a pregnancy test report would be reported as "negative" when the woman is, in fact, pregnant. In either case, a wrong decision or error in judgment occurs, with deleterious healthcare consequences.

Chart representation of Bayesian ("two by two table") analysis of Type I and Type II Error type

	Not Reject Null Hypothesis	Reject Null Hypothesis
Null Hypothesis is true	(TP)	Incorrectly reject the null = Type I Error (FP)
Alternative Hypothesis is true	Incorrectly not reject the null = Type II Error (FN)	(TN)

2.13.3 BAYESIAN ANALYSIS — FALSE NEGATIVE (FN) AND FALSE POSITIVE (FP) RATE, AND STATISTICAL POWER

False Negative (Type-II error) and False Positive (Type-I error) rates and their relationship to Sensitivity, Specificity, and Power of a Statistical test:

- False positive rate (α) = FP / (FP + TN) = 18 / (18 + 182) = 9% = 1 − specificity
- False negative rate (β) = FN / (TP + FN) = 1 / (2 + 1) = 33% = 1 − sensitivity

- Power = sensitivity = 1 − β (False negative rate)

2.13.4 BAYESIAN ANALYSIS — EXAMPLES
(A. IN EVERYDAY LIFE, B. IN MEDICINE, AND C. IN BUSINESS)

a. *In Everyday Life*: Suppose you want to determine the probability of rain tomorrow. Based on historical data, your prior belief is that the chance of rain on any given day is 20 percent. However, you hear a weather forecast that states there is a 70 percent chance of rain (parenthetically, this happens a lot in Southwest Florida). Using Bayesian Statistics, you can update your belief by combining the prior probability with the new evidence. Applying Bayes' theorem, you can calculate the revised posterior probability of rain tomorrow based on the recent weather forecast.

b. *In Medicine*: Bayesian Statistics are crucial in medical diagnosis and treatment decisions. For instance, consider a diagnostic test for a disease wherein the prior probability of an individual having the disease could be estimated based on the prevalence of the disease in the general population. As the test results become available, Bayesian analysis allows the incorporation of the test's sensitivity and specificity to update the probability of disease presence, which helps to inform treatment decisions.

A Bayesian Analysis calculation was performed on Fecal Occult Blood (FOB) findings used in 203 patients to look for Bowel Cancer. Positive Predictive Value (PPV) and Negative Predictive Value (NPV), as well as Sensitivity and Specificity of testing, were additionally determined for this sample:

The Fecal Occult Blood (FOB) screening test used in 203 people to look for bowel cancer yielded the following after Bayesian analysis:

		Patients with Bowel Cancer (as confirmed on endoscopy, GOLD Method)		
		Positive Test	Negative Test	
	Positive (disease present)	TP = 2	FP = 18 [TYPE I error]	···→ Positive predictive value = TP / (TP + FP) = 2 / (2 + 18) = 2 / 20 = 10%
FOB test	**Negative** (Disease absent)	FN = 1 [TYPE II error]	TN = 182	·· Negative predictive value = TN / (FN + TN) = 182 / (1 + 182) = 182 / 183 ≈ 99.5%
		↓ Sensitivity = TP / (TP + FN) = 2 / (2 + 1) = 2 / 3 ≈ 66.67%	↓ Specificity = TN / (FP + TN) = 182 / (18 + 182) = 182 / 200 = 91%	

Calculations:

PPV = TP/(TP+FP) = 2/ (2+18) = 10%
NPV = TN/(FN+TN) = 182/ (1+182) = 99.5%

Sensitivity = TP/(TP+FN) =2/ (2+1) =66.67%
Specificity = TN/(FP+TN) = 182/ (18+182) = 182/200 = 91%

The patients with Bowel Cancer (as confirmed by endoscopy) were deemed the "Gold" standard or method.

In this elucidatory example, with large numbers of False Positives (FP) but few True Positives (TP), a positive FOB screen test result is, by itself, poor at confirming suspect bowel Cancer (Positive Predictive Value

(PPV) = 10%) and further investigations must be undertaken, especially is suspicion is high, if there is a familial history of Bowel Cancer or other reason that would cause an increased prevalence or likelihood of disease. Notwithstanding, the FOB test will pick up 66.67% of all Bowel Cancers (the test's sensitivity). As a screening test, a negative test result is superior and very good at reassuring that a patient *does not* have Cancer (Negative Predictive Value NPV) = 99.5%), and, at this initial screening, correctly identifies 91 percent of those who *do not* have Bowel Cancer (the Specificity of the test, or "Negativity in Health").

c. *In Business:* Bayesian Statistics can be applied in various Business contexts, such as market research and Decision-Making. For example, a company launching a new product may have prior beliefs about product marketability and consumer acceptance. By collecting customer feedback and sales data, Bayesian Statistical methods can update the company's views about the product's success, estimate future demand, and make informed decisions concerning anticipated production levels, pricing, and future marketing strategies.

2.14 MACHINE LEARNING (ML)

Machine Learning (ML) uses algorithms and Statistical modeling that enable computational systems to analyze data and provide probability regarding future performance. ML subtends a broad, multidisciplinary field that utilizes concepts from Statistics, computer science, computer digital vision, mathematics, and natural language processing (NLP) to enable ML systems to learn from and make predictions or decisions based on large data sets. The utility of Machine Learning relates to an ability to extract meaningful patterns, trends, interrelationships, and forecasts from vast and complex datasets that would be challenging for humans to analyze manually. ML algorithms can identify obscure, hidden relationships and insights within data, categorize and classify objects, make Decision-Making recommendations, and perform various other tasks. ML has found applications in many fields beyond those just mentioned, including finance, healthcare, marketing, and autonomous vehicle systems. One practical example of Machine Learning is in healthcare, specifically in the early detection of diseases, where researchers' algorithms analyze patient medical records data, Pathology and Cyto-Pathology images, and genomic information. ML models have been trained to identify pre-neo-plastic (pre-Cancer) disease patterns. Earlier interventions and better patient care can result.

One question often asked—can Machine Learning replace the Delphi technique as applied to Problem Analysis in Business?

Machine Learning can complement and enhance the use of the Delphi technique in Problem Analysis, but it is unlikely to replace it entirely in the near short term. Recall that the Delphi technique is a structured, organized method for gathering opinions and insights from a panel of domain experts or stakeholders to reach a consensus of opinions to make informed decisions. It involves multiple rounds of iterative feedback and anonymous input. Machine Learning, on the other hand, is a data-driven approach that involves training algorithms on exceptionally large datasets to find patterns, make predictions, or automate Decision-Making. It relies on historical data to learn and generalize from. While Machine Learning can provide valuable insights and help analyze large volumes of data, it has limitations regarding subjective or qualitative aspects that the Delphi technique captures and analyzes instead.

Additional points to ponder regarding ML versus the Delphi technique:

- *Expert judgment and subjectivity*: The Delphi technique relies on participants' collective wisdom and expertise. It captures diverse perspectives, insights, and subjective opinions that may not be easily represented in structured data. Machine Learning algorithms, on the other hand, typically rely on quantifiable, very large, and measurable data sets.

- *Contextual understanding*: The Delphi technique allows for a contextual understanding of the problem by capturing nuances, complexities, and domain-specific knowledge. Machine Learning models, in contrast, while powerful in analyzing patterns, may lack the intuitive, human deliberative ability to grasp the broader context or make sense of complex, unstructured, and primarily abstract information.

- *Iterative feedback loops*: The Delphi technique leads to a singular consensus of opinions used for Decision-Making. The Delphi technique employs iterative feedback loops to refine and converge on a consensus of opinions, resulting in Decision-Making. Discussions, Arguments, and the exchange of ideas are encouraged. Machine Learning models, on the other hand, typically operate in a more static, sterile, programmed manner. Once trained, they function without the same capacity for dynamic, back-and-forth consensus building that the Delphi technique is known for. The latter offers transparency, as participants' opinions and reasoning can be understood, dissected, scrutinized, and critiqued.

- *Interpretation and miscellaneous concerns:* Machine Learning, mainly using complex deep learning models, can have challenging outputs. They need more transparency, making understanding the reasoning behind their predictions or decisions easier. Only a software engineer programs the Machine Learning source code and understands the Logic sets employed.

Machine Learning techniques, instead, can be used alongside the Delphi technique to augment or complement analysis. Machine Learning models can help process and analyze copious amounts of data, identify patterns and trends, or generate insights that inform the discussions within the Delphi technique. The complementary combination of human domain expertise and judgment, coupled with the power of Machine Learning, can be integrated to inform problem-solving and Decision-Making.

2.15 ARTIFICIAL INTELLIGENCE (AI)

Artificial Intelligence (AI): AI focuses on creating intelligent systems that can autonomously perceive, "reason," and act upon data to achieve specific goals. It involves designing algorithms, employing Neural Networks, simulation models, and architectures that enable machines to exhibit "intelligent behavior." AI uses various methods and techniques, including Machine Learning, Natural Language Processing (NLP), computer digital vision, robotics, expert systems, and more. These methods emulating human cognition are used to develop models and algorithms to learn from data, "reason," and make predictive decisions. AI has numerous applications across numerous fields, including but not limited to healthcare, finance, manufacturing, transportation, and customer service. It can be used for tasks such as speech recognition, digital image topology and classification, autonomous automated vehicles, recommendation systems (product suggestions to users based on their internet browsing history, preferences, and behavior), and fraud detection.

As mentioned above, one sub-field of AI is Natural Language Processing (NLP), which embraces enabling computational systems to interact with and understand human language. NLP employs various techniques, including Machine Learning and Neural Networks, to parse, analyze, and generate text or speech through the application of algorithms such as Recurrent Neural Networks (RNNs) that require sequential data to be processed in order and Transformers designed to handle sequential data, such as Natural Language, for translation and text summarization operating without the need for sequential data. Deep learning architectures, such as the former

Recurrent Neural Networks (RNNs) and the latter Transformer models like BERT (Bidirectional Encoder Representations from Transformers), have revolutionized language understanding and generation tasks. These models excel at tasks like machine translation, text summarization, and question answering by leveraging large-scale pre-training on extensive textual corpora. NLP systems can capture contextual nuances, syntactic structures, and semantic meaning in written or spoken language. This enables various applications, from language translation and sentiment analysis to chatbots and speech recognition systems.

The amalgamation of Neural Networks and NLP, in turn, has led to extraordinary advancements. Even so, challenges must be addressed with both Neural Networks and NLP. Neural Networks require substantial computational resources for training and deployment, and their seemingly "black box" nature can limit interpretability. NLP systems often face difficulties understanding context, humor, sarcasm, and double entendre. Ethical concerns also arise due to Biases in language data and the potential misuse of AI-generated content.

In an earlier discussion above describing the complementary nature of Machine Learning and the Delphi technique, one would additionally have to include AI, a triumvirate, notwithstanding that AI (as well as ML), compared to iterative analysis, are distinct concepts, they can be related and act synergistically in specific contexts. AI focuses on creating intelligent systems that can exhibit human-like Intelligence. Iterative analysis, in contrast, is a broader approach used to improve understanding, refine insights, and solve problems through repetitive cycles of analysis and refinement, especially using the Delphi technique. Lastly, AI is the simulation of human Intelligence in machines programmed to perform tasks and make decisions. It aims to develop systems that mimic or replicate human cognitive abilities, such as learning, problem-solving, and pattern recognition.

An advancement in technology or a threat?

My prediction, looking at the long term, is that Machine Learning and Artificial Intelligence (AI) are poised to transform the landscape of Problem Analysis and Decision-Making, regretfully becoming a means to what will result, at the end, of subverting human intervention, imagination, autonomy, and interaction.

Various problem-solving frameworks and methodologies have been examined primarily in this Chapter, demonstrating their practical utility in different contexts, particularly everyday Life, Business, and Medicine. The processes are intertwined, yielding to the recognition of problems, their analysis, and the exploration of various solutions. Maximizing the utility of these processes empowers individuals, Organizations and Enterprises to arrive at informed, effective decisions, contributing to achieving their goals and objectives. However, a "one-size-fits-all" approach or paradigm does not exist, nor should it!

CHAPTER 3

"NO MATTER WHAT ANYONE SAYS, IT IS SAFE TO STATE THAT THERE IS GOOD EVIDENCE IN THE LITERATURE, SOMETIMES PEER-REVIEWED AND SUPPORTED BY STATISTICS, TO SUPPORT WHATEVER"

3.1 "LIES, DAMNED LIES, AND STATISTICS"

The phrase *"Lies, Damned Lies, and Statistics"* is often attributed to British Prime Minister Benjamin Disraeli (1804-1881). Yet, an earlier known use of a similar phrase can be traced back to the British politician Charles Wentworth Dilke (1789-1864) in the late nineteenth century. Dilke was reported to have said there are three kinds of lies – "Lies, Damned Lies, and Statistics." However, this attribution is not universally accepted, and the exact wording may have changed over time. In his 1907 autobiography, Mark Twain (1835-1910), an American writer, humorist, and journalist, attributed this phrase to Disraeli.

Relevant is that the above Aphorism conveys a skeptical view of the more universally accepted, compelling majority opinion of the veracity of Statistics. It suggests that Statistics can be manipulated or misrepresented to support any Argument or position, leading to deceptive or misleading conclusions. This is a reminder that Statistics can easily distort the truth and mislead if used improperly or selectively. Regardless of the Aphorism's precise origin, the phrase has become popular in usage and widely used to express skepticism toward the trustworthiness of Statistical information and the potential for data manipulation.

3.2 GENERATING AND TESTING A HYPOTHESIS

How do you generate and test a Hypothesis?
Generating and testing a Hypothesis is fundamental to the scientific method and problem-solving process.

There are *key steps involved in generating and testing a Hypothesis:*

- *Identify the problem:* Clearly define the problem or question you want to investigate. Understand the context, background information, and relevant factors related to the problem.

- *Formulate a research question:* Based on the problem, develop a research question that states what you want to explore or investigate. The research question should be specific, limited, clear, and focused. As well as measurable and quantitative.

- *Generate a Hypothesis:* Formulate a Hypothesis that provides a potential explanation or prediction for the research question. A Hypothesis is a statement that proposes a relationship between Factors and Variables or suggests an outcome. It should be testable and based on existing knowledge or observations.

- *Define Factors and Variables:* Identify the Factors and Variables involved in your Hypothesis. Variables are the indispensable factors that you believe may significantly influence the outcome or relationship(s) stated in the Hypothesis. Distinguish between independent Variables (the X-axis, the ones you manipulate, otherwise known as "The Cause") and the dependent Variables (the Y-axis, the ones you measure or observe, otherwise known as "The Effect").

- *Design an experiment or study:* Determine your experiment's method and case study design. Consider the appropriate data collection techniques, eliminate Bias, and determine the proper sample size, control groups, randomization, and other factors necessary to test your Hypothesis effectively. Ensure that your case study design allows you to measure and analyze the Variables involved.

- *Collect data:* Implement your experiment or study to collect relevant data. Follow your case study design protocol and procedures, avoid Biases, and collect data, measurements, observations, or responses according to your case study design plan.

- *Analyze data:* Analyze the collected data using appropriate Statistical or analytical methods. Use a graphic output to discover and reveal patterns, relationships, interrelationships, or trends that provide insights into the investigated Variables and their potential effects.

- *Draw conclusions:* Based on the data analysis, evaluate whether the evidence supports or rejects your primary Hypothesis. Consider the importance of the results, Statistical and Practical significance, and any limitations or Alternative Hypothesis (explanation).

- *Communicate findings:* Summarize and communicate the findings of your Hypothesis testing. Present the results, Statistical analysis, Statistical significance (p-value), practical (real-world) significance, and the implications of the outcomes. Be transparent about the limitations, constraints of the study, and potential areas for further research.

- *Iterate and refine:* If your Hypothesis is rejected or inconclusive, revise and refine the initial Hypothesis based on the preliminary findings. Consider redefining or modifying the Variables to investigate, changing the experimental case study design, or research question to investigate the problem further.

It is important to note that testing a Hypothesis is an iterative process, and multiple iterations may be required to arrive at robust and conclusive results that withstand logical, intellectual scrutiny. Throughout the process, maintain objectivity and integrity, adhere to ethical guidelines, and critically evaluate the validity and reliability of your data, methods, collection method, and Statistical analysis.

3.3 EVALUATING AS WELL AS CRITIQUING QUANTITATIVE RESEARCH AND EXPERIMENTAL DATA

Regardless of the quantitative research design, Statistical or experimental modeling, research results, and final analysis, one must systematically appraise the case study design. The rigors of the sample size chosen, attributes and the population from which it was derived, identification of Factors and Variables, avoidance of Bias, the definition of Statistical and practical significance, the meaning of the "Null" and Alternative Hypotheses, Confounding Factors, validation, and more must be addressed. Coughlin and his colleagues (2007) have provided an excellent, integrated, holistic step-by-step methodical guide to assessing, as well as critiquing quantitative research:

Table 1. Research questions - guidelines for critiquing a quantitative research study

Elements influencing the believability of the research

Elements	Questions
Writing style	Is the report well written – concise, grammatically correct, avoid the use of jargon? Is it well laid out and organized?
Author	Do the researcher(s') qualifications/position indicate a degree of knowledge in this particular field?
Report title	Is the title clear, accurate and unambiguous?
Abstract	Does the abstract offer a clear overview of the study including the research problem, sample, methodology, finding and recommendations?

Elements influencing the robustness of the research

Elements	Questions
Purpose/research Problem	Is the purpose of the study/research problem clearly identified?
Logical consistency	Does the research report follow the steps of the research process in a logical manner? Do these steps naturally flow and are the links clear?
Literature review	Is the review logically organized? Does it offer a balanced critical analysis of the literature? Is the majority of the literature of recent origin? Is it mainly from primary sources and of an empirical nature?
Theoretical framework	Has a conceptual or theoretical framework been identified? Is the framework adequately described? Is the framework appropriate?
Aims/objectives/ research question/ hypotheses	Have aims and objectives, a research question or hypothesis been identified? If so are they clearly stated? Do they reflect the information presented in the literature review?
Sample	Has the target population been clearly identified? How were the sample selected? Was it a probability or non-probability sample? Is it of adequate size? Are the inclusion/exclusion criteria clearly identified?
Ethical considerations	Were the participants fully informed about the nature of the research? Was the autonomy/ confidentiality of the participants guaranteed? Were the participants protected from harm? Was ethical permission granted for the study?
Operational definitions	Are all the terms, theories and concepts mentioned in the study clearly defined?
Methodology	Is the research design clearly identified? Has the data gathering instrument been described? Is the instrument appropriate? How was it developed? Were reliability and validity testing undertaken and the results discussed? Was a pilot study undertaken?
Data Analysis / results	What type of data and statistical analysis was undertaken? Was it appropriate? How many of the sample participated? Significance of the findings?
Discussion	Are the findings linked back to the literature review? If a hypothesis was identified was it supported? Were the strengths and limitations of the study including generalizability discussed? Was a recommendation for further research made?
References	Were all the books, journals and other media alluded to in the study accurately referenced?

3.4 SCATTERPLOTS AND ANSCOMBE'S QUARTET

An example of how *Mean, Standard deviation, Pearson Correlation Coefficient (r), Linear Regression, and Slope can be the same. However, the distribution of Variables is very different and is visualized in Anscombe's Scatterplot Quartet.*

Anscombe's quartet shows the caution one must exercise in analyzing Statistical data!

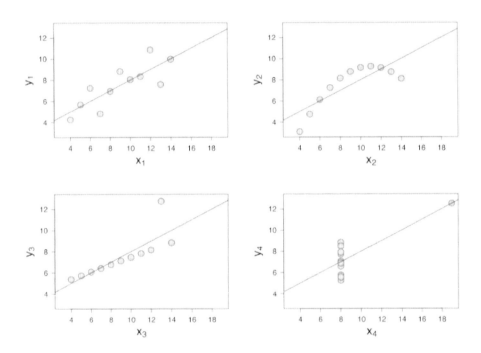

3.5 STATISTICS CAN BE MISLEADING FOR MULTIPLE REASONS – THE SPECIAL PROBLEM OF SELECTION BIAS

Various types of Bias exist, in particular, Selection Bias:

Selection Bias (or effect) is a type of Bias that occurs when the selection process for participants or data points in a study is not random or representative of the target population. It can distort the findings and conclusions of an investigation, leading to inaccurate or misleading results. Statistics are often derived from a sample rather than an entire population. If the sample is not representative of the population or suffers from selection Bias, the resulting Statistics may not accurately reflect the actual characteristics of the population. Biased samples can lead to misleading conclusions and generalizations.

Selection Bias is the rubric for several subordinate Biases:

- *Sampling Bias*: A type of Selection Bias that involves the same fundamentals, occurring when a sample is selected, influenced by selection Bias.

- *Non-random sampling*: If participants or data points are not selected using a random sampling method, Bias can be introduced. For example, using convenience sampling, where participants are selected based on their accessibility or convenience, may lead to a Biased sample that does not accurately represent the entire population of interest.

- *Self-selection Bias*: When individuals have the choice to participate in a study voluntarily, it can lead to self-selection Bias. Those who participate may differ systematically from those who decline, resulting in a non-representative sample. This Bias is commonly seen in surveys or studies that rely on self-reporting.

- *Survivorship Bias:* Survivorship Bias occurs when the analysis or conclusions are based only on the data of those individuals or entities that have "survived" or made it through a specific process. By excluding data from those who were unsuccessful or dropped out, the resulting sample may not accurately represent the entire population, leading to Biased conclusions.

- *Pre-screening Bias*: Pre-screening or pre-selection of participants based on specific characteristics or criteria can introduce Bias. If the pre-screening criteria are related to the studied outcomes, it can distort the results by selectively including or excluding particular individuals.

- *Berkson's Bias:* Berkson's Bias can occur when the study participants are selected based on a specific characteristic or condition related to the exposure and the outcome being investigated. This can create an artificial association or correlation that may not exist in the general population from which the sample was derived.

- *Publication Bias*: Publication Bias occurs when studies with Statistically significant or positive results are more likely to be published than those with nonsignificant or negative results. This can lead to distortion and overrepresentation of specific Statistical findings and skew the overall body of published literature.

To minimize selection Bias, researchers should aim for random sampling methods and strive to ensure that the sample truly represents the target population. Transparent reporting of the sampling methods and inclusion and exclusion criteria is crucial for assessing potential Biases. Awareness of selection Bias and careful study design are essential to obtaining valid, trustworthy, and reliable Statistical results.

3-5.1 SMALL SAMPLE SIZE INFLUENCES RESEARCH OUTCOMES

When the sample size is small, the Statistics may lack Statistical *Power*, leading to an imprecise estimate and increased chances of random variation affecting the results. Small samples can result in unstable or unreliable Statistics that may not represent the entire population.

3.5.1.1 THE CONCEPT OF BETA, THE "NULL" HYPOTHESIS, IMPLICATIONS OF SAMPLE SIZE, VARIANCE, AND TYPE-II (FN) ERROR

A. Beta:

Conceptually, in Statistics, *Beta refers to the probability of committing* a *Type-II (FN) error, which occurs when we fail to reject the "Null" Hypothesis that is actually false.*

B. Definition of the ***"Null" Hypothesis***:

The Hypothesis is that there is <u>no</u> significant Statistical difference (defined by the p-value) between the specified samples or populations, any observed difference being due to sampling, chance, coincidence alone, or experimental error. The term itself relates to the finding of no relationship; therefore, the usage of the term "Null" precedes the word Hypothesis. Succinctly, the "Null" Hypothesis is used to assess the credibility of a Hypothesis by interrogating sample data. It is deemed *"true" until proven wrong"* at a specified Statistical probability value (p-value) based on the Statistical analysis of the experimental data.

C. Sample size:

Implications of Sample Size:

- *Inverse relationship between Sample Size and Beta*: As the sample size increases, the probability of committing a Type-II (FN) error (Beta) decreases. With a larger sample, more information is available to estimate population parameters accurately, making it easier to detect differences or effects if they exist.

- *Statistical Power of the test*: Beta is directly related to the Power of a Statistical test. Power is the probability of *correctly* rejecting a "Null" Hypothesis when it is false (i.e., avoiding a Type-II (FN) error). A larger sample size increases the Power of a test, leading to a lower Beta and a better ability to detect actual effects or differences.

- *Effect size:* The magnitude of the effect being tested also affects Beta. Thus, more significant effects are generally easier to detect, even with smaller sample sizes. Conversely, smaller effects may require larger sample sizes to achieve sufficient Statistical Power and reduce the risk of a Type-II (FN) error. Effect sizes help determine the practical importance of a finding by providing a standardized measure of the observed effect relative to the variability in the data.

- *Variance (Variability)*: The degree of variability or dispersion around the mean in the data can influence Beta.

The Variance or Variability ($\sigma 2$ or s^2) is the average squared standard deviation of a random Variable as measured from its mean. By definition, the square root of the variance is its standard deviation (σ or s)

The variance measures a sample's variability (spread, scatter, or dispersion). Variability is most commonly measured with the following descriptive Statistics:

1. Range: the difference between the highest and lowest values.

2. Interquartile range: the middle half of a distribution.

3. Standard deviation: average distance from the mean.

4. Variance: average of squared distances from the mean (the mean symbol is x̄).

The symbol σ2 or s2 represents variance, so the variability of sample data is:

σ2 or s² = (Σ (x-x̄)²) / n-1

Note: dividing by n-1 corrects the Bias since we are using the sample mean (x̄) instead of the population mean (μ) to calculate the variance. Here, since Variance is dependent on the calculation of the sample means, we have one constraint: the degree of freedom (D.O.F.) is n-1. Therefore, if you divide by n-1, the standard deviation (s, or σ) becomes an unbiased estimate.

A greater degree of variability makes it more challenging to detect effects, increasing the probability of committing a Type-II (FN) error. Increasing *the sample size can help mitigate this concern by reducing the influence of random variation and providing a more accurate estimate of the population parameters.*

D. Type II (FN) Error:
The type-II error produces a False Negative (FN), also known as an error of omission. It is important to note that while increasing the sample size can reduce Beta and improve the Statistical Power of a test, there may be practical constraints (such as cost and time to perform the study) or diminishing returns associated with extremely large sample sizes, attempting to attain Statistical Power. Statisticians need to balance the desired level of Statistical Power, available resources, and feasibility when determining the appropriate sample size for a study.

3.5.1.2 CONFOUNDING FACTORS AND VARIABLES

Statistics may fail to account for Confounding Factors, which are Variables that influence both the independent Variable (the Variable being studied or manipulated, X-axis or the "Cause") and the dependent Variable (the outcome of interest, Y-axis, the "Effect:). Ignoring Confounding Factors can lead to false associations of causal, non-Statistical, or chance relationships. Failing to consider important Variables can distort the Statistical analysis and lead to incorrect conclusions. These Variables can introduce a systematic Bias into the analysis and make it difficult to determine the true relationship between the independent (X) and dependent (Y) Variables. Confounding Factors can lead to incorrect or misleading conclusions if they are not adequately accounted for in the Statistical case study design analysis.

There are a few key aspects of Confounding Factors and Variables in Statistics to be aware of:

- *Relationship with Independent (X) and Dependent (Y) Variables*: Confounding Factors are associated with both the independent (X-axis, the "Cause") and dependent (Y-axis, the "Effect") Variables. They can have an impact on the outcome, making it challenging to determine whether the observed relationship between the independent (X) Variable and the outcome (Y, "The Effect") Variable is genuinely causal or if it is influenced by the confounding Factor(s).

- *Distortion of associations*: Confounding Factors can distort the associations between the independent (X) and dependent (Y) Variables, leading to a spurious or false conclusion. They can create the appearance of a relationship when none actually exists or alternatively mask an actual relationship.

- *Intervening Variables*: Confounding Factors can function as intervening Variables that mediate or explain the relationship between the independent (X) and dependent (Y) Variables. They can obfuscate the actual mechanism of causality and make it difficult to establish a direct relationship between the Variables of interest.

- *Impact on Selection Bias*: Confounding Factors can be related to the selection process or characteristics of the study participants, leading to Biased samples. Suppose the Confounding Factors are unequally distributed across separate groups or conditions. In that case, it can create differences in the outcome that are not solely due to the independent (X-axis, the "Cause") Variable.

- *Statistical analysis*: Confounding Factors must be accounted for in Statistical analysis to obtain unbiased estimates of the relationship between the independent (X) and dependent (Y) Variables. This can be done through techniques such as stratification, matching, or Statistical modeling, such as multiple regression, Analysis of Variance (ANOVA), or Analysis of Covariance (ANCOVA). (As a footnote, ANCOVA, a generalized form of ANOVA, has the additional advantage of controlling for the effects of certain Factors and Variables, which ANOVA does not).

To address Confounding Factors effectively, researchers should carefully design their investigative studies, consider potential confounders during case study design planning, and collect data on relevant Variables. Analytical techniques, such as Statistical adjustment or matching, should be employed to control Confounding Factors. Additionally, replication of findings and conducting sensitivity analyses can help assess the robustness of results to potential confounding effects.

3.6 THE COMMON PROBLEMS WITH STATISTICAL ANALYSIS THAT NEED RECONCILING

- *Misinterpretation of correlation and causation*: Statistics often measure correlations between Variables, but *correlation does not necessarily imply causation*. For instance, inferring a causal relationship solely based on Statistical association or Pearson correlation coefficient (r) can be misleading. Other factors, such as common causes or coincidences, may be responsible for the observed Statistical relationship.

- *Incomplete data or missing data*: Incomplete or missing data can introduce Bias and compromise the validity of the Statistical analysis. If data is selectively excluded or unavailable for specific groups or Variables, the resulting Statistics may not accurately represent the entire population or the phenomena under investigation.

3.7 STATISTICAL SIGNIFICANCE VERSUS PRACTICAL SIGNIFICANCE

- *Statistical significance vs. Practical significance*: Statistical significance measures the likelihood of obtaining an observed result by chance alone. However, Statistical significance does not always equate to practical (or real-world) significance or importance. Small or trivial effects can be Statistically significant and seemingly impactful if the sample size is large enough, leading to misinterpretation of the practical implications of the findings. Conversely, an effect may appear considerable but not reach the Statistical significance threshold due to a limited or small sample size or variability. *Practical significance and Statistical significance are, indeed, two distinct concepts* used to evaluate the importance and meaningfulness of research findings; the differences are further expanded upon below:

    1. *Statistical significance*: Statistical significance is a measure of the likelihood that an observed effect or difference in data is not due to random chance or coincidence alone. It is typically assessed using Statistical tests like Hypothesis testing or p-values. Statistical significance indicates

whether the observed results are unlikely to occur by random variation or chance alone. Use the p-value as the probability of obtaining a test Statistic "at least" as extreme as the one that was actually observed, assuming that the "Null" Hypothesis is true.

2. *Practical significance*: Practical significance refers to the real-world importance or relevance of a research finding. It focuses on whether the observed effect or difference has practical implications or a meaningful impact in the context of the research question or problem being investigated. Practical significance considers factors such as the magnitude of the effect, its relevance to the target population or domain, and the potential practical applications or consequences of the finding.

Researchers should always strive to report both Statistical and practical significance that provides a comprehensive understanding of the findings and their implications.

3.8 P-VALUE AND THE "NULL" HYPOTHESIS

In Statistical Hypothesis testing, *the p-value is the Statistical significance, that is, the probability of obtaining a test Statistic "at least" as extreme as the one that was actually observed, assuming that the "Null" Hypothesis is true. The fact that p-values are based on this assumption is crucial to their correct interpretation.* The extent to which the test in question supports the postulated or conjectured Hypothesis, which has (or has not) been nullified, is called its Statistical "significance level." T*he more stringent the Statistical significance level is set, the less likely the phenomenon in question could have been produced by chance or coincidence alone.* Therefore, the lower the p-value, the less likely the result is by chance or coincidence alone, assuming the "Null" Hypothesis. The more

Statistically "significant" the result, the more the likelihood that there is a real difference between the populations or samples being studied. One often rejects the "Null" Hypothesis (a proposition that <u>no</u> Statistical significance exists in a set of given observations) if the p-value is less than 0.05 (five percent) or 0.01 (one percent, an even more stringent value), respectively, of an outcome, at least that extreme, given the "Null" Hypothesis.

One rejects the "Null" Hypothesis if the p-value is smaller than or equal to the Statistical significance level set, often represented by the Greek letter alpha (a). If the alpha level is 0.05, for instance, then results that are only five percent likely or less, given that the "Null" Hypothesis is true, are deemed extraordinary and not due to chance or coincidence alone.

Alpha Significance level	Odds	"Null" Hypothesis Rejection	Interpretation
p<=0.05	1:20	Yes	Significant
p>0.05	N/A	No	Not Significant

To reinforce the concept of the "Null" Hypothesis—The "Null" Hypothesis is that there is <u>no</u> significant difference between the specified samples or populations, any observed difference being due to random sampling, chance, coincidence alone, or experimental error. The term itself relates to the finding of no relationship. Therefore, the usage of the "Null" term precedes the word Hypothesis. So, the *"Null" Hypothesis is used to assess the credibility of a stated or claimed Hypothesis by interrogating sample data. It is deemed "true" until proven "wrong" at a specified Statistical probability value (p-value) based on the experimental data.*

It is crucial to approach Statistics with a critical, discerning mindset, considering the limitations and potential Biases, especially sampling Bias, parameters under investigation, Confounding Factors and Variables, and miscellaneous and contextual factors that can influence the interpretation and validity of the Statistical analysis. Transparent reporting, careful case study design, and robust Statistical analytical methods are essential for minimizing misleading or false Statistics.

3.9 KEY FORMULAS AND ANALYTICAL PROCESSES IN STATISTICAL ANALYSIS — LINEAR REGRESSION

One common Statistical analytical technique utilizes Linear Regression (LR) analysis. Linear Regression is specifically used to examine the relationship between a dependent Variable (Y-axis, "The Effect") and one or more independent Variables (X-axis, The "Cause").

The Linear Regression ("Least Squares") method of analysis uses the algebraic straight-line equation:

Graphic of the LINEAR REGRESSION ("least squares") ANALYSIS

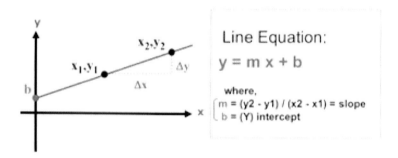

The formula for Linear Regression:

The relationship between the dependent Variable (Y) and independent Variable(s) (X) is modeled by fitting a straight-line equation to the observed data.

The general form of a simple Linear Regression model using the algebraic straight-line equation is:

$$Y = \beta_0 + \beta_1 X + \varepsilon$$

Where:

Y is the dependent Variable

X is the independent Variable

β_0 is the Y-intercept (the value of Y when X = 0)

β_1 is the regression coefficient (slope, representing the change in Y for a unit change in X)

ε is the error term, representing the random variability or unexplained portion of the relationship between the Variables

The objective of Linear Regression is to estimate the regression coefficients (β_0 and β_1) that best fit the data. This estimation is typically done using the "Least Squares method," where the sum of the squared differences between the observed and predicted Y values is minimized.

The "Least Squares" method estimate of the regression coefficients is calculated as follows:

$$\beta_1 = (\Sigma ((X_i - \bar{X})(Y_i - \bar{Y}))) / \Sigma ((X_i - \bar{X})^2)$$
$$\beta_0 = \bar{Y} - \beta_1\bar{X}$$

Where:

X_i and Y_i are the observed values of the independent (X-axis) and dependent (Y-axis) Variables, respectively.

$\bar{X}$ and $\bar{Y}$ (X bar and Y bar) are the means of X and Y, respectively

Σ denotes the summation of values across all observations

Linear Regression analysis is a widely used Statistical analytical technique that aims to model and examine the relationship between a dependent (Y-axis, "The Effect") Variable and one or more independent (X-axis, "The Cause") Variables. It is a powerful tool for understanding and predicting the impact of changes in independent Variables on the outcome (Y-axis, the "Effect") Variable of interest in the investigation.

In Linear Regression analysis, the dependent (Y-axis) Variable represents the response, "The Effect," or outcome Variable, while the independent (X-axis) Variables are the predictors or explanatory Variables. The goal is to estimate the relationship between the dependent Variable and the independent Variables, allowing for the quantification of the effect of each independent Variable on the dependent Variables while controlling for all other factors.

The Linear Regression model assumes that a mathematical equation can represent the relationship between the dependent (Y-axis) Variable and the independent (X-axis) Variables. Linear Regression is the most common form of regression analysis, which assumes a linear (algebraic straight line) relationship between the Variables. However, there are also other regression models, such as polynomial, logistic, and multiple regression (designating several explanatory Variables to predict the outcome of a response Variable), whose models accommodate different mathematical types of relationships and data structures.

Estimating the regression coefficient involves minimizing the sum of squared differences between the observed values of the dependent Variable and the predicted values based on the regression equation. The average difference, or the calculated sum of the squares of the distances of each point from the line that compares the "new method" to the "reference method," is optimized at a minimum. Thus, the term "Least Squares" represents the correlation coefficient that is sought where the slope (m) is ideally equal to a value of one (1), and the Y-intercept goes through zero (0). In the usual "Least Squares" graphic plot, the "new method" is plotted on the Y-axis and the (old) "reference method" is plotted on the X-axis. The equation has two constants: m (the slope of the algebraic straight line) and b (the Y-intercept). An optimized, ideal correlation between the X and Y Variables will have a slope, m = one (1), and b (Y-intercept) will be zero (0). How well the various data points "fit the line" and display the aforementioned is the correlation coefficient (r). In summary, this estimation of the regression coefficient using *the "Least Squares" (LS) regression method provides the "best-fit" line that minimizes the sum of squared errors:*

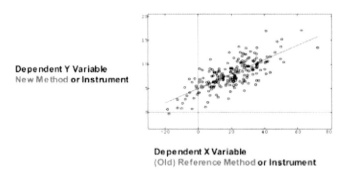

Dependent Y Variable
New Method or Instrument

Dependent X Variable
(Old) Reference Method or Instrument

Linear Regression Statistical analysis provides several important out-puts and insights. The regression coefficients indicate the magnitude and direction of the relationship between the dependent (Y-axis, "the "effect"") Variable and each independent (X-axis, the "Cause") Variable. These coefficients can be used to estimate the expected change in the dependent Variable associated with a unit change in the corresponding independent Variable. In addition, regression analysis allows for Hypothesis testing to assess the relationships' Statistical significance (p-value). This involves evaluating whether the regression coefficients significantly differ from zero, indicating that the independent Variable(s) significantly impact the dependent Variable. Consequently, *Linear Regression analysis enables the assessment of model fit and predictive performance.* As a parametric testing model, it assumes homogeneity of Variance (homoscedasticity): The size of the error in our prediction does not change significantly across the values of the independent (X) Variable.

Measures such as R-squared (Coefficient of Determination (R^2)) and adjusted R-squared provide insights into the proportion of Variance (variability) in the dependent (Y-axis, the "Effect") Variable that can be explained by the independent (X-axis, the "Cause") Variables.

These measures help evaluate the "goodness-of-fit" of the regression model and the predictive nature of the model for future observations (vide infra, 3-10.5).

Regression analysis and the commonly utilized Linear Regression model provide a fundamental Statistical tool in various fields, including finance, economics, marketing, Sociological—Psychological and Behavioral sciences, and Healthcare. It provides a quantitative framework for understanding, Statistical modeling, and simulation, predicting relationships between dependent (Y-axis, the "Effect") outcome and independent (X-axis, "the Cause') Variables, allowing Statisticians, researchers, and analysts to make informed Decision-Making, based on objective, empirical evidence.

3-10 MULTIPLE LINEAR REGRESSION AND EXAMPLE (MEDICAL)

Title of Hypothetical Case Study: "Examining the Relationship between Physical Activity and Cardiovascular Health in Older Adults: A Multiple Linear Regression Analysis"

Abstract: Using a Multiple Linear Regression analysis, this study investigates the relationship between physical activity and cardiovascular health among older adults. A sample of five hundred participants aged sixty-five and above was recruited for the study. Physical activity, measured in minutes per week, was the independent (X-axis, the Cause") Variable, while cardiovascular health (assessed using a composite score based on blood pressure, cholesterol levels, and body mass index) defined the dependent (Y-axis, the "Effect") Variable. After controlling for age, gender, and smoking status, a multiple Linear Regression Statistical model was fitted to the data. The model included physical activity as the predictor (X) Variable and cardiovascular health as the outcome (Y-axis, the "Effect') Variable. The analysis accounted for potential Confounding Factors and aimed to quantify the association between physical activity and cardiovascular health in older adults. The Multiple Linear Regression analysis revealed a Statistically significant positive relationship between physical activity and cardiovascular health (β (slope = 0.32), and

Statistical significance level at p < 0.001). This relationship means that for every additional minute of physical activity per week, the composite cardiovascular health score increased by 0.32 units. This finding suggests that higher levels of physical activity are associated with better cardiovascular health outcomes among older adults. Furthermore, the multiple regression model utilized demonstrated a "good fit" to the data, with an R-squared (Coefficient of Determination (R^2)) value of 0.40, indicating that 40 percent of the variability in cardiovascular health could be explained by physical activity and the covariates (complementary or related to the dependent Variable) included in the Statistical model. The results of this multiple regression analysis contribute to the growing body of evidence supporting the beneficial effects of physical activity on cardiovascular health in older adults. These findings highlight the importance of promoting and encouraging regular physical activity among older populations to improve cardiovascular outcomes and overall health. This study provides valuable insights for healthcare professionals, policymakers, and researchers in the geriatric health field. The multiple regression analysis, in this example, offers a robust Statistical data analytical approach to understanding the relationship between physical activity and cardiovascular health, aiding in evidence-based Decision-Making and the development of targeted interventions for older adults.

3.10.1 MULTIPLE LINEAR REGRESSION AND EXAMPLE (MEDICAL) – INTERPRETATION AND OVERVIEW

Instead of using the one sole Variable utilized in simple Linear Regression, Multiple (linear) regression (MLR) uses several Variables to predict the outcome of a response Variable. Multiple regression is, therefore, an extension of the linear "Least Squares" regression method previously discussed. It increases reliability and Statistical inquiry completeness by avoiding dependency on only one Variable by having more than one independent (X, the "Cause") Variable to explain an event. Multiple regression requires at least two independent

Variables (nominal, ordinal, or interval/ratio level Variables). It allows the investigator, by experimental design, to account for all of these potentially important factors in a singular Statistical model. The advantages of this approach are that it typically leads to a more accurate and precise understanding of the association of each individual Factor with the outcome. Generally, the Variable with the greatest value correlation coefficient is identified as a good ("best") predictor. One can also compare and calculate the R-squared value (Coefficient of Determination). As a general rule of thumb, one can assume that the predictor (X_i) Variable with the largest standardized multiple regression correlation coefficient corresponds to the most important Variable, the predictor (X_{ii}) Variable with the next largest standardized regression correlation coefficient is the next, following important Variable, and so on …

And, regarding sample size, while Statistical significance is generally accorded to a sample size (N) of at least 20, to preferably 30 observations when dealing with a single X and a single Y Variable, most Statisticians suggest adding at least an additional Ten (10) observations for each additional independent Variable added to a multiple point regression analysis.

Beyond sample size, many difficulties arise when there are more than five independent Variables in multiple regression analysis:

1. The most frequently cited problem is that two or more independent Variables are highly correlated, termed multicollinearity.

2. Another disadvantage of using a multiple regression model is incomplete data, leading to unreliable results.

3. Falsely concluding that a correlation is causation (also commonly mentioned with linear regression).

4. "Overfitting" can occur when the Statistical model includes too many independent Variables, leading to complex and unreliable predictions.

As described, the multiple regression model is complex.

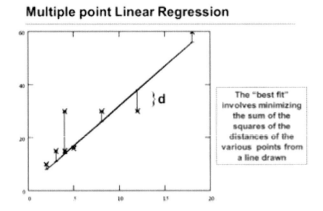

Multiple point Linear Regression

The "best fit" involves minimizing the sum of the squares of the distances of the various points from a line drawn

Five main assumptions underlie multiple regression models that must be satisfied and include: (1) linearity, (2) independence of errors, (3) normality, (4) independence of independent Variables, and (5) homoscedasticity (also termed homogeneity of Variances, an assumption of equal or similar Variances in distinct groups being compared). This is an essential assumption of parametric Statistical tests because they are sensitive to any dissimilarities (uneven Variances in samples result in Biased and skewed test results).

For validation, scatterplots can assist in detecting nonlinear relationships, while residual plots are useful for detecting homoscedasticity violations and errors' independence.

It is important to note that Statistical analysis and interpretation should be made by domain experts, providing quantitative and qualitative interpretive considerations and the specific problem context. Statistical techniques provide the quantitative framework for evaluating and prioritizing solutions. Still, they should be used in conjunction with other relevant analytical tools, methodologies, and techniques to make a definitive, well-informed decision. The analysis should conclude with the distinction between Statistical and practical significance and applicability to the problem investigated within the case study design.

Once the regression correlation coefficients (the estimates of the unknown population parameters describing the relationship between a predictor (X) Variable and the response) are estimated, we can assess the Statistical significance of the relationship between the Variables using "Null" Hypothesis testing, recalling that the "Null" Hypothesis (H_0) assumes that there is <u>no</u> relationship between the Variables ($\beta_1 = 0$). In contrast, the Alternative Hypothesis (H_1) suggests a Statistically significant relationship ($\beta_1 \neq 0$).

Statistical tests, such as T-tests or F-tests, can be performed to determine if the estimated regression coefficient is Statistically significantly different from zero.

3.10.2 T-TEST AND STATISTICAL INTERPRETATION

T-test (t-test):

The t-test is a Statistical test to assess the significance of the determined differences between the means of two groups or conditions. It is commonly employed when comparing the means of two independent groups or when examining the effects of a single independent (X) Variable with two levels (e.g., in Medicine, comparing experimental or treatment vs. control group).

The t-test is based on the t-distribution and calculates the t-value, representing the standardized difference between the means of the two groups or conditions. The t-value is determined by considering the sample means, sample sizes, and Variances (variabilities) of the groups being compared.

There are two main types of t-tests:
  A. *Independent Samples t-Test (3-10.2.1)*
  B. *Paired Samples t-Test (3-10.2.2)*

3.10.2.1 INDEPENDENT SAMPLES T-TEST

Independent Samples t-test: This *t-test is used when comparing the means of two independent groups.* The "Null" Hypothesis (H_0) assumes that there is no significant Statistical difference between the population means, while the Alternative Hypothesis (H_1) suggests that a Statistically significant difference exists.

The Independent samples t-test formula:
$t = (M_1 - M_2) / [\text{square root}[(s_1^2/n_1) + (s_2^2/n_2)]]$

Where:
M_1 and M_2 are the sample means of the two groups
s_1^2 and s_2^2 are the sample variances of the two groups
n_1 and n_2 are the sample sizes of the two groups

3.10.2.2 PAIRED SAMPLES T-TEST

The Paired Samples t-test: This t-test is used when comparing the means of two related or paired groups. It examines the differences within each pair and determines if the mean difference is significantly different from zero. The "Null" Hypothesis (H_0) assumes that there is <u>no</u> significant difference, while the Alternative Hypothesis (H_1) suggests a significant difference.

The paired samples t-test formula is:
$t = (M - \mu_0) / (s / \text{square root}(n))$

Where:
M is the mean of the differences between the paired observations
μ_0 is the hypothesized mean difference (often zero)
s is the standard deviation of the differences
n is the number of pairs

Statistical Significance of the T-Value:
To assess the Statistical significance of the t-value, researchers and Statisticians refer to the t-distribution or consult Statistical tables to determine the critical value for a given alpha level (typically 0.05 or 0.01 (even more stringent)).

Suppose the calculated t-value exceeds the critical value. In that case, *the "Null" Hypothesis is rejected* in favor of the Alternative Hypothesis, suggesting that a significant difference exists between the means of the groups or conditions being compared.

T-tests provide a valuable tool for assessing differences between groups or conditions in various investigative settings. They allow researchers to determine if observed differences in group or sample means are Statistically significant and provide evidence of meaningful distinctions' presence or absence.

3.10.3 HYPOTHESIS TESTING, STATISTICAL SIGNIFICANCE, TYPE-II (FN) AND TYPE-I (FP) ERRORS, AND STATISTICAL MODELING

1. The *first step* in Statistical modeling is to specify the "Null" Hypothesis:

For a two-tailed test (a method in which the critical area of distribution is two-sided and tests whether a sample mean is greater than or less than a specific range of values), the "Null" Hypothesis is typically given that a parameter equals zero, although there are exceptions.

The usual statement for the "Null" Hypothesis is $\mu1 - \mu2 = 0$ (which is equivalent to $\mu1 = \mu2$).

Where:
u1 = mean of the first population
u2 = mean of the second population

For a One-Tailed test, the "Null" Hypothesis is either a parameter that is greater than or equal to zero or a parameter that is less than or equal to zero.

If the prediction is that μ1 is larger than μ2, then the "Null" Hypothesis (the reverse of the prediction) is μ2 - μ1 ≥ 0. This is equivalent to μ1 ≤ μ2.

2. The *second step* is to specify the alpha or α (Statistical significance) level.

Typical values are p = 0.05 and 0.01 (even more stringent).

3. The *third step* is to compute the probability value, also known as the p-value.

This is the probability of obtaining a sample Statistic as different or more different from the parameter specified in the "Null" Hypothesis, given that the "Null" Hypothesis is *true*.

4. The *fourth step* is to compare the probability value with the chosen alpha (α)

Statistical significance level. If the probability value is lower, then you REJECT the "Null" Hypothesis (i.e., REJECT that there is <u>no</u> difference).

Remember that rejecting the "Null" Hypothesis is not an all-or-none decision.
The lower the probability (p) value, the more confidence you have that the "Null" Hypothesis is false. However, if your probability value is higher than the conventional alpha (α) level of 0.05, most Statisticians will consider the findings inconclusive. The alpha (a) level is the threshold (lower) level utilized to determine whether to reject the "Null" Hypothesis. Failure *to reject the "Null" Hypothesis does not constitute support for the "Null" Hypothesis. It just means you do not have sufficiently robust data to reject the "Null" Hypothesis!*

The One-Tail distribution example with the "Null" Hypothesis and alpha (a) significance level are graphically represented below.

3.10.3.1 THE T-DISTRIBUTION TABLE PROVIDES THE CRITICAL T-VALUES FOR BOTH ONE-TAILED AND TWO-TAILED T-TESTS AND CONFIDENCE INTERVALS

The t-distribution table provides the critical t-values for both One-Tailed and Two-Tailed t-tests and confidence intervals. The t-test distribution at the 95th percentile with 29 degrees of freedom (D.O.F., sample size less than 30) has a critical value of 1.699; the ("Null" Hypothesis) rejection region is, therefore, any t-Statistic greater than 1.699. Of note, since the "test Statistic" is within the Statistical significance (p-value defined) area, that is, beyond (to the right of the critical value of 1.699 in this One-Tail graphic (3-10.3)) of the alpha critical level, then the "Null" Hypothesis (H_0) is rejected.

t-distribution

					Confidence Level					
	60%	70%	80%	85%	90%	95%	98%	99%	99.8%	99.9%
					Level of Significance					
2 Tailed	0.40	0.30	0.20	0.15	0.10	0.05	0.02	0.01	0.002	0.001
1 Tailed	0.20	0.15	0.10	0.075	0.05	0.025	0.01	0.005	0.001	0.0005
df										
1	1.376	1.963	3.133	4.195	6.320	12.69	31.81	63.67	—	—
2	1.060	1.385	1.883	2.278	2.912	4.271	6.816	9.520	19.65	26.30
3	0.978	1.250	1.637	1.924	2.352	3.179	4.525	5.797	9.937	12.39
4	0.941	1.190	1.533	1.778	2.132	2.776	3.744	4.596	7.115	8.499
5	0.919	1.156	1.476	1.699	2.015	2.570	3.365	4.030	5.876	6.835
6	0.906	1.134	1.440	1.650	1.943	2.447	3.143	3.707	5.201	5.946
7	0.896	1.119	1.415	1.617	1.895	2.365	2.999	3.500	4.783	5.403
8	0.889	1.108	1.397	1.592	1.860	2.306	2.897	3.356	4.500	5.039
9	0.883	1.100	1.383	1.574	1.833	2.262	2.822	3.250	4.297	4.780
10	0.879	1.093	1.372	1.559	1.813	2.228	2.764	3.170	4.144	4.586
11	0.875	1.088	1.363	1.548	1.796	2.201	2.719	3.106	4.025	4.437
12	0.873	1.083	1.356	1.538	1.782	2.179	2.682	3.055	3.930	4.318
13	0.870	1.079	1.350	1.530	1.771	2.160	2.651	3.013	3.852	4.221
14	0.868	1.076	1.345	1.523	1.761	2.145	2.625	2.977	3.788	4.141
15	0.866	1.074	1.341	1.517	1.753	2.131	2.603	2.947	3.733	4.073
16	0.865	1.071	1.337	1.512	1.746	2.120	2.584	2.921	3.687	4.015
17	0.863	1.069	1.333	1.508	1.740	2.110	2.567	2.899	3.646	3.965
18	0.862	1.067	1.330	1.504	1.734	2.101	2.553	2.879	3.611	3.922
19	0.861	1.066	1.328	1.500	1.729	2.093	2.540	2.861	3.580	3.884
20	0.860	1.064	1.325	1.497	1.725	2.086	2.529	2.846	3.552	3.850
21	0.859	1.063	1.323	1.494	1.721	2.080	2.518	2.832	3.528	3.820
22	0.858	1.061	1.321	1.492	1.717	2.074	2.509	2.819	3.505	3.792
23	0.857	1.060	1.319	1.489	1.714	2.069	2.500	2.808	3.485	3.768
24	0.857	1.059	1.318	1.487	1.711	2.064	2.493	2.797	3.467	3.746
25	0.856	1.058	1.316	1.485	1.708	2.060	2.486	2.788	3.451	3.725
26	0.856	1.058	1.315	1.483	1.706	2.056	2.479	2.779	3.435	3.707
27	0.855	1.057	1.314	1.482	1.703	2.052	2.473	2.771	3.421	3.690
28	0.855	1.056	1.313	1.480	1.701	2.048	2.468	2.764	3.409	3.674
29	0.854	1.055	1.311	1.479	1.699	2.045	2.463	2.757	3.397	3.660
30	0.854	1.055	1.310	1.477	1.697	2.042	2.458	2.750	3.386	3.646
40	0.851	1.050	1.303	1.468	1.684	2.021	2.424	2.705	3.307	3.551
50	0.849	1.047	1.299	1.462	1.676	2.009	2.404	2.678	3.262	3.496
60	0.848	1.045	1.296	1.458	1.671	2.000	2.391	2.661	3.232	3.460
70	0.847	1.044	1.294	1.456	1.667	1.994	2.381	2.648	3.211	3.435
80	0.846	1.043	1.292	1.453	1.664	1.990	2.374	2.639	3.196	3.417
90	0.846	1.042	1.291	1.452	1.662	1.987	2.369	2.632	3.184	3.402
100	0.845	1.042	1.290	1.451	1.660	1.984	2.365	2.626	3.174	3.391
∞	0.842	1.036	1.282	1.440	1.645	1.960	2.327	2.576	3.091	3.291

Again, in this one-trail test graphic, the shaded area, that is, below (to the left of the critical value of 1.699 in this one-tail graphic (3-10.3)) of the alpha critical level, does NOT reject the "Null" Hypothesis.

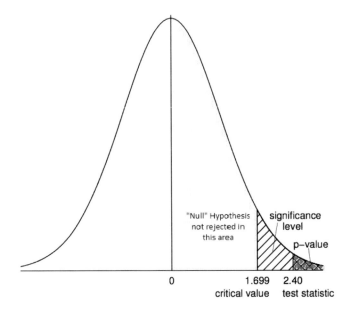

British Statistician Sir Ronald Aylmer Fisher (1890-1962) stressed that the "Null" Hypothesis "… is never proved or established, but it is possibly disproved in the course of experimentation. Every experiment may be said to exist only in order to give the facts a chance of disproving the "Null" Hypothesis."

1. The "Null" Hypothesis (H_0) is often stated Statistically as the assumption that "there is _no_ change, that is, _no_ difference between two groups, or samples, _no_ relationship between two Variables."

2. The Alternative Hypothesis (H_1), on the other hand, is the statement that there is a change, a difference exists, or there is a relationship between the Variables.

Rejecting the "Null" Hypothesis means that a relationship does exist between a set of Variables and that the effect is Statistically significant (for example, at a designated, defined value of $p > 0.05$ or $p > 0.01$ (even more stringent)).

3.10.4 F-TEST

In contrast to the t-test, an F-test is a Statistical test that assesses the equality of variances or the significance of the overall variation among the means of multiple groups or conditions. Stated differently, the F-test determines whether two population's Variances are equal. Additionally, it is used to examine the Hypothesis that a population's mean values are normally distributed. Finally, it can be employed to determine whether a suggested regression model accurately predicts the data.

The F-test is commonly used in the Analysis of Variance (ANOVA) to determine if there are significant differences between the means of two or more groups.

The F-test is based on the F-distribution, a probability distribution that arises when comparing Variances or ratios of Variances.

The F-test calculates an F-value, representing the ratio between-group and *within-group variation.*

In ANOVA, there are two main types of F-tests:

1. One-Way ANOVA test (3-10.4.1)

2. Two-Way ANOVA test (3-10.4.2)

3.10.4.1 F-TEST AND ONE-WAY ANOVA TEST

- *One-Way ANOVA*: This F-test compares the means of more than two independent groups. The "Null" Hypothesis (H_0) assumes that the means of all groups are equal, namely, that there is <u>no</u> difference. In contrast, the Alternative Hypothesis (H_1) suggests that at least one mean is significantly different.

The One-Way ANOVA F-test formula is calculated by dividing the ratio of the between-group Variance (SSB / dfB) by the ratio of the within-group Variance (SSW / dfW). Suppose the calculated F-value exceeds the critical value based on the chosen alpha (a) level of Statistical significance. The "Null" Hypothesis is rejected in that case, indicating significant differences between the group means.

$$F = (SSB / dfB) / (SSW / dfW)$$

Where:
SSB is the sum of squares between groups
dfB is the degrees of freedom for between-group Variance
SSW is the sum of squares within groups
dfW is the degrees of freedom for within-group Variance

3.10.4.2 F-TEST AND TWO-WAY ANOVA TEST

- *Two-Way ANOVA:* This F-test is used when comparing the means of multiple groups across two independent Variables, also known as "Factors." It examines the main effects of each Factor and their interaction. The F-value in two-way ANOVA assesses the Statistical significance of the main effects and interactions.

The role of F-tests in Statistical analysis is to determine if there are significant differences or relationships between groups or conditions. They provide a measure of the overall Variance explained by the independent Variables and can help identify the sources of Variance in the data.

F-tests are valuable in Hypothesis testing, determining the significance of effects, and assessing the adequacy of Statistical models in explaining the observed variation. By conducting F-tests, investigators can determine if the differences among groups or conditions are Statistically significant, supporting or refuting research hypotheses and providing insights into the relationships and differences between Variables.

3.10.5 THE COEFFICIENT OF DETERMINATION (R²), PEARSON CORRELATION COEFFICIENT (R), AND STATISTICAL MODEL "GOODNESS OF FIT"

Coefficient of Determination (R²): Other Statistical measures can be derived from the Linear Regression analysis. For instance, the Coefficient of Determination (R^2) represents the proportion of the total Variance in the Y (dependent, "The Effect") Variable that the Linear Regression model explains. It is calculated as the ratio of the explained sum of squares (ESS) to the total sum of squares (TSS):

R^2 = ESS / TSS = **Explained Variance Total Variation R2=Total Variance Explained**

It is also commonly calculated as:
R2 = 1−Residual Variance Total Variance $R2$ = 1−Total Variance Residual Variance

The explained Variance in the first equation is the sum of squares due to the regression (that is, how well the regression line fits the data), and Total Variance is the total sum of squares (that is, how much the data points vary from the mean).

In the second equation, Residual Variance is the sum of squares of the residuals (the differences between observed and predicted values).

Notably, the Coefficient of Determination (C.O.D., or R^2) is not exactly the same as the Pearson Correlation Coefficient (r) but is related.

Pearson Correlation Coefficient (r):
While the *Pearson* Correlation Coefficient (r) measures the strength and direction of the linear regression relationship between two Variables, the Coefficient of Determination (C.O.D., or R^2) quantifies the proportion of the total Variance or variation in the dependent (Y) Variable that can be

explained by the independent Variable(s). R^2 represents the proportion of the total Variance in the dependent Variable (Y) that is accounted for by the independent Variable (X). R^2 is expressed as a value between 0 and 1 or as a percentage between 0 and 100 percent. The Coefficient of Determination (R^2) ranges from zero when the independent Variable(s) explains none of the Variance or variability in the dependent Variable to one when it explains all (100 percent or value = one (1)) of the variation.

R^2 is calculated by squaring the Pearson Correlation Coefficient (r) determined between the independent and dependent Variables:

$R^2 = r^2$

Where:

r represents the Pearson Correlation Coefficient that quantifies the strength and direction of the linear regression relationship between the Variables.

The equation is valid when only one intercept is included.

The significance of R^2 lies in its ability to provide information about the "goodness-of-fit" of a regression model. It indicates how well the independent (X) Variable(s) explains the variation in the dependent (Y) Variable. A higher value of R^2 suggests a better fit, implying that a larger proportion of the total Variance or variation (variability) in the dependent (Y) Variable is accounted for by the independent (X) Variable(s). However, it bears repeating that *R^2 does NOT indicate the causal relationship between Variables, nor does it provide information about the Statistical significance of the relationship. R^2 is ultimately used to identify the strength of the model ("Goodness of Fit"), whereas r (Pearson correlation coefficient) is used to identify patterns, strengths, mutual relationships, directions, or correlation of two Variables in the Statistical analysis.*

    In summary, to determine the Statistical significance, "Null" Hypothesis testing or other Statistical modeling methods need to be employed: Samples are analyzed, and the results are graphically plotted. The Linear Regression

Statistical method minimizes the distance between the individual points, and the 'best fit" line ("Least Squares" method) is selected.

To cite a specific illustrative example, where the algebraic linear equation is $Y = 0.96X + 0.5$, the slope of the line, $m = 0.96$, means or translates to the result from method Y is ninety-six (96) percent (0.96) of the effect from method X. The Y-intercept, $b = 0.5$, means that method Y has a constant Bias of 0.5 relative to the result (ninety-six percent of method X value). The Pearson Correlation Coefficient (r) determined for the above data was calculated at 0.991, indicating that the two Variables (X and Y) are highly correlated. If necessary, the Statistician or investigator analyst could use the results of the Linear Regression method using an algebraic linear equation ($Y = mX + b$) to convert results from reference (new) method Y and make them virtually identical (equivalent) to those of an existing (old) method X, (the independent, the "Cause") Variable. The slope, in this case, makes the methods essentially interchangeable. As an anecdotal annotation to this topic, the latter is commonly done with Statistical correlative analysis when, for example, comparing and contrasting two Hospital laboratory instruments/analytical methodologies to one another, often to provide a backup instrument/methodology (old to new). Their relationship and Statistical equivalence or agreement to one another are established utilizing the Linear Regression model, in particular, derivative values, such as the Pearson Correlation Coefficient (r) and Coefficient of Determination (C.O.D., or R^2), to determine the suitability of the instrument/methodology as a backup for clinical laboratory patient testing, all things being equal.

These above formulas and equations taken together are Statistical methods providing a resource for understanding the relationship between Variables employing Statistical modeling. The Pearson Correlation Coefficient (r) and Coefficient of Determination (R^2) are estimated, and Statistical significance (p-value) is assessed. Linear Regression is a versatile, widely used method that allows for exploring and quantifying relationships between Variables obeying a parametric, normal distribution.

CHAPTER 4

"IRRELEVANT AND ERRONEOUS INFORMATION OR BOTH CAN NOT BE REPEATED OFTEN ENOUGH"

4.1 REPEATING ERRONEOUS AND IRRELEVANT INFORMATION OR BOTH AND THEIR CONSEQUENCES

When irrelevant information is repeated, it can lead to miscommunication, misaction, confusion, inefficiency, and impairment of the Decision-Making process.

There are many potential consequences of repeating irrelevant information:

- *Distraction:* Repeating irrelevant information can divert attention away from critical points or relevant details, causing confusion and making it more challenging to understand Corporate and Enterprise goals and objectives. It may hinder effective communication and lead to misunderstandings.

- *Information overload:* Repeating irrelevant information can contribute to information overload, where excessive or unnecessary details make extracting essential and pertinent useful information challenging. The idiom, "separating the wheat from the chaff," is a metaphor. Repeating irrelevant information can impede the Decision-Making processes, as relevant information may get lost amidst repetition.

- *Loss of productivity*: Repeating irrelevant information can waste valuable time and resources. It prolongs discussions or meetings unnecessarily and contributes to "meeting fatigue," leading, in turn, to decreased productivity and delayed progress on important, already prioritized tasks, assignments, or projects.

- *Reduced clarity*: Repeating irrelevant information can obscure the clarity of the message or objective being communicated. It may dilute the essential points, making it harder for the recipients to discern the critical information and take appropriate actions.

- *Frustration and disengagement*: Repeating irrelevant information can cause frustration and disengagement among the individuals involved in the communication or Decision-Making process. It can be perceived as a lack of preparation, organization, or focus, diminishing the motivation and interest of the participants.

In contrast to the aforementioned but related—what happens when input information (received) is erroneous and repeated often? This scenario can also lead to numerous adverse outcomes, including Misinformation, confusion, Disinformation, and the perpetuation of inaccuracies.

There are several potential consequences when erroneous information is repeated often:

- *Difficulty in correcting misconceptions: When erroneous information is repeatedly reinforced, correcting the misconceptions and replacing them with accurate information is an uphill struggle and becomes more challenging. The more an incorrect belief is reiterated, the more resistant or obstinate individuals may become to accepting correct information when presented.*

- *Inaccurate Decision-Making: If erroneous information is relied upon for Decision-Making, the decisions may be flawed, misguided, or overtly incorrect. This can negatively affect various domains, including personal, professional, Organizational, and Enterprise contexts.*

- *Loss of credibility: Repeating erroneous information consistently can undermine credibility. When individuals finally realize that the information being shared is inaccurate or false, it can erode trust and credibility in the source or even the messenger or transmitter of that information.*

- *Confusion and inefficiency: Erroneous information repeated often can create confusion and inefficiency. It can misdirect efforts, waste intellectual and other resources, and hinder progress, as individuals may be working on tasks premised on incorrect assumptions or presented "facts."*

- *Misinformation: Repeating erroneous information can perpetuate false or incorrect Facts," leading to Misinformation being disseminated. This can misguide individuals who rely on the information, potentially affecting their beliefs, Decision-Making, or subsequent actions.*

4.2. EFFECTIVE COMMUNICATION STRATEGIES

To avoid the negative consequences of repeating irrelevant information, it is important to practice effective communication strategies:

- *Clear and concise communication*: Ensure the shared information is relevant and concise. Focus on conveying the key message without unnecessary repetition or extraneous details (frills or fluff).

- *Active listening*: Encourage active listening among all participants to ensure that the conveyed information is understood correctly. Active listeners can help identify and address irrelevant information and repetition while redirecting the conversation toward the essential, incisive points.

- *Structure and organization*: Maintain a structured and organized approach to communicating and implementing the Decision-Making process. Clearly define the objectives, create an agenda, and establish guidelines to ensure the discussion stays focused and on track relative to the relevant topics.

- *Feedback and course correction*: Encourage open feedback and constructive criticism to address any repetition of irrelevant information. This can help identify areas for improvement and promote more effective communication in the future. By minimizing the recurrence of unrelated information, individuals can enhance communication clarity, streamline discussion regarding Decision-Making processes, and promote more productive and efficient interactions at all levels. "The Ability to Problem Solve, and Course Correct, Makes for Forward Progress."

4.3 DISINFORMATION — AN OVERVIEW, AND CONSEQUENCES OF ERRONEOUS INFORMATION

Disinformation is deliberately spreading false or misleading information to deceive or manipulate others. This is not to be confused with irrelevant or erroneous information mentioned above. Disinformation is, however, shared similarly to the above scenarios. The dissemination of inaccurate and fabricated content or both is decidedly designed to shape public opinion, sow discord, dissuade, or achieve specific, for example, political, social, or economic objectives. Disinformation can take various forms, including written articles, social media posts, memes, videos, manipulated images, and contrived images or audio. It bears mentioning that the absence of information and the blocking, withholding, or obfuscating information can also be utilized to dissuade, deceive, disseminate, and even forge opinion. Disinformation is orchestrated to distort reality with fabrication, the selective presentation of "facts," and manipulation of the contextual "surround." According to The Washington Post, Misinformation and Disinformation research has recently become "radioactive" (Nix, N. September 23, 2023).

Several key aspects characterize the concept of Disinformation:

- *Intent and malicious intentions*: Disinformation is, as described, created, and disseminated with a deliberate intent to deceive, mislead, or manipulate. Those behind the creation and distribution of Disinformation have specific goals, an agenda to influence public opinion, undermine trust in institutions, government, or political parties, and promote a particular ideology or otherwise lead the audience astray.

- *Exploitation of Cognitive Biases*: Disinformation takes advantage of various Cognitive Biases and vulnerabilities ingrained in human psychology. It may appeal to emotions, reinforce pre-existing held beliefs, belief systems, political or religious, or even exploit Confirmation Bias, making it more likely for individuals to accept and share false information before its critical evaluation and validation.

- *Erosion of trust and polarization*: Disinformation undermines trust in once-held credible, validated, and reliable sources of information, such as major media outlets, scientific institutions, or government and regulatory agencies. It can contribute to a polarized society by promoting alternative narratives, fostering division, tribalism, and factions, thereby creating echo chambers where individuals are exposed only to information that aligns with their (pre)existing beliefs. Confusion and inaccuracy are sown.

- *Amplification and "virality:"* Disinformation spreads rapidly and widely, facilitated by the speed and reach of today's digital world wide Web internet platforms and social media. It often relies on the viral nature of information sharing, leveraging algorithms, Search Engine Optimization (SEO) of keywords, or using phrases, bots, or coordinated networks of accounts to amplify its visibility, transmission, and impact. It can become "viral" in its dissemination.

- *Lack of fact-checking and verification*: Disinformation often bypasses traditional fact-checking processes, relying on the speed of spread and sensationalism to capture one's attention and enhance transmission. This can lead to rapidly disseminating false or misleading information before its accuracy is appropriately assessed and contradicted by fact-checking.

- *Influence on political elections and societal discourse*: Disinformation can impact political processes, including elections, by manipulating public opinion or spreading false information about candidates or issues. It can also fuel social tensions, contribute to conspiracy theories, and undermine public discourse on critical societal matters.

Addressing the situation of Disinformation requires concerted efforts from various stakeholders, including individuals, policymakers, major mainstream media (MSM) outlets, Organizations, and Enterprises, as well as companies utilizing digital technology-based platforms. Fact-checking initiatives, media literacy programs, improved algorithms, and legislative regulation of digital platforms are some strategies employed to combat Disinformation and promote accurate and trustworthy information sources.

In the end, verifying the information before sharing or relying on it is essential to mitigate the negative impact of erroneous information and Disinformation. Verifying its accuracy from credible, validated, and reliable sources is necessary. Fact-checking and cross-referencing information can help prevent the spread of inaccurate data. Promoting Critical Thinking[2] skills among individuals is vital to help them question and evaluate information. Encouraging skepticism, the willingness to seek out corroborating, supporting references, and the use of expert consultants with varying perspectives may be required before a conclusion is reached. An environment where individuals feel comfortable questioning and challenging the presented information represents the promotion of open dialogue. Encouraging open discussions and respectful debates to allow for the correction of erroneous information needs to be a "best-established practice." Notwithstanding, when incorrect information is identified, it is crucial to correct and clarify the inaccuracies promptly. Communicate the correct information to employees, Management, and the Organization and Enterprise, and expeditiously address any misunderstandings or misconceptions that may have arisen. By actively addressing and rectifying erroneous information, Misinformation, and Disinformation, individuals, Organizations and Enterprises can achieve more accurate and reliable information sharing, leading to better Decision-Making, enhanced understanding and knowledge, and improved Business outcomes and profitability. If the opposite occurs, the repetitive dissemination of the described irrelevant or erroneous information, Misinformation, or Disinformation, without acknowledging or correcting inaccuracies, can ostensibly contribute to untoward effects or actions. The spokesperson promoting or promulgating irrelevant, erroneous, or inaccurate Misinformation or Disinformation may exhibit arrogance or an inflated ego. A dismissive attitude toward others' perspectives and positions can arise. Attempts at making factual corrections may lead to conflict. It is important to note that narcissistic self-importance can occur in the latter situation. Certain associated attitudes and behaviors, such as arrogance or the direct link to pomposity, are not always definitive or universal.

4.4 THE MISUSE OF GRAPHICS OUTPUT DATA TO DISPLAY ERRONEOUS INFORMATION, MISINFORMATION, AND DISINFORMATION

Erroneous information, Misinformation, and Disinformation can be displayed visually using graphics output data, such as the (purposeful?) truncating of the Y-axis and the use of a non-zero-baseline, to skew the displayed data, as in the bar chart depicted. In this instance, if the Y-axis does not start at zero, then minor or negligible changes become hyperbolic and create a Bias in the observer's perspective, as well as the interpretation of the bar chart:

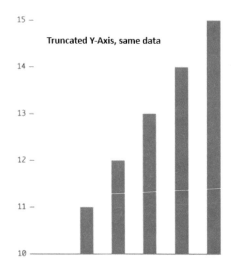
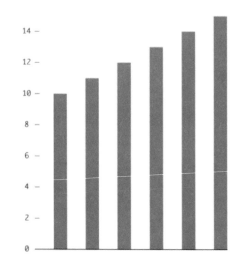

Truncated Y-Axis, same data

A Pie chart can be expository, adding meaning to a statement or Statistic, such as, in this example: "Suicides accounted for more than half of U.S. gun deaths in 2021 (percent of U.S. gun deaths by type-2021)," in contrast to the more commonly (mis)represented Mainstream Media (MSM) exaggeration: "Guns were implicated in (fill in the blank) number of deaths in 2021." The former garnered less attention than the sensationalized headline: "gun-related deaths," Suicides accounted for 26,328 deaths, while actual murders were 20,958, according to the Centers for Disease Control (CDC) in 2021. The graphic in the former also reveals that three percent of U.S. deaths in that year were for "Other" causes, namely, gun deaths due to accidents (549), law enforcement (537), or undetermined circumstances (458). In summary, eight in ten U.S. murders in 2021, or 81 percent, involved a firearm. All those Statistics mentioned above are factual and accurate, varying only on "how the story is told," as well as how it is conveyed to an audience. The CDC recorded that the 81 percent figure marked the highest percentage since at least 1968, the earliest the CDC had online records. Remarkably, buried deeper in the report is that "Despite the increase in such fatalities, the rate of gun deaths—a Statistic that accounts for the nation's growing population – remained *below* the levels of earlier decades (Pew Research Center Analysis of Data from the CDC, the FBI, and other sources).

Pie charts, as just one example of a graphic, can be quite misleading and are responsible for erroneous information, Misinformation, and Disinformation. It should be noted that when looking at a pie chart, donut graph, or gauge chart, it is difficult to tell how much more significant one portion of a graphic is than another since human perception is much better at comparing lengths or linear distances than comparing areas. Data manipulation can yield false impressions or conclusions using the pie chart. The disadvantages of interpreting pie charts also relate to failing to reveal key assumptions, causes, effects, or patterns. Changes over time and the exclusion of exact values are other cited disadvantages of the graphic.

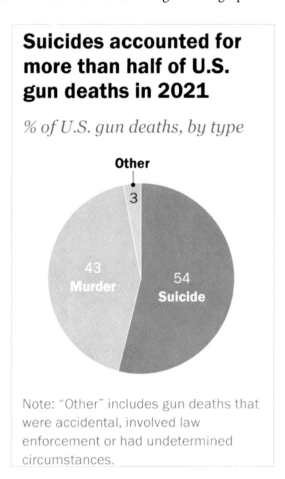

Suicides accounted for more than half of U.S. gun deaths in 2021

% of U.S. gun deaths, by type

Other
3

43
Murder

54
Suicide

Note: "Other" includes gun deaths that were accidental, involved law enforcement or had undetermined circumstances.

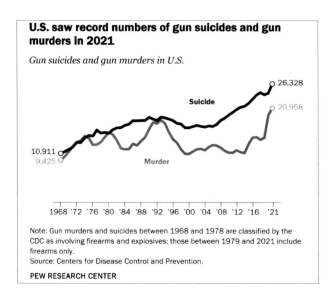

An instance where graphic data may be correct and factual but may show inverted or skewed axes that would intentionally or not confuse a reader is depicted in the following example:

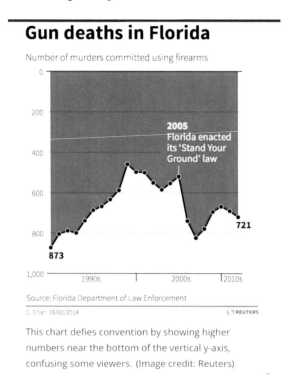

This chart defies convention by showing higher numbers near the bottom of the vertical y-axis, confusing some viewers. (Image credit: Reuters)

4.5 GASLIGHTING

The unique situation of Gaslighting deserves particular mention and refers to the deliberate distorting of information. Gaslighting is a form of Psychological manipulation in which one person or entity systematically undermines another person's perception of reality, causing them to doubt their thoughts, emotions, and reality experiences. Gaslighting uses denial, distortion, contradiction, and manipulation tactics to gain power and control over the subject. Gaslighting can occur in several types of relationships, including personal, professional, political, or even societal contexts. "Straight-up" lies, "reality manipulation," "scapegoating," and "coercion" are some of the puppet master's modes of control.

Gaslighting behavior and techniques are defined by:

- *Consistently denying events or occurrences that the victim clearly remembers or experienced.* Some expressions used: "That never happened," or "You're making things up."

- *Deliberately withholding essential information or conveniently "forgetting" contextual details*, making the victim question their memory or understanding of a situation.

- *Manipulating facts and presenting them distortedly to confuse and disorient* the victim. They may twist the truth, selectively omit important and consequential information, or make false accusations. The omission of correct (exculpatory) information especially needs to be recognized as another "distortion" of the truth.

- *Contradicting the victim's statements, beliefs, or emotions* makes them doubt their judgment. Expressions used: "You're overreacting," or "You're being too sensitive."

- *Deflecting responsibility for their actions and behaviors by blaming the victim.* Expressions used: "You're the problem," or "It's your fault this happened."

- *Intentionally creating a sense of confusion and uncertainty* by constantly changing one's story or making inconsistent statements. This can make the victim question their sanity and grasp on reality.

- *Attempting to isolate the victim from support and information validation sources,* such as friends, family, or other trusted individuals or authorities. By cutting off these interpersonal connections, Gaslighting increases the victim's dependence on the perpetrator and further undermines the victim's self-confidence.

Gaslighting can have severe Psychological effects on the recipient or victim, leading to self-doubt, anxiety, depression, and a veritable distorted sense of reality. It is essentially abusive behavior aimed at exerting power and mind control over the recipient (victim) of the so-called "information." Recognizing Gaslighting behavior is essential in order to protect oneself, seek support from trusted, credible individuals or professionals, and establish the veracity of transmitted, conveyed, and shared information.

4.6 THE DISTINCTION BETWEEN "TRUTHS AND FACTS" — GENERAL

The author closes with the following caveat: a person's perspective, own beliefs, belief system, and context can conceptually determine "Truth" and, therefore, the possibility of their existing "Multiple Truths!" On the other hand, a *"Fact" is undeniable, indisputable, and singular, not relying on perspective.* A "Fact" or constellation of "Facts" must be what drives Decision-Making.

Epistemology is a branch of philosophy dealing with the Theory of knowledge, including its sources. The term is derived from the Greek epistēmē ("knowledge") and logos ("reason" or "plan"). The Theory of Epistemology involves the typology of knowledge, its nature, the categorization of beliefs, knowledge sources themselves, and their justification. Limitations or constraints are further examined within this framework. Epistemology intends to explain just what "Truth" is.

Schommer (1990), who helped conceptualize the pillars of knowledge, defined epistemological beliefs as consisting of four independent, non-hierarchical, non-developmental dimensions (modified):

1. Certain knowledge employing Logic and reason

2. Intuitive knowledge

3. Omniscient knowledge (divine revelation authority)

4. Experience

Epistemological considerations influence Problem Analysis and Decision-Making within the realm of Business. One invokes epistemology by exploring how knowledge is acquired, justified, and applied in Business settings. In the deliberative evaluation of evidence, an individual's perception plays a role, ranging from certainty to doubt. The offsetting effect of Cognitive Bias impacts problem identification, framing, and analysis.

The philosophy of what is "Truth "broadly encompasses the following theories:

1. *The Correspondence Theory of "Truth"*

2. *The Performance Theory of "Truth"*

4.6.1 THE DISTINCTION BETWEEN "TRUTHS AND FACTS" — THE CORRESPONDENCE THEORY OF "TRUTH"

The Correspondence Theory of Truth is a classical, traditional, and broadly accepted Theory positing that a statement or belief is considered "true" if it accurately corresponds to incontrovertible, objective reality. The proposition of "Truth" means that the Claim must accurately represent or reflect the contemporary state of affairs. Testing a Hypothesis or accepting or rejecting the "Null" Hypothesis in Statistics is an example of the proposition of "Truth." When an experiment is conducted, and we verify (or disprove) a Hypothesis, we effectively use the Correspondence Theory of Truth. What we observe in the investigation is what is "True." This Theory is Aristotelian in its origins. Contemporary philosophers such as Donald Davidson, Hilary Putnam, and Simon Blackburn have supported this viewpoint. The justification for this interpretation of "Truth" is the relationship between the actual language and linguistics employed or thought and the external world. When a statement corresponds to the "Facts" or accurately depicts the same or reflects reality, it is, then, deemed "True" ("Truth"). Conversely, incongruence or disconnection between the Claim or statement and reality is definitionally considered false.

4.6.2 THE DISTINCTION BETWEEN "TRUTHS AND FACTS" — THE PERFORMANCE THEORY OF "TRUTH"

The Performance Theory of Truth is relatively modern, challenging "Truth" as mere correspondence with objective reality. The advocates of this Theory instead argue that "Truth" is dynamic and "context-dependent," constructed through human actions and social practices. According to this view, "Truth" has no independent, assertive meaning. Proponents, Theorists, and Philosophers such as P. F. Strawson, Jean-François Lyotard, and Richard Rorty have argued that "truth" is not simply a matter of accurately reflecting reality but is metamorphosed by the performance or enactment of statements within specific social and cultural environments. When you say, "It is "true" that … "you agree with, accept, or endorse a statement." The Performance Theory of Truth would argue that "Truth" emerges from how individuals and the collective community engage with language and symbols, and it can thus vary across different contexts and cultures. P.F. Strawson (1919-2006), for instance, in his essay "Truth (1950b)," holds that to say that a statement is true is not to make a statement about a statement but to perform the act of agreeing with, accepting, or endorsing a statement. So, does that mean— multiculturalism and diversity [(of) opinions] = multiple "Truths?"—Think about it…

4.7 SPINNING THE SPOOF, SPAMOUFLAGE, AND AI MISINFORMATION PUSHED BEYOND JUST MEMES

Generative Artificial Intelligence (AI) software can produce Text, Images, Video, and Audio files that are deceptively realistic. Examples—Image generators like labs.openai.com DALL-E2 product, Midjourney, and Stable Diffusion yield AI-generated images, while OpenAI's chatbot, ChatGPT software product, generates text.

Deepfakes are digitally manipulated media consisting of Images, Audio, and similar cloned replicas or, worse, actual duplicates. AI can and has propagated and disseminated Disinformation and propaganda. On Tuesday, February 7, 2023, the Graphika Lab Team reported an instance of pro-China bots during late 2022 sharing propaganda and "fake news," especially Avatar Videos (Spamouflage) featuring AI-generated news anchors on Facebook and Twitter! Canada recently saw a Spamouflage campaign that enlisted a network of new or hijacked social media accounts to post propaganda messages across various platforms, such as Facebook, X/Twitter, Instagram, YouTube, Medium, Reddit, TikTok, and LinkedIn—all to curb criticism of the Chinese Communist Party (CCP). This Disinformation assault was extraordinary in that it was linked to State-sponsored manipulation of information targeting Prime Minister Justin Trudeau, Conservative Leader Pierre Poilievre, and almost fifty Members of Parliament (MP) in August and September, according to Global Affairs Canada (Tunney, C. China Linked to Propaganda Campaign-Global Affairs, CBC-Politics section. October 23, 2023).

4.7.1 THE PROBLEM OF DEEPFAKES AND RECOGNITION... THE ACHILLES HEEL OF IMAGE DEEPFAKES

What happens when Deepfakes become ubiquitous? This may, indeed, become the case as early as 2024, according to Vandehei, A. and Allen, M. (November 8, 2023). Trusting your "lyin eyes" will be confounding. And, what if "Tech layoffs ravage the teams that fight online misinformation and hate speech" (Field, Hayden and Vanian, Jonathan in MSNBC Tech News section, May 27, 2023)? Consider the following scenario – ninety (90) plus percent (%) of online content is expected to be generated by AI, particularly that generated by open-source models, into 2025—not only will National Security but the integrity of our political process, as well as jobs and more, will be threatened. Both open-source and proprietary AI models will be confronted by legal inquiry over the existence of copyrighted material within the vast data sets incorporated to train them.

Researchers (Shunailov, I. et al., May 2023) using Large Language Models (LLM) / LLaMA (Large Language Model Meta AI) posit that "use of model-generated content in training causes irreversible defects in the resulting models… tails of the original (human-inspired as well as derived) content distribution can disappear over time"—an effect termed "Model Collapse." If you make AI tools that create and amplify Intelligence, then edit and eventually evaluate social media, text, images, and video, you have a quandary on your hands, the likes of which have never been seen before! My take on this is that it is time to put on your wading boots.

Notwithstanding, the counterweight and hallmark of detecting Deepfakes is the lack of output details. In fact, the lack of details is a recognizable consequence of current Deepfake AI generative software. One can usually identify most instances by focusing on facial and head and neck anatomy, such as: "dull shadows around the eyes, unrealistic facial hair, overly smooth or wrinkled skin, fictitious moles and unnatural lip color" (Telefónica Communication Team, March 2023).

Technology has risen to the recognition challenge—Intel has introduced a real-time Deepfake detector, designated "FakeCatcher"—A technology that can detect fake videos with a 96 percent (viz., not 100 percent) accuracy rate, returning results in milliseconds. The detector analyzes blood flow pixel alterations (algorithmically translated into spatiotemporal maps using deep learning analysis applied to video images). FakeCatcher was designed in collaboration with Umur Ciftci from SUNY at Binghamton, New York, using Intel hardware and software running on a server and interfacing through a web-based platform. Tools and Technology aiding in Deepfake detection have "almost" caught up with the AI platforms used to produce the Deepfakes themselves (McFarland, A. October 2023).

CHAPTER 5

"IF YOU ARE TOTALLY CONFUSED, BORDERING ON BEWILDERMENT, THEN YOU PROBABLY HAVE A COMPLETE GRASP OF THE COMPLEX CONCEPT"

SO, YOU THINK YOU HAVE PROBLEMS? NO SURPRISE: LIFE IS complicated …

Here are a few examples of highly complex concepts and problems, some without solutions.

5.1 QUANTUM ENTANGLEMENT

Quantum entanglement is a fundamental concept in quantum physics whose central tenet is a peculiar correlation between particles, regardless of the distance between them. It is characterized by an intimate and inseparable connection that defies classical notions of physics' cause-and-effect phenomenon. In Quantum physics, two or more particles become correlated to the extent that their states are intertwined, regardless of the distance between them. Changes in the state of one particle instantaneously affect the state of the other, even if vast distances separate them. Quantum entanglement cannot be understood using conventional physics logic. At the heart of Quantum entanglement lies the *superposition principle*, which states that Quantum particles can exist in multiple states simultaneously until they are measured. When two or more particles become entangled, their states become entwined, and the properties of one particle become instantaneously connected to the properties of the others, regardless of the spatial (distance) separation between them.

The complexity of Quantum entanglement arises from several aspects:

- *The first is non-locality*, challenging the concept of locality, which suggests that information cannot be transmitted faster than the speed of light. Entangled particles exhibit a form of non-locality, where changes to one particle's state "instantaneously" affect the other particle's state, even if they are light-years apart. This non-locality correlation defies our classical understanding of causality and challenges our intuitive notions of space and time.

- *Secondly is the concept of uncertainty and measurement.* Quantum entanglement is intricately linked to Quantum systems' inherent uncertainty and indeterminacy. Until measured, the entangled particles exist in a superposition of possible states whose properties are not well-defined. It is only upon measurement that the state of one particle collapses into a definite value, instantaneously determining the state of the entangled partner. The probabilistic nature of measurement outcomes adds an element of unpredictability and complexity to entangled systems.

- *Thirdly, conservation laws and conservation of information:* When particles become entangled, their combined state forms a new composite state that retains specific attributes and correlations. These correlations persist regardless of the spatial separation between the particles. Understanding how information is conserved and transmitted through entangled systems poses complex questions and challenges our understanding of information Theory.

- *Fourthly, Quantum information processing* lies at the core of Quantum information processing and Quantum computing. Harnessing entanglement allows for the creation of Quantum bits (qubits) that can represent and process information in ways that surpass classical processing and computational systems. Exploiting the potential of entanglement in practical applications requires dealing with complex phenomena such as Quantum error correction, entanglement distillation, and entanglement swapping. One powerful quantum computational system is Google's Sycamore 53 qubit chip, whose processing speed is reportedly more potent than the Cray Supercomputer.

Without a doubt, the complexity of Quantum entanglement stems from its departure from classical physics concepts and its fundamental departure from deterministic cause-and-effect relationships. It defies our classical understanding of physical systems and requires a sophisticated mathematical and imaginative conceptual framework to describe and comprehend its properties fully. Quantum entanglement continues to be an active research area, deepening our understanding of the Quantum world and its potential applications in Quantum communication, cryptography, and Quantum computing. Extraordinarily, the actual, incremental, albeit exponential speedup achieved by quantum computers can vary widely based on the algorithm used, problem complexity, the quantum computer's hardware's quality, stability of the environment, and error rates, not to mention error correction. Exploring multiple possibilities simultaneously is achievable and is the amplification of the processing power of quantum computing. Indeed, quantum computing efficiently factors large numbers, forming the basis of many encryption methods and unsolvable problems. The latter, in turn, raises concerns about the security of existent encryption methods, leading to the exploration of new quantum-impervious cryptographic techniques. One advance begets the requirement for another.

5.2 QUANTUM COMPUTING

Quantum computing leverages the principles of Quantum Mechanics to perform computations. It utilizes Quantum bits (Qubits), which can exist in superposition states of zero (0) and one (1) simultaneously, enabling parallel processing and exponential computational power. Quantum computing has the potential to revolutionize fields such as cryptography, optimization programs, drug discovery, materials science, logistics, Machine Learning, Artificial Intelligence (AI), and scenario simulation. Quantum computing is a rapidly advancing field at the convergence of Quantum Mechanics, computer science, and information Theory. It explores the use of Quantum mechanical phenomena to perform computations far beyond classical computers' capabilities. By leveraging the principles of superposition and entanglement, Quantum computers have the potential to solve some complex issues more efficiently than classical supercomputer computations. The basic units of information, the qubits (unlike traditional classical bits), can exist, as stated, in superposition states, that is, both states simultaneously. This superposition allows Quantum computers to process and manipulate multiple computational states simultaneously, exponentially increasing their arithmetic operations' throughput power. The power of Quantum computing also stems from the underlying phenomenon of entanglement. Entanglement occurs when qubits become highly correlated, such that the state of one qubit is intimately linked to the state of another, even if they are physically separated. Through entanglement, Quantum computers can perform parallel computations and process information in ways that are not achievable with traditional computers. Quantum algorithms, furthermore, exploit the unique properties of qubits and entanglement to solve specific complex computational problems more efficiently. As a baseline, the eight-bit classical computer processing power can represent only a single number from zero to two hundred and fifty-five (total = 256 bits). Still, an eight-bit Qubit computer can simultaneously represent every number from zero to two hundred and fifty-five. Shor's algorithm demonstrates the potential of Quantum computers to factor mathematically large numbers exponentially faster than classical algorithms. This has implications for cryptographic systems that rely on the difficulty of factoring large numbers. Nonetheless, employing Quantum computers poses significant implementation challenges due to the delicate, ephemeral nature of qubits and the sensitivity of Quantum systems to "noise and decoherence." Researchers regularly explore different physical platforms to realize qubits, including superconducting circuits, trapped ions, topological systems, etc. In parallel, error correction techniques and fault-tolerant architectures are being developed jointly to mitigate noise's effects and ensure reliable Quantum computational analyses. Overall, Quantum computing has the potential to revolutionize various fields of study and solve complex, convoluted problems that are currently unmanageable or intractable for traditional computers. While Quantum computing is still in its preliminary developmental stages, progress is being made in scaling up Quantum hardware, designing Quantum algorithms, and exploring new applications. As the field progresses, it is expected to have a transformative impact on computing and unlock novel, previously unknown, innovative possibilities in scientific research, technological innovation, and problem-solving.

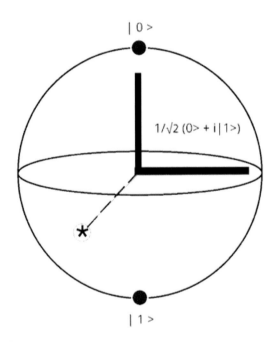

● A bit can only take on a state of 0 or 1

✳ **QUBIT** can take on any state

5.3 CHAOS THEORY

Chaos Theory is a branch of mathematics and physics that deals with complex systems characterized by sensitive dependence on initial conditions. It explores the behavior of nonlinear systems that exhibit unpredictable and chaotic behavior. Slight changes in initial conditions can lead to dramatically different outcomes, making long-term predictions challenging. Conceptually, it seeks to understand and describe the patterns and dynamics of random and unpredictable phenomena. Chaos Theory has applications in various fields, including weather forecasting, economics, physics, and biology. At the core of Chaos Theory is deterministic Chaos, where a system's future behavior is determined by its initial conditions and a set of deterministic equations governing its dynamics. However, even though the equations are deterministic, the long-term behavior of chaotic systems appears random and quite unpredictable. This behavior arises due to the amplification of minor uncertainties in the initial conditions, often called the "butterfly effect."

Chaos Theory emphasizes that specific complex systems can exhibit simple deterministic rules leading to intricate and complex random behavior. These systems are sensitive to initial conditions, meaning that even a slight change in the starting conditions can lead to vastly different outcomes over time. This property is commonly visualized through the notion of "strange attractors," geometric shapes that describe the long-term behavior of chaotic systems. An example of Chaos Theory can be seen in weather system behavior. Numerous Variables, such as ambient and oceanic temperatures, humidity, precipitation, cloud coverage, wind speed and direction, wind shear, atmospheric barometric pressure, and additional Variables, influence weather patterns. Minor changes in these Variables can significantly and dramatically impact weather conditions over time. This sensitivity to initial conditions makes it challenging to predict long-term weather patterns accurately. A slight variation in the initial measurements or the input data can lead to drastically different weather forecasts. A separate experimental illustration of Chaos Theory is the so-called double pendulum system. A double pendulum consists of two connected pendulums, each swinging back and forth. The system's behavior can quickly become chaotic, even though the underlying equations governing the pendulums' motion are deterministic. A minor change in the pendulum's initial momentum angles or velocities can result in wildly different trajectories and motions over time.

Chaos Theory provides insights into the complexity and unpredictability inherent in many natural and artificial systems. Understanding and studying chaotic systems can aid in developing better theoretical and real-world models, making more accurate predictions, and gaining a deeper understanding of the underlying dynamics of complex phenomena.

5.4 GENERAL RELATIVITY

General Relativity is a Theory of Gravitation developed by Albert Einstein. It describes gravity as the curvature of space-time caused by the distribution of mass and energy. According to General Relativity, massive objects like planets and stars deform the fabric of space-time, causing other objects to move along curved paths. The Theory has successfully explained phenomena such as the bending of light by gravity and the Gravitational Waves observed in more recent experiments. The first directly observed Gravitational Waves phenomenon was made in 2015, and researchers K. Thorne and B. Barish, both of Caltech, and R. Weiss of MIT, were awarded the Nobel Prize in Physics for their decisive contributions to the Laser Interferometer Gravitational-Wave Observatory (LIGO) detector and observation of Gravitational Waves in 2017. Thus, the ripples in space-time, initially predicted by Albert Einstein's Field Equations, confirmed their existence and opened a new field of observational astronomy. Bear in mind that the General Relativity Theory of Gravitation was formulated by Albert Einstein one hundred years earlier in 1915. Singularly, it provided a comprehensive description of the existent gravitational force phenomenon and its effect on the structure of space-time.

General Relativity has revolutionized our understanding of gravity, replacing Newton's classical Theory with a framework that accounts for the curvature of space-time caused by the presence of mass and energy. According to General Relativity, massive objects such as stars, planets, and galaxies deform the fabric of space-time, creating a gravitational field. In turn, the motion of objects in this field is determined by the curvature of space-time, which influences the paths they follow. Rather than the traditional gravitational force acting instantaneously across distances, General Relativity, in contrast, portrays the force of gravity as a consequence of the curvature of space-time. The mathematical formulation of General Relativity is based on the principles of differential geometry and Field Equations known as Einstein's Field Equations. These equations relate the distribution of matter and energy in space-time to the curvature of the metric tensor, which characterizes space-time geometry. Solving these equations provides insights into the gravitational field and the behavior of matter and light in its presence. The formula for General Relativity is the Einstein Field Equations, which describes the relationship between the curvature of space-time and the distribution of matter and energy within it. These equations are at the core of Einstein's Theory of General Relativity and provide a mathematical framework for understanding gravity as the curvature of space-time.

Einstein Field Equations

$$G_{\mu v} + \Lambda g_{\mu v} = \frac{8\pi G}{c^4} T_{\mu v}$$

The left-hand side of the equation represents the curvature of space-time, while the right-hand side represents the distribution of matter and energy. In essence, the Einstein Field Equations inform us how the presence of mass and energy curves space-time, and this curvature, in turn, affects the motion of particles and the propagation of light, giving rise to the force we perceive as gravity. One of the key predictions of General Relativity is the bending of light in the presence of a gravitational field. This effect was confirmed through observations of starlight passing close to the Sun during a solar eclipse, providing supporting empirical and observational evidence for the Theory. General Relativity also predicts the existence of Black Holes, which are regions of space-time with powerful gravitational fields from which nothing, including light, can escape. General Relativity has successfully explained various phenomena and has withstood the test of time with numerous confirmatory experimental tests. It has implications for our understanding of cosmology, astrophysics, and the universe's nature. The Theory has been instrumental in explaining the expansion of the universe, the dynamics of galaxies, and the formation, as well as the scalar effects of large structures. Without a doubt, General Relativity represents a profound shift in our understanding of gravity, space-time, and the fundamental nature of the universe. Its mathematical and conceptual complexity requires sophisticated tools and techniques, making it a cornerstone of modern physics and an essential component in our quest to comprehend the fundamental workings of the cosmos.

5.5 GAME THEORY

Game Theory is a branch of mathematics that studies strategic interactions between individuals or groups. It provides a framework for analyzing Decision-Making in situations where the outcome depends on the choices of multiple entities. Game Theory models can be used to understand various scenarios, such as pricing decisions in economics, resource allocation, political science, voting machine behavior, military strategy and analysis of strategic interactions, Business negotiations, conflict resolution, cooperation computer science, and evolutionary biology. Game Theory studies Decision-Making in situations where the outcome of an individual's choice depends on the choices made by other participants. It provides a formal framework for analyzing and predicting the behavior of rational individuals or entities in competitive or cooperative situations.

Game Theory models interactions as "games" where players have different strategies to choose from, and the payoffs or outcomes of the game depend on the strategies chosen by all players. It aims to understand how rational Decision-Making optimizes choices while considering the actions and strategies of others. The foundational concept in Game Theory is the namesake *Nash equilibrium*," named after mathematician John Nash (1928-2015). In a Nash equilibrium, no player can unilaterally deviate from their chosen strategy and improve their outcome. It represents a "stable state" where all players' strategies are mutually the best responses given the strategies of others. An example of Game Theory is *the "Prisoner's Dilemma."* In this scenario, two suspects are arrested for a crime but are held separately and cannot communicate. Each suspect is given the option to either confess or remain silent. The outcomes and associated penalties are as follows:

1. *Scenario one.* If both suspects remain silent, they receive a minimal sentence.

2. *Scenario two.* If one suspect confesses while the other remains silent, the confessor receives a reduced sentence, while the one who remained silent receives a severe penalty.

3. *Scenario three.* If both suspects confess, they both receive a moderately harsh sentence.

The prisoner's dilemma illustrates a situation where the optimal strategy for each player is to confess, even though both players' outcomes would be better if they remained silent. This scenario highlights the tension between individual rationality and collective optimal results. Researchers employ mathematical models and techniques such as extensive-form games, strategic-form games, and repeated games to analyze and predict the behavior of rational Decision-Making in complex social and economic situations. By providing a rigorous framework for understanding strategic interactions, Game Theory offers valuable insights into human behavior and Decision-Making processes in a wide range of scenarios.

5.6 NEURAL NETWORKS

Neural Networks are computational models inspired by the structure and function of biological Neural Networks in the human brain. They consist of interconnected artificial neurons that process and transmit information. Neural Networks can learn from data and make predictions or classifications based on patterns and relationships. They have been successfully applied in various domains, including their early application in digital image recognition, Natural Language Processing (NLP), finance, healthcare, robotics, and autonomous automatic vehicles. Neural Networks have also proven to be highly effective as Convolutional Neural Networks (CNNs), a specialized type of Neural network, which has achieved remarkable performance in tasks such as object detection and facial recognition. CNNs learn to identify hierarchical visual features, such as edges, textures, and shapes, enabling them to accurately classify and locate objects within images. Recurrent Neural Networks (RNNs) and transformer-based architectures, such as the popular "Transformer" model, have revolutionized machine translation, text generation, sentiment analysis, and language understanding (comprehension) tasks. These models capture contextual dependencies and learn the underlying structures of language, allowing for a more accurate and nuanced analysis of textual data. Neural Networks excel in tasks involving complex and non-linear patterns, where traditional algorithms may struggle. Their ability to learn from data and generalize to unseen, unanticipated, unforeseen, and unexpected examples has made them a powerful tool for solving a wide range of problems. Overall, Neural Networks offer a versatile and adaptable approach or conduit to Machine Learning. Artificial Intelligence (AI) enables computers to process and interpret data to mimic human Intelligence. Their capacity to learn and recognize patterns and inputs of vast amounts of data has made them an indispensable tool in various scientific, industrial, informatics, and technological domains. These complex concepts require a deeper understanding of underlying principles and involve advanced mathematics or theoretical frameworks. However, these concepts provide intriguing insights into the fundamental workings of human behavior, the development of advanced technologies, and the universe. Neural Networks are extraordinary computational models consisting of interconnected artificial neurons or "nodes" that mimic the behavior of biological neurons. Neural Networks can learn from data, recognize patterns, and make predictions or classifications based on the learned knowledge. The fundamental building block of a Neural Network is an artificial neuron, also known as a "perceptron." Each artificial neuron receives input signals, applies a mathematical transformation to those inputs, and produces an output signal. The strength or weight assigned to each input determines its impact on the neuron's output. This weight is adjusted through a process called "training," which allows the Neural Network to learn and adapt to the specific task or problem at hand. The artificial neurons are organized into different layers within the Neural Network. The input layer receives the initial input data, while the output layer produces the final output or prediction. There can be one or more "hidden layers" of interconnected neurons in between. The hidden layers enable the network to learn complex representations and extract meaningful features from the input data. The connections between neurons, represented by weights, form the structural and functional basis of the Neural Network's architecture. During the preliminary training process, the network adjusts these weights to minimize the difference between the predicted and desired outputs using various optimization algorithms. This process is often referred to as "backpropagation," where errors are propagated backward through the network to update and revise the allocated weights.

5.7 STRING THEORY

String Theory is a theoretical framework in physics that attempts to explain particles' fundamental nature and interactions. It posits that the universe's fundamental building blocks are tiny vibrating strings or loops rather than point-like particles. String Theory seeks to unify Quantum Mechanics and General Relativity and has implications for our understanding of gravity, high-energy physics, and the structure of space-time. These strings exist in multiple dimensions, and their various vibrational modes give rise to the diverse particles and interactions observed in nature. At its core, String Theory seeks to reconcile two fundamental pillars of modern physics: Quantum Mechanics and General Relativity. It attempts to describe the behavior of particles at the smallest scales, where Quantum effects dominate, while also accounting for the gravitational interactions that occur at larger scales. String Theory incorporates the principles of Quantum Mechanics to describe the vibrational modes and energy levels of the strings while also incorporating the curved space-time framework of the General Relativity theorem. The "strings" vibrate at different frequencies and amplitudes, metaphorically akin to the harmonics of a musical instrument. The vibrational modes of the strings correspond to other particle types, such as photons, electrons, and quarks, as well as force-carrying particles, like gravitons. One of the more remarkable features of String Theory is its requirement for extra dimensions beyond the three spatial dimensions and another singular time dimension that we perceive in everyday Life. On the face of it, Life, as we know it, is constrained by these four ordinary dimensions. In solid geometry, length (L), width (W), and depth (D) define the first three dimensions, while time or direction through space creates the fourth dimension. Interestingly, as the dimension of depth applied to a two-dimensional square creates the cube, adding a fourth dimension to the latter creates the Tesseract (the "hypercube"). String Theory predicts the existence of yet additional dimensions, usually "compactified" or curled up at extremely small scales. These extra dimensions, along with the vibrational modes of the strings, contribute to the richness and diversity of particle physics and the interactions between them. Moreover, String Theory suggests that other configurations or solutions, known as "string vacua," represent different universes with different physical laws and constants. This notion of a "landscape" of possible universes has led to the concept of a "multiverse" in which our universe is just one of many realizations within the larger framework of String Theory. Due to its mathematical complexity and the lack of experimental confirmation, the Theory remains a subject of active research and academic debate. Its proposition has led to various advancements, including the discovery of duality symmetries related to String and Gauge theories. String Theory has also found connections with other areas of physics, such as Black Hole physics and condensed matter physics. While still a work in progress, String Theory offers another promising theoretical construct for understanding the fundamental nature of the universe, unifying the forces of nature, and resolving long-standing puzzles in theoretical physics. Its potential implications for cosmology, Quantum gravity, and the nature of space-time continue to be explored by physicists and astrophysicists worldwide.

5.8 FRACTALS

Fractals are intricate and infinitely self-repeating patterns that exhibit self-similarity, possessing the property of being detailed and complex, regardless of the level of magnification. They are created through recursive mathematical equations and manifest in natural phenomena such as coastlines, clouds, and snowflake patterns. Fractals have applications in computer science and graphics, art, data compression, physics, chaotic dynamics, biology, and the study of complex systems. Fractal geometry explores the idea that these complex and irregular shapes can emerge from simple rules and recursive processes.

Examples:

- *Fractal geometry of coastlines*: Coastal lines often exhibit fractal characteristics, with intricate shapes and irregularities at different scales. The jaggedness and self-repeating patterns of coastlines can be quantified using fractal dimension, a measure of the complexity of a fractal. Fractal geometry has been employed to study and model coastal erosion, shoreline dynamics, and the behavior of sediment deposits.

- *Fractal patterns in nature*: Fractals can be observed in various natural phenomena. Examples include the branching patterns of trees, the intricate shapes of snowflakes, the structure of fern leaves, the arrangement of blood vessels in the human body, and the intricate patterns found in geological formations like mountains and coastlines. Fractal patterns in nature often arise from the iterative growth processes and self-replicating structures found in biological and physical systems.

- *Fractals in Chaos Theory*: Fractals are closely connected to Chaos Theory. Chaotic systems often exhibit fractal patterns, with sensitive dependence on initial conditions leading to intricate and unpredictable dynamics. The famous "Lorenz attractor" is a chaotic system with a fractal structure, representing the strange and intricate behavior of a simplified model of atmospheric convection.

- *Fractal antennas*: Fractal geometry has been applied to the design of telecommunication antennas. Fractal antennas possess self-similar patterns and can efficiently transmit and receive electromagnetic signals across a broad range of frequencies. The fractal design allows for miniaturization, wide bandwidth, and enhanced performance compared to traditional antenna designs.

A single individual did not discover fractals as a mathematical concept, but their study and popularization can instead be attributed to mathematicians and scientists over several decades. One distinguished figure in the development and popularization of fractal geometry was Benoit Mandelbrot (1924-2010), a Polish-born French American who worked as a mathematician at the IBM Thomas J. Watson Research Center. Mandelbrot introduced and coined the term "fractal" in the 1970s. He expanded upon the work of earlier mathematicians and researchers who explored self-repeating patterns and irregular shapes. The most well-known and widely studied fractal is the namesake, *Mandelbrot Set* (called "God's thumbprint"), which is generated by iterating a simple mathematical equation in the complex plane:

$$Z_n + 1 = Z_n^2 + C$$

In this equation, Z_n represents a complex number, and C is a constant. By repeatedly applying this equation to different values of Z, the Mandelbrot Set is constructed. Each point in the complex plane is assigned a value based on how the iterated equation behaves. Points that remain bounded under iteration are considered part of the set, while points that escape to infinity are considered outside the set. The iterative process continues for each point in the complex plane, revealing the intricate and self-similar patterns that characterize the Mandelbrot Set. The process of repeatedly applying a set of mathematical operations or transformations to generate new points or shapes based on previously calculated values results in the fractal's intricate and detailed patterns. The complex, elaborate structures and shapes emerge at different magnification levels or scales, displaying the self-repeating nature of fractals.

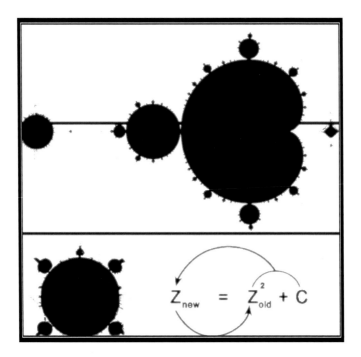

$$Z_{new} = Z_{old}^2 + C$$

It is important to note that numerous other types of Fractals have different equations and generation methods. For instance, Fractals can be created using algorithms such as the Julia Set, Sierpinski Triangle, Koch Snowflake, and many others. Each Fractal has a specific equation or iterative process defining its unique shape and properties. The study of Fractals is a broad and active field of research, and mathematicians and scientists continue to explore and develop new fractal-generating equations, algorithms, geometric forms, and applications.

Fractals have been and will continue to be extensively studied. Beyond the aforementioned, Mandelbrot has been credited for bridging the gap between art and mathematics and demonstrating that these two worlds are not mutually exclusive. Put succinctly, Fractals provide a mathematical language to describe and understand complex and irregular patterns in nature, from the microscopic to the macroscopic scale. They offer insights into the self-similarity and intricate structures that emerge from simple rules and recursive processes.

5.9 BLACK HOLES

Black Holes are regions in space where gravity is so strong that nothing, including light, can escape their gravitational pull. They are formed from the remnants of massive stars that have undergone gravitational collapse. Black Holes have properties such as event horizons and singularities, and they play a crucial role in our understanding of General Relativity, astrophysics, and cosmology. Black Holes are fascinating and enigmatic objects in the universe that arise from the just-mentioned gravitational collapse of massive stars. The intense gravitational forces preclude light from escaping once it passes a specific boundary called the event horizon. The study of Black Holes has profoundly impacted our understanding of gravity, space-time, and the extreme conditions of the universe. One of the fundamental concepts described in black hole physics is the Schwarzschild radius, named after the German physicist Karl Schwarzschild (1873-1916). This radius defines the size of the event horizon of a non-rotating black hole. The Schwarzschild radius is directly proportional to the mass of the black hole: the larger the mass, the larger the event horizon. Inside the event horizon, the curvature of space-time becomes so extreme that all paths lead towards the central singularity, a point of infinite density. Black Holes have several intriguing properties elucidated from the Theory of General Relativity, developed contemporaneously by Albert Einstein. One such property is the "no-hair" theorem, which states that Black Holes can be characterized by only three observable properties: mass, charge, and angular (spin) momentum. This theorem suggests that all other information about the matter that formed the black hole is lost within the event horizon. Elaborating further, *Black Holes can be classified into distinct types based on their properties.*

- *Non-rotating Black Holes, also known as Schwarzschild Black Holes,* are characterized solely by their mass.

- *Charged Black Holes, or Reissner-Nordström Black Holes*, possess an electric charge in addition to their mass.

- *Rotating Black Holes, or Kerr Black Holes*, exhibit angular momentum and mass.

- *Kerr-Newman Black Holes,* whose formation is due to the combination of charge and rotation.

The behavior and dynamics of matter falling into Black Holes have been extensively studied. As matter approaches the event horizon, it undergoes intense tidal forces and is subjected to extreme superheating and compression. This process gives rise to the formation of an accretion disk, a swirling disk of superheated gas and dust spiraling into the black hole. The accretion disk emits radiation, including X-rays, which astrophysicists can detect and study. Black Holes certainly play a critical role in studying astrophysics and cosmology. Their immense gravitational pull influences the motion of nearby stars and galaxies. Observations of the orbital dynamics of stars around a compact invisible object have provided compelling indirect evidence for the existence of Black Holes. More fundamentally, Black Holes are thought to play a crucial role in the formation and evolution of galaxies, contributing to the understanding of large-scale cosmic structures. In recent years, detecting Gravitational Waves has opened a new window into the study of Black Holes. Gravitational Waves are ripples in space-time caused by the acceleration of massive objects, such as the merging of Black Holes. Advanced gravitational wave detectors, such as Laser Interferometer Gravitational-Wave Observatory (LIGO) and Variability of solar IRradiance and Gravity Oscillations (Virgo), have observed the merger of Black Holes, confirmed their existence, and provided valuable insights into their properties and behavior. Despite our growing knowledge, many mysteries still surround Black Holes, such as the nature of the singularity within the event horizon and the possibility of Quantum effects near the Black Hole boundary.

The study of Black Holes continues to push the limits of our understanding of gravity, space-time, and the extreme physics of the universe, captivating the attention of scientists and inspiring ongoing research and exploration.

As an aside, dispelling the myth or fear regarding *Conseil Européen pour la Recherche Nucléaire* (CERN) and any possible generation of a Black Hole is warranted. There is a misconception that the Large Hadron Collider (LHC) at CERN, the European Organization for Nuclear Research, could create or inadvertently generate a Black Hole that could threaten Earth or humanity. However, this concern is not supported by scientific evidence and is, therefore, incorrectly based on misunderstandings of the physics involved. Some concerned citizens have raised concerns that the high-energy collisions in the LHC could potentially create microscopic Black Holes that would grow and consume matter, posing a danger to Earth. However, these concerns are not justified for several reasons:

- *Energy scale*: The energy produced in the LHC collisions is still several orders of magnitude below the energy scale required to create Black Holes. In fact, the energies involved in the LHC experiments are comparable to those observed in ordinary cosmic ray interactions with Earth's atmosphere, which have been occurring naturally for billions of years without any catastrophic consequences.

- *Hawking radiation:* Even if microscopic Black Holes were produced in the LHC, the late theoretical physicist Stephen Hawking (1942-2018) proposed they would dissipate quickly due to the namesake Hawking radiation phenomenon. According to this theoretical construct, Black Holes emit photons, neutrinos, and other particles and lose mass over time until they eventually dissipate entirely.

- *Conservation of energy and momentum:* The laws of physics, such as the conservation of energy and momentum, would prevent microscopic Black Holes from growing uncontrollably. They would be extremely short-lived and rapidly decay into other particles before they could cause any significant untoward, catastrophic effects.

- *Astrophysical evidence:* Black Holes exist naturally in the universe and are formed through the gravitational collapse of massive stars. Observations of Black Holes in astrophysical settings, such as in binary star systems or at the centers of galaxies, provide evidence for their existence and behavior. These naturally occurring Black Holes have not posed a threat to Earth or humanity to date. Nonetheless, the LHC is undeniably the world's most powerful particle accelerator, designed to study the fundamental cosmic particles and forces of nature, and that fact alone is undisputed. The LHC collides particles, such as protons, at extremely high energy levels to recreate the conditions that existed shortly after the "Big Bang." These artificially provoked collisions allow scientists to investigate the properties of matter and explore the frontiers of particle physics.

- *Safety:* It is important to note that the safety of experiments conducted at CERN, including those at the LHC, is thoroughly assessed, reviewed, and subject to rigorous scrutiny with periodic inspections by the scientific community. Extensive studies, including safety assessments, have been conducted to ensure safety and security.

In summary, the fears and misconceptions regarding Black Holes possibly being created at CERN's LHC and posing a threat to Earth and humanity are unfounded. The experiments conducted at CERN are conducted with the utmost care, based on well-established physics principles and protocols, and supported by extensive scientific research and safety inspections. The scientific and regulatory community continuously monitors and evaluates the safety of experiments conducted to ensure the above.

5.10 THE DIGITAL PRIVACY PARADOX — INTRODUCTION

Not Astrophysics or mathematics, but it may be just as unsolvable—Data Integrity and Privacy—The Digital Privacy Paradox:

"Too Much Data" and "Too Little Security," or the Reliance on Digital Information, Technology, and How It Relates to the Digital Privacy Paradox

In the fast-paced and interconnected worldwide web of the twenty-first century, Businesses have come to rely heavily on digital technology to enhance their operations, improve communication, data capture, billing, and integral efficiency, and better understand their customer base. However, this reliance on data-driven processes has given rise to a profound and unsolvable Business dilemma, the *Digital Privacy Paradox.* This Paradox revolves around the tension between two fundamental aspects of modern Business: Data-driven insights and privacy concerns. In today's digital landscape, Businesses gather vast amounts of data from their customers, employees, and various other sources. This data is invaluable in gaining insights, identifying trends, and making data-driven decisions. It allows companies to personalize customer experiences, optimize marketing strategies, and create and track innovative products and services. Simultaneously, consumers and regulatory bodies are growing increasingly concerned about the potential misuse of personal data.

Data mining as a tool (using computer languages, such as R or Python) can uncover patterns in exceptionally large data sets to optimize information and customers' (habits) product choices, services provided, and more. Detecting trends and opportunities for improved market competitiveness, solving problems, and mitigating risks such as fraud give permanence and a "place at the table" to this adjunct data-gathering tool. So, what is wrong with this?

Amazingly, almost two megabits of data enter the digital space each second, according to datagrail.io.

5.10.1 THE DIGITAL PRIVACY PARADOX —
DATA SUSCEPTIBLE TO PRIVACY BREACHES
(SELECT EXAMPLES LISTING) AND ADDITIONAL INFORMATION

Data susceptible to privacy breaches include, but are not limited to:

- *General data*

- *Local Area Network and Cloud data*

- *Authentication and access control – Login*

- *Encryption data*

- *Products purchased online*

- *Search Engine and Browser history*

- *Location information.*

- *Financial and banking information.*

- *Employee records and benefits profile data (Social Security Insurance information, Health Savings Account data, administrative employ-ment information, and retirement account data).*

- *Personal data, especially employee messaging, Social Media com-munication, and similar.*

To be sure, personal identity theft, fraud, data loss, and data "hostaging" (the selling of one's (tracked) shopping preferences and purchases, as well as related) are significant data security and personal privacy concerns. Recent high-profile data breaches and scandals involving major corporations have eroded public trust in Businesses' ability to safeguard sensitive information. As a result, governments worldwide are enacting strict data protection laws and regulations, like the General Data Protection Regulation (GDPR) in Europe and the California Consumer Privacy Act (CCPA) in the United States. The Digital Privacy Paradox creates an unsolvable dilemma for Businesses. On the one hand, Businesses recognize the immense potential of data-driven insights to gain a competitive marketing edge and meet customer expectations. Failing to leverage this data could put them at a disadvantage compared to more data-savvy competitors. On the other hand, complying with strict data privacy regulations and addressing consumer concerns about data security breaches requires Businesses to collect, store, and handle data with the utmost care. But even with robust security measures, there is always the risk of data breaches, potential data loss, and reputational damage. The unsolvable aspects of this Paradox relate to balancing data utilization and privacy rights. Striking this equilibrium is an ongoing challenge, as data-driven insights often require voluminous amounts of personal information, making it difficult to respect individuals' privacy fully. Meanwhile, rapidly evolving technology presents Businesses with constant new challenges as they adapt to innovative technologies like Machine Learning, Artificial Intelligence (AI), and the Internet of Things (IoT). The last mentioned, the Internet of Things (IoT), has led to the rise of "edge and fog computing," where computation and data processing occur close to the data source, even in devices. This reduces latency and bandwidth requirements, but the challenge remains in maintaining security, managing decentralized systems, and ensuring cross-platform compatibility. These technologies offer unparalleled potential for data analytics, yet privacy risks are always in the background, pervasive, and seemingly unresolved. Struggling to keep up with evolving technology can create gaps in privacy protection. Complicating matters, different countries have varying data protection laws, which can be inconsistent and sometimes contradictory. For Businesses operating on an international, global scale, navigating these complexities while maintaining regulatory and privacy compliance becomes an obstacle. The consumer has different expectations, increasingly demanding personalized experiences that rely on copious data and data analysis. Nonetheless, consumers expect companies to be transparent and responsible with their data as they become more privacy-conscious. Balancing these two almost contradictory demands is an accountability tightrope act for Businesses. While Businesses can take measures to mitigate and minimize risks, if not eliminate privacy risks, they turn to implement robust security protocols, anonymization techniques, and the obtaining of explicit consent, that is, End-User Authorizations (EUA), from users. The end-user needs help to read, absorb, digest, and comprehend the EUAs provided by Businesses, multipage, legalese formal and technical language, and small font documents. Indeed, there needs to be more clarity between individuals' concerns about online privacy and their actual consumer behaviors in the digital realm. The evolving landscape and contemporary trends of digital privacy, coincident contributing factors developments, reinforce the complex interplay between individual privacy apprehensions and especially network, worldwide activities. The Digital Privacy Paradox encapsulates the contentious relationship between users' professed concerns about online privacy and their seemingly contradictory consumer behaviors in engaging with those digital platforms. As the digital data-driven ecosystem expands exponentially, understanding this paradox is crucial for legislative policymakers, Businesses, and individuals to ensure a balanced, rational approach to privacy Management that recognizes both positions. The end-users often complain about data breaches, surveillance, information misuse, and theft. Yet, they frequently engage in activities that compromise their privacy, such as sharing personal data on social media or utilizing data-intensive services that oblige the usage of identifier data platforms and networks. Cognitive Biases, convenience-driven choices, trust in the inherent security of digital platforms, and the perceived benefits versus risks of sharing digital information all contribute to this paradoxical phenomenon. In 2023, the Digital Privacy Paradox continues to shape user interactions with digital technologies. The widespread adoption of Internet of Things (IoT) devices, Artificial Intelligence (AI) driven services, and personalized advertisements have intensified the paradox. While regulatory efforts have heightened awareness about data protection, users' consumer behaviors remain complex and contradictory. Contemporary trends and developments indicate an evolving consciousness of digital privacy among end-users. The data breaches affecting prominent corporations, Organizations and Enterprises, industry-sector high-profile cases of data mishandling (even by major Banks), and unauthorized data sharing have fueled public discourse, anger, and calls for more legislative regulation related to privacy concerns.

The scale of the problem is enormous. Cyentia's Information Risk Insights Study 20/20—"Extreme Edition" (IRIS Xtreme) meta-analysis of the five years before 2021 analyzed the hundred most significant cyber loss events during the study period. It showed $18 billion in reported losses and ten billion in compromised records.

In response, some users adopt privacy-centric tools, employ encryption algorithms, and demand transparency from internet service and digital platform providers. Even with the wide prevalence of data-driven digital services and the allure of personalized, boutique experiences continue challenging the alignment or reconciliation of digital privacy concerns and consumer behaviors. Privacy education and policy formulation are next. Businesses must strike a balance between data-driven innovation and respecting end-user privacy preferences. Policymakers should consider fostering an environment that promotes informed Decision-Making, transparency, and end-user empowerment. Technological advancements, such as decentralized identity solutions, quantum computing, encryption, and differential privacy mechanisms, promise to address the Digital Privacy Paradox by empowering users to retain greater control over their personal information. Today, our society navigates the intricate interplay between digital innovation and consumer privacy preservation. Users' attitudes and behaviors reflect an evolving awareness of digital privacy implications, driven by a combination of incidents in the mainstream media, legislative regulations, and emerging technological solutions. Navigating this digital paradox necessitates a purposeful approach encompassing ethical considerations, technological advancements, and informed end-user consumer engagement.

The Digital Privacy Paradox remains a quagmire due to the inherent conflict between data-driven requirements and benefits versus end-user privacy concerns. As technology advances, this perplexing dilemma will only become exacerbated, challenging Businesses to continually adapt, change, transform, and find innovative ways to navigate and juggle the ever-changing landscape of digital privacy while providing value to their customers. Ultimately, it calls for continuous dialogue between Businesses, government regulators, and consumers to strike a balance that respects privacy without stifling the potential benefits of data-driven information and innovation. Can this be solved?

CHAPTER 6

"IF IT APPEARS THAT A LOGIC-BASED ARGUMENT IS BEING PURSUED, AN IRRELEVANT QUESTION WILL BE ASKED"

6.1 THE CIRCUMSTANCE OF A LOGIC-BASED ARGUMENT

A Logic-based Argument refers to a sequence of inquiry and Argumentation or both underscored by Critical Thinking[2] and deliberation that follows rational principles, adheres to logical reasoning, and is supported by evidence. It involves structuring ideas and information coherently and systematically, ensuring that each step or premise logically leads to the next.

Key characteristics of a Logic-based Argument or Claim:

- *Logical coherence*: The Logic-based Argument or Claim follows a clear and logical stepwise progression, where each step coherently builds upon the earlier one. The ideas flow logically and are connected in a way that makes intuitive and overt sense.

- *Clear premises*: The Logic-based Argument or Claim is based on well-defined premises or assumptions. These premises should be clear, specific, and supported by evidence or logical reasoning.

- *Reasoned Arguments or Claims*: Each step in the Logic-based Argument or Claim is supported by reasoned Arguments or evidence. It involves presenting logical explanations, making deductive inferences, and providing justifications that support the overall Argument or Claim or conclusion.

- *Avoidance of Logical Fallacies*: A Logic-based Argument or Claim avoids Logical Fallacies, which are reasoning errors that can undermine an Argument's or Claim's validity. Logical Fallacies include, for instance, Ad Hominem attacks and others, such as circular reasoning, false analogies, and other invalid or deceptive reasoning tactics.

- *Critical Thinking[2]*: The analysis of information, evaluating the strengths and weaknesses of Arguments or Claims, and considering alternative viewpoints or counterarguments are foundational.

- *Evidence-based*: The Logic-based Argument is grounded in evidence or relevant, pertinent information. It relies on facts, data, research findings, reference citations, or other credible, validated sources to support Argumentative Claims or Claims and conclusions.

- Clarity and precision of communication: The Logic-based Argument or Claim is communicated succinctly and precisely, using well-defined terms and concepts. Ambiguity or vagueness is minimized to ensure the ideas are effectively conveyed and understood.

- *Objective and impartial*: A Logic-based Argument or Claim aims to be objective and impartial. It avoids personal Biases, emotional appeals, jargon (unless explained), or subjective judgments that could undermine the rationality of the Argument or Claim.

Overall, a Logic-based Argument or Claim and reasoning demonstrates a structured, rational, and evidence-based approach to thinking, reasoning, and Argumentation. It ensures that ideas are presented clearly, logically, coherently, and well-supported, leading to more effective communication and Decision-Making. An evidence-based approach to Problem Analysis involves systematically gathering, evaluating, and using relevant, pertinent evidence to understand and solve a problem. It emphasizes the importance of relying on data, research findings, domain expert opinions, and other credible, validated sources of information to inform problem-solving processes and Decision-Making.

6.2 DECOMPOSING" A PROBLEM AND USING AN EVIDENCE-BASED APPROACH TO PROBLEM ANALYSIS

"Decomposing" a problem is the process of breaking down a complicated, compound problem into smaller, more manageable components or sub-problems. By "decomposing" a problem, you can better understand its various dimensions, scale, and characteristics, identify the underlying causes, and develop effective solutions.

- *Define the problem:* Start by clearly defining the problem or issue you want to solve. Ensure that the problem is well-defined, specific, and focused. This will provide the parameters for the "decomposing" process.

- *Identify the key components and relevant information:* Identify the major components or elements contributing to the problem. Consider the distinct aspects, Factors, or Variables involved or affected by the situation. This step requires identifying the critical areas of focus and subsequent brainstorming.

- *Gather data:* Collect and gather the necessary data and information to support the Problem Analysis. This may involve conducting surveys, conducting interviews, doing observations, photography, videography, reviewing social media and podcasts, and reviewing research studies, case studies, industry reports, expert consultant's (third-party) opinions, or other pertinent sources of data and evidence. Consider both quantitative and qualitative data, current existent data, previous historical data, and alternative sources. Ensure that the data is credible, validated, reliable, and representative of the problem area.

- *Evaluate the quality of evidence*: Assess the quality and credibility of the data and evidence sources. Evaluate factors such as the methodology used in the data collection or research studies, the experience, educational background, credentials, and expertise of the authorities or consultants, and any potential Biases that could impact the validity of the evidence.

- *Analyze relationships and dependencies*: Examine the relationships and dependencies between the identified components. Identify how they interact and determine if any dependencies, interdependencies, or causal relationships exist. This preliminary analysis helps understand each element's interconnectedness and potential impact and the problem's sub-components. Use inferential reasoning and analytic methodologies to extract meaningful information pari passu data interpretation. Patterns and trends will emerge from this introspection.

- *Generate Hypotheses or proposed solutions*: Based on the analysis of the evidence, develop Hypotheses or potential solutions that address the root cause(s). Use the data and evidence to support or validate the proposed Hypotheses or solutions.

- *Test and refine solutions*: Implement and assess the proposed Hypotheses or solutions. Monitor the outcomes, determine whether they effectively address the identified root cause(s), and make adjustments or refinements as necessary based on ongoing evaluation and feedback.

- Communicate findings and recommendations: Communicate the conclusions of the data and evidence-based analysis, along with the recommended actions or proposed solutions, to relevant stakeholders, shareholders, Leaders, Team Leaders, and employees. Provide a clear rationale and evidence-based justification for making the recommendations.

- *Break down into sub-problems:* Once the key components are identified, break down the problem into more minor, more manageable sub-problems. These sub-problems should represent specific aspects that can be readily and independently addressed. Each sub-problem itself should be well-defined and focused. Then, prioritize the sub-problems. Evaluate the importance and urgency of each sub-problem. Prioritize them based on their impact on the major problem or situation, the feasibility of solving them, or any other relevant criteria. This step helps determine where to allocate resources and draws attention to the problem-solving process.

- *Analyze root causes, Factors, Variables, and effects:* Analyze each sub-problem to identify the underlying causes and effects. Understand what factors contribute to each sub-problem and how they are connected. This additional analysis helps develop targeted and effective solutions for each sub-problem component.

- *Develop solutions for sub-problems:* Brainstorm and develop potential solutions or strategies for each sub-problem. Consider the specific context, constraints, and desired outcomes for each sub-problem. The solutions should be tailored to address the causes and effects identified in the previous steps.

- *Integrate solutions and assess impact:* Once solutions are developed for each sub-problem, consider how they can be integrated to form an overarching, comprehensive solution for the overall major problem, assessing the potential impact of the integrated solution(s).

- *Evaluate if any modifications or refinements are needed* to ensure experimental case study design coherence and effectiveness.

- *Implementation:* Implement the solutions for each problem and associated sub-problem(s) and monitor their implementation and effectiveness. Continuously evaluate the progress being made and adjust as necessary. Measure the impact of the solutions and assess if the problem(s) has (have) been adequately addressed.

- *Continue to monitor and evaluate*: Continuously monitor and evaluate the effectiveness of the implemented solution(s). Gather feedback, measure outcomes, and adjust as needed, to ensure ongoing continuous improvement. Gather ongoing feedback to ensure continuous improvement and quality improvement.

In the end, by "decomposing" a problem into smaller sub-problems, you can analyze each component in a more focused and systematic way. This approach allows for a more targeted Problem Analysis and enables the development of specific solutions that address the underlying causes and effects of the major problem and sub-problems.

Adopting an evidence-based approach makes Problem Analysis more rigorous, objective, and informed. It helps mitigate or eliminate Biases, improves Decision-Making, and increases the likelihood of finding effective solutions to complex problems.

6.3 IRRELEVANT QUESTIONS AND INQUIRY

In the realm of questioning and inquiry, the relevance of a question varies depending on the context, goals of the case study design, and the specific subject matter being discussed. What may be irrelevant in one context could be highly relevant in another. However, it is essential to note that some questions may be considered less relevant or valuable than others in certain situations.

Scenarios where a question might be perceived as irrelevant:

- *Lack of connection:* A question may be considered irrelevant if it does not have a clear connection or relationship to the topic or problem. Irrelevant questions may divert focus and resources away from the main discussion or issue or fail to contribute to the understanding or resolution of the problem.

- *Lack of importance or priority:* In some cases, a question may be deemed irrelevant if it does not address significant aspects of the subject matter or if it is not essential or peripheral to the goals and objectives of the discussion. Questions that do not contribute to the primary purpose or desired outcomes may be considered less relevant or irrelevant.

- *Lack of applicability:* Questions that do not apply to the specific context or situation may be considered irrelevant. For example, asking a question about a particular technology in a discussion about historical events may be considered irrelevant because it does not align with the specific contemporaneous subject under consideration.

- *Lack of timeliness:* Questions that are not timely or appropriate within the given context or defined chronological time limitations could be considered irrelevant. For instance, asking about past events when focused on future planning may not be relevant to the current discussion.

While some questions may be perceived as irrelevant, it is essential to approach them with an open mind and consider the potential underlying motivations or intentions behind the question. Sometimes, irrelevant questions can spark new insights, revelations, alternative perspectives, or creative thinking that can enrich the discussion. It is often helpful to evaluate the relevance of a question based on the context, purpose, and objective of the forum or inquiry.

6.4 LOGIC AS A DISCIPLINE – GENERAL

Logic is a discipline that studies and analyzes the principles of valid reasoning. An Argument and rationale are valid if and only if it would be contradictory for the conclusion to be false if all the premises are true. The validity, therefore, does not require and necessitate the truth of the premise(s). Instead, it merely demands that the conclusion follows from the former without violating the correctness of the Logical construct. This provides a framework for understanding how to evaluate Arguments or Claims, draw conclusions, and make sound judgments, playing a crucial role in Problem Analysis and problem-solving by helping to structure, navigate, and assess the reasoning process.

6.5 LOGIC PRINCIPLES APPLIED TO BUSINESS AND PROBLEM ANALYSIS

In this application, Logic refers to the set of rules, their execution, and fundamental operational processes that govern the conduct and operations of a Business, Organization and Enterprise. The essential aspects of workflows and Decision-Making frameworks that guide how the Business operates and interacts with stakeholders, shareholders, Leaders, and employees are encompassed by this rubric. The principles by which objectives are achieved are encapsulated within the discipline of Logic, which forms the backbone of an Organization's and Enterprise's functionality, as seen by the visibility of its operations and the underlying processes that drive them. At its core, it defines how data and outputs are processed, transformed, and utilized within an Organization and Enterprise. The rules for data validation, data integrity, calculations, Statistics, transactions, and the overall flow of operations are within the definition of Business Logic. Implementation occurs through computer software applications, Structured Query Language (SQL) relational databases, and various technology solutions that automate and streamline operational processes. The requisite, essential contribution of Business Logic is its alignment with the strategic goals and objectives of the Organization and Enterprise. It ensures that day-to-day activities and Decision-Making are maintained within the Business's core and that these align with its plenary goals and objectives, as well as its mission, vision, and value statement. Business Logic evolves as the Organization and Enterprise grow, adapting to market changes, opportunities, challenges, threats, and governmental regulations and refining its operational strategies. Ultimately, this is the intellectual underpinning or framework that defines a Business's operational essence and lifeblood. Logic combines the rules of conduct, processes, and data flows to create a structured and efficient operating model that translates to the proper functioning of an Organization and Enterprise.

6.5.1 LOGIC PRINCIPLES APPLIED TO BUSINESS AND PROBLEM ANALYSIS — THE UTILITY OF LOGIC

- *Clear thinking:* Logic promotes clear and systematic thinking. It helps to organize ideas, identify relevant information, and recognize logical connections and interconnections between different facets of knowledge. This clarity of thought enables problem-solvers to analyze problems more effectively and make better-informed decisions.

- *Identifying and evaluating Arguments:* In Problem Analysis and problem-solving, assessing the strength and validity of different Arguments or Claims is essential. Logic provides the tools to assess the reasoning behind tendered Arguments or Claims. It helps to discern Logical Fallacies, errors in reasoning, or unsupported

Arguments or Claims, enabling Problem Analysis to distinguish between sound and unsound Arguments or Claims. To digress somewhat but illustrative, consider that while the shortest distance between two Euclidean points is a straight line, the closest distance between two points on a sphere does not necessarily follow the geometric rule and obeys the "great circle" (geodesic) construct, and so with Logic …

- *Creating, testing, and assessing Hypotheses: Logic aids in creating, testing, and evaluating Hypotheses during problem-solving.* It helps in formulating Hypotheses that are logical and testable. By applying Logical reasoning, Problem Analysis can identify the necessary evidence and experimental case study design to accept or reject the "Null" Hypothesis.

- *Deductive and inductive reasoning:* Logic encompasses mainly deductive and, less so, inductive reasoning, which are both crucial in problem-solving:

  1. *Deductive ("top-down") reasoning* involves drawing specific conclusions based on general principles or premises. This type of reasoning significantly relies on the initial premise(s) being correct. The final Argument is invalid if even one premise is found to be incorrect.

  2. *Inductive ("bottom-up") reasoning* involves inferring general conclusions from specific observations or evidence.

Applying these forms of reasoning allows Problem Analysis to draw meaningful inferences and make predictions based on available data or information.

- *Problem Analysis and "decomposing (vide infra):"* Logic assists in breaking down complex problems into manageable parts. It allows Problem Analysis to identify and correlate the logical relationships between different components, ensuring a systematic approach to the Problem Analysis. By "decomposing" a problem Logically, it becomes easier to identify the underlying causes and develop effective solutions.

- *Systematic Decision-Making:* Logic gives credence and rationality to systematic decisions. It facilitates Problem Analysis to consider relevant information, weigh varied Factors or Variables, and evaluate potential outcomes or consequences. By applying Logical principles, the Decision-Making process can minimize Biases, assess solution trade-offs and options, and make choices that align with problem-solving objectives.

- *Communication and persuasion:* Logic aids in effectively communicating ideas and persuading others. It helps Problem Analysis by presenting coherent Arguments, supporting their Argumentative Claims with Logical evidence, and anticipating counterarguments or rebuttals. Rational communication enhances the clarity and persuasiveness of problem-solving deliberations and Argumentative presentations.

By incorporating Critical Thinking[2] and employing Logic principles into Problem Analysis and problem-solving processes, individuals can enhance their ability to analyze complex, convoluted problems, make informed decisions, and thereby effectively communicate their reasoning. Logic provides a structured approach to Problem Analysis and problem-solving, ensuring that reasoning is sound and evidence-based and leads to rational conclusions and qualified, eligible options for Decision-Making.

The discussion now takes us to a formal review of Argumentation or debate and Logic employing the Toulmin method.

6.6 LOGIC VERSUS FACT, ARGUMENTATION OR DEBATE, AND THE TOULMIN METHOD

British philosopher Stephen E. Toulmin (1922-2009) conceived a method of Argumentation style in his 1958 publication, "*The Uses of Arguments*," that breaks Arguments or debates down into six components:

1. *Claim*
2. *Grounds*
3. *Warrant*
4. Qualifier
5. *Rebuttal*
6. *Backing*

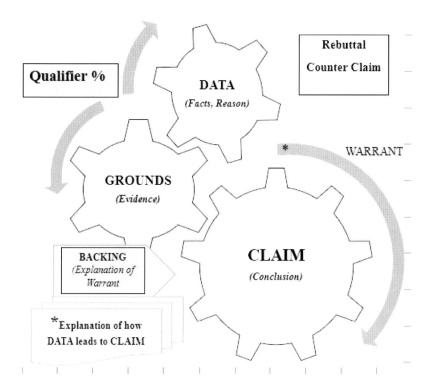

In Toulmin's method, every Argument begins with the three critical fundamentals (the Claim, the Grounds, and the Warrant), as well as three additional parts:

- The *Claim* is the assertion one would like to prove to an audience. It is, in other words, the main Argument or conclusion.

- The *Grounds* (reasons and evidence) of an Argument are the supportive evidence and facts addressing the Claim.

- The *Warrant* is finally implied or stated explicitly and is the assumption(s) that links the Grounds to the Claim.

The Toulmin method is structured to analyze and Logically argue a Claim, conclusion, or assertion. The organization and categorization of Arguments are developed by way of the process. The Argument itself is separated and deconstructed into its constituent parts, and each part is, in turn, evaluated in terms of how well it contributes to the whole, how valid the Argument or Claim or assertion is, and how effective. The analysis is orderly and linear, with one idea leading to another in an orderly, stepwise, organized manner. The Arguments are bolstered, strengthened, or improved upon as to any specific weaker points. The first three components, as described, are obligatory. At the same time, the last three (Qualifier (percentage), Rebuttal, and Backing (explanation of the Warrant or how Data leads to the Claim) are optional and may be presented in any order (rearranged) or omitted. However, the more complex or nuanced Arguments or Claims may call for their inclusion.

In Argumentation:

The four basic types of Claims:

1. *Claims of fact* (Claims that assert their main idea as a matter of fact, supported by relevant, sufficient, and reliable Grounds).

2. *Claims of value* (Claims that assert their main idea as a matter of morals, values, or beliefs, supported by appeals to the shared beliefs and values of the audience).

3. *Claims of policy* (Claims that assert their main idea as a matter of changing policy, supported by relevant, sufficient, and reliable Grounds *AND* appeals to the audience's values).

4. *Claims of definition* (Claims that assert their main idea as a matter of defining a concept or term, supported by relevant, sufficient, and reliable Grounds that justify and fortify the proposed definition).

The support offered to justify a given Argument or Claim, counterclaim, and Rebuttal considerations:

- Is the support offered to defend the Argument or Claim sufficient, relevant, reliable, and authoritative? How can it be improved?

- Does the support offered in defense of the Argument or Claim match the kind of Argument or Claim being argued? In other words, if it is an Argument or Claim of fact, value, policy, or definition, does the arguer provide the right kind of supportive evidence to defend that particular kind of Argument or Claim?

- Are alternative points of view considered and given fair treatment?

- Anticipated counterclaims and Rebuttals and their support?

- Adding to the Grounds (Data) that would help to further support or challenge the assertion of the main Argument or Claim?

The Six Types of Warrants:

- *Warrant-based generalization*: A generalization is a broad statement applied to various circumstances, situations, or individuals.

A Warrant-based generalization assumes that if your Grounds and Argument or Claim apply to a sample population, they also apply to the entire population from which the sample is derived.

- *Warrant based on principle* is related to a common moral or value. For example, "many individuals believe it is important to tell the truth."

- *Warrant based on analogy* is a comparison between two seemingly different ideas, individuals, or circumstances. A Warrant based on an analogy equates stating something is true or valid for one situation and is, in all likelihood, valid for a distinct event or situation with fundamental commonalities.

- *Warrant based on means* indicates that the occurrence or presence of one idea or construct indicates another idea or construct. For example, "someone who owns an automobile likely also has a garage, State mandated car insurance, and likely car cleaning and maintenance items."

- *Warrant based on authority* establishes the truth based on an expert professional or group within the field. For example, "many medical education experts say it's important for medical students to undergo a rigorous internship."

- *Warrant based on causality* is when one matter can influence or directly cause a particular outcome. For example, "studying and passing a Department of Motor Vehicles (DMV) exam and road test, not to mention driver education and regular practice, can help improve your driving skills."

Turning to the backside of the model: The Qualifier, Rebuttal, and Backing:
These three elements are not fundamental to a Toulmin Argument but may be added as needed, rearranged, or not even utilized, as already mentioned.

The Qualifier shows that an Argument or Claim may *not* be true or valid in all circumstances.

A Qualifier is a word or phrase that indicates the degree (percentage) of certainty or scope of your Argument or Claim. Terms like—"Presumably," "Sometimes," "Some," "Most," "Usually," "Many," "Probably," "In Most Cases," and "For Our Target Segment"—underscore to your audience that you understand there are instances, that is, exceptions, where your Argument or Claim may *not* be correct. On the contrary, using too broad and especially absolute Qualifiers such as "Always" or "Never" can have the opposite effect, making Arguments or Claims challenging to support.

The Rebuttal is acknowledging another valid perspective or viewpoint of the situation. Including a Rebuttal or Qualifier in an Argument or Claim builds one's ethos or credibility. When one realizes that your stance is not always accurate or when you provide multiple perspectives of a situation, you signal to the audience, opposing debater, discussant, or Corporate and Enterprise Leadership that you are building upon an image of being careful, prudent, balanced and being an unbiased Critical Thinker, rather than of someone unthinkingly pushing as well as promoting a singular interpretation of a circumstance or situation. The debater can use a Rebuttal to pre-empt counterarguments, strengthening the original Argument or Claim. The Rebuttal is the counterargument that continues the dialogue, comprising an Argument or Claim, Warrant, or Backing.

The Backing refers to any additional factual and relevant data or informational support of the Warrant. In many cases, the Warrant is implicit, and therefore, the Backing provides support for the Warrant by giving a specific example and rationale that justifies the Warrant.

6.7 UTILITY OF THE TOULMIN METHOD IN BUSINESS

The Toulmin method for Argumentation and its use of Logic in Problem Analysis is an effective way of getting to the "*How* and *Why*" levels of an Argument or Claim in debating. In most instances, the Argument or Claim is anatomically "dissected" (a figurative forensic autopsy of sorts, done prospectively rather than retrospectively). The Toulmin method of Argumentation can be utilized to improve Critical Thinking[2] by in-depth evaluation using a high level of Logical reasoning skills. The Toulmin method can be used effectively in routine and board committee meetings, leveraging debating to make compelling Arguments and arrive at solid conclusions and eventual decisions. Getting the Decision-Making step right is a mission-critical accomplishment for a Business Leader, CEO, and Organization and Enterprise. To employ Toulmin's model for your Business proposal or Argument, you need to identify your Argument or Claim first and then gather evidence to support it. Explain the Warrant by connecting the Data to the Argument or Claim using Logic or authority. Provide Backing to reinforce the Warrant and add a Qualifier to express your level of certainty. Lastly, address any objections, counterarguments, or rebuttals to your Argument or Claim.

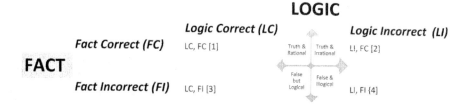

6.8 DISCUSSION – DEBATE QUESTIONNAIRE (MODEL)

CLAIM:

QUALIFIER AND EXCEPTIONS:

REASON OR POSITION 1

What makes this reason relevant?

What makes this reason effective?

What evidence supports this reason?

Is this evidence sufficient?

Is this evidence credible?

Is this evidence accurate?

REASON OR POSITION 2

What makes this reason relevant?

What makes this reason effective?

What evidence supports this reason?

Is this evidence sufficient?

Is this evidence credible?

Is this evidence accurate?

REASON OR POSITION 3

What makes this reason relevant?

What makes this reason effective?

What evidence supports this reason?

Is this evidence sufficient?

Is this evidence credible?

Is this evidence accurate?

OBJECTION:

QUALIFICATION: *(*Specifying limits to Claim, Warrant, and Backing with the degree of conditionality asserted).

According to the famous satirist Jonathan Swift, "Argument is the worst sort of conversation."

CHAPTER 7

"NO MATTER HOW SIMPLE OR MUNDANE A PROBLEM INITIALLY SEEMS, IT INVARIABLY MAY BECOME TOO COMPLEX TO BE UNDERSTOOD OR SOLVED"

7.1 THE CHRONIC FATIGUE SYNDROME/ MYALGIC ENCEPHALOMYELITIS — GENERAL

While fatigue is a common symptom, identifying the underlying cause can be challenging due to the numerous potential factors involved when it becomes chronic and persistent. Chronic Fatigue Syndrome (CFS), also known as Myalgic Encephalomyelitis (ME), is a complex and poorly understood condition characterized by persistent fatigue that is not alleviated by rest and is often accompanied by a range of other co-morbid associated symptoms. The causes of CFS/ME are not yet fully known or understood, and research is still ongoing to uncover its underlying mechanisms.

7.1.1 THE CHRONIC FATIGUE SYNDROME/ MYALGIC ENCEPHALOMYELITIS — CAUSES?

While there are no definitive and universally accepted causes, *several factors have been implicated or studied concerning CFS/ME:*

- *Viral infections*: Some studies have suggested that certain viral infections, such as Epstein-Barr Virus (EBV), Lyme disease, Human Herpes Virus 6 (HHV-6), and Enteroviruses, may trigger or contribute to the development of CFS/ME. However, no specific viral cause has been definitively identified to date.

- *Immune dysfunction*: Abnormalities in the immune system have been observed in individuals with CFS/ME. These include altered cytokine profiles, decreased T-lymphocyte natural killer (NK) cell function, and autoimmune responses. It remains unclear whether immune dysfunction is a cause or a consequence of the condition.

- *Neuroendocrine dysfunction*: Dysregulation of the Hypothalamic-Pituitary-Adrenal (HPA) axis, which controls the body's stress response, has been observed in some individuals with CFS/ME. This may contribute to chronic fatigue and other associated symptoms.

- *Genetic predisposition*: Evidence suggests that certain genetic factors may increase the susceptibility to CFS/ME. However, no specific genes have been identified as definitive causal factors.

- *Environmental triggers*: Some environmental factors have been suggested as potential triggers for CFS/ME, including exposure to toxins, chemicals, or mold. However, more research is needed to understand their putative role.

- *Psychological factors*: Psychological stress, trauma, depression, and certain predisposing personality traits have been proposed as potential contributors to the development or persistence of symptoms of CFS/ME. However, it is essential to note that Psychological factors alone cannot account for the complexity of the condition.

- *Dysautonomia*: Autonomic nervous system dysfunction, specifically orthostatic intolerance (problems with blood pressure and heart rate regulation upon standing), has been observed in some individuals with CFS/ME. This may contribute to some associated symptoms, such as dizziness and cognitive impairment.

- *Mitochondrial dysfunction*: Some studies have indicated that impaired mitochondrial function, which affects whole-body cellular energy production, may play a role in CFS/ME. However, further research is needed to confirm this putative association.

- *Sleep Disorders*: Sleep disturbances, such as disrupted sleep patterns, insomnia, and non-restorative sleep, as well as sleep deprivation, are common in individuals with CFS/ME. However, it is unclear whether sleep abnormalities are a cause or a consequence of the condition.

- *Multifactorial causes*: CFS/ME can be attributed to many physical, Psychological, and lifestyle components. Determining the primary cause or combination of causes requires a comprehensive evaluation of the patient's medical history, lifestyle habits, sleep patterns, stress levels, and potential underlying medical conditions. The latter, some already mentioned, such as chronic infections (e.g., viral diseases), autoimmune disorders (e.g., Systemic Lupus Erythematosus, Fibromyalgia), hormonal imbalances (e.g., thyroid dysfunction), or mental health conditions (e.g., depression, anxiety). Accurately diagnosing these conditions often requires ruling out other potential etiological causes through extensive examinations, ancillary laboratory testing, and consultations with various specialists.

- *Overlapping symptoms*: CFS/ME often coexists with other symptoms, such as pain, cognitive impairment, and sleep disturbances. These overlapping symptoms can further complicate the diagnostic process as they may indicate different underlying causes or epiphenomena.

- *Subjective nature*: Fatigue, in the end, is a subjective experience, and its semi-quantifiable clinical assessment relies heavily on the patient's self-reporting. However, different individuals may describe chronic fatigue differently, making it challenging to objectively measure and compare chronic fatigue levels within and between patients. This subjectivity can add a layer of perplexity to the diagnosis and monitoring of CFS/ME.

It is important to note that this list represents putative etiological or associated factors that have been investigated or theorized to be involved in the development or persistence of CFS/ME. The condition is complex, the list may be incomplete, and individual experiences and contributing factors may vary. Further research is needed to establish a more comprehensive understanding of the causes and underlying mechanisms of CFS/ME.

7.1.2 THE CHRONIC FATIGUE SYNDROME/MYALGIC ENCEPHALOMYELITIS — IMPACT ON THE QUALITY OF LIFE AND TREATMENT APPROACHES

Due to the complexity of CFS/ME, no universal treatment regimen works for all patients. Treatment plans often involve a multidisciplinary approach, including lifestyle modifications (e.g., sleep hygiene, stress Management), medications (e.g., pain relievers, antidepressants), and targeted therapies (based on the underlying cause, if identified). Finding the most effective treatment strategy may require trial and error, personalized therapeutic plan adjustments, and long-term Management. CFS/ME can significantly impact a person's quality of Life through impairments of their physical and mental well-being, leading to reduced productivity, social withdrawal, and decreased quality of Life. Understanding and addressing the broader implications of CFS/ME on an individual's Life requires a comprehensive clinical approach beyond diagnosing and treating the symptoms alone. CFS/ME may initially seem like an ordinary, mundane medical problem on its surface. Still, its complexity stems from the multitude of putative causes, overlapping symptoms, and the subjective nature of the condition, with a need for a multidisciplinary approach. Accurate diagnosis and effective Management of Chronic Fatigue Syndrome/Myalgic Encephalomyelitis (CFS/ME) require thorough evaluations, collaboration between healthcare specialist professionals, and a patient-centered approach to address the underlying factors contributing to the condition.

7.2 THE PATHOLOGICAL DIAGNOSIS OF CANCER — INTRODUCTION

An otherwise daily, routine problem encountered in Diagnostic Pathology, the diagnosis of Cancer belies this notion due to its inherent, actual, and potential diagnostic complexity. It begins with the interpretation of prepared histopathological slides.

Histopathology embraces the preparation and microscopic examination of tissue samples to determine the presence, type and subtype, grade, and stage of Cancer in this diagnosis. While the process seems straightforward enough, several factors can complicate and compound the diagnostic interpretation of these slides.

7.2.1 WHY INTERPRETING HISTOPATHOLOGICAL SLIDES FOR CANCER DIAGNOSIS CAN BE CHALLENGING — GENERAL CONSIDERATIONS AND USE OF ANCILLARY TESTING

- *Morphological variations*: Cancerous tissues can exhibit a wide range of morphological variations, making it difficult to differentiate between normal and abnormal cells. This challenge is amplified when dealing with poorly differentiated or rare types of Cancer, where characteristic features may be subtle or atypical.

- *Interobserver variability*: Different Diagnostic Pathologists may have varying expertise and experience, and subjective interpretations can vary. This variability can lead to discrepancies in diagnosing Cancer and even the grading of its aggressiveness or predictive behavior. Achieving consensus among Pathologists through internal quality control measures and external (second or even third opinion) consultations can obviate this issue.

- *Mimickers and overlapping features*: Some non-cancerous conditions and benign tumors can mimic the appearance of Cancer cells and tissues under the microscope. Distinguishing between these entities and true malignancy can be complex and daunting, requiring a comprehensive understanding of the subtle differences between cellular morphology and cyto-histoarchitecture.

- *Sampling Bias:* The accuracy of Cancer diagnosis relies heavily on the correct selection, adequacy, and viability of the cellular or tissue sample obtained during the Surgical biopsy procedure or Surgical resection. In some cases, the sample may not be viable, sampling necrotic tissue, and therefore may not be representative of the entire tumor, leading to the possibility of missing important diagnostic and prognostic features by sampling (error) only a less representative area of cancer.

- *Ancillary techniques*: The interpretation of histopathological slides may require the use of ancillary techniques, such as immunohistochemistry, immunofluorescence, diagnostic molecular testing, next-generation gene sequencing, and ultrastructure (to name a few), that aid in diagnosing Cancer or in sub-classifying malignant tumors. The selection and interpretation of these various ancillary tests themselves can be complex, requiring expertise in understanding their indications, limitations, and usage, as well as interpretation of testing or reaction nuances and correlation with the initial Hematoxylin and Eosin (H and E) stained histopathological slide findings. There are existent biomarkers with both prognostic and therapeutic implications. Further testing may involve, but is not limited to, using, for example, KRAS, HER2, EGFR, and ALK mutations. The latter also possesses the benefit of having therapeutic implications and even a role in diagnosing carcinomas of unknown origin, especially adenocarcinoma. In particular, therapeutic and prognostic consequences for the patient may be disclosed. Additionally, genomic technologies elucidate large-scale gene expression or profiles based on mRNA and microRNA or both. These are exquisitely applicable to the assay of very small (micro) biopsy samples available in Formalin-Fixed Paraffin-Embedded (FFPE) tissue using a quantitative Reverse Transcriptase Polymerase Chain Reaction (RT-PCR) platform. RT-PCR has, more recently, revolutionized genetic expression profiling or "*footprinting*" as a means of Problem Analysis and Decision-Making; this, for all intents and purposes, represents the 'nth" degree of diagnostic Cancer investigation (Alshareeda, 2020).

Commercially available molecular assays using gene-expression profiling for cancer of unknown primary site

Supplier	Test	Platform	Material	No. of genes profiled	No. of tumour classes
Pathwork Diagnostics	ResponseDX Tissue of Origin™ Test	RNA extraction/ microarray	Fresh	2000	10
BioTheranostics	CancerTYPE ID®	RT-PCR	FFPE	92	54
Rosetta Genomics-Prometheus	miRview_ mets (ProOnc Tumour SourceDxT)	RT-PCR for microRNA	FFPE	48	42

Notwithstanding the above use of ancillary testing, certain types of Cancers can especially pose intransigent diagnostic challenges to their nosological and taxonomic classification due to their intrinsic complex nature or their histopathologic features, overlapping similarities to other conditions, many discussed or alluded to as diagnostic dilemmas:

- *Undifferentiated or poorly differentiated tumors*: These are Cancers that lack clear ontogenetic differentiation or may resemble (mimicry) other types of Cancer. Determining the tumor's precise cellular origin, type, or specific subtype may be difficult, as the tumor cells and H & E cyto-histoarchitecture may not exhibit distinct characteristics.

- *Sarcomas:* A diverse group of malignancies arising from mesenchymal connective tissues. They can exhibit various phenotypic patterns and cellular characteristics, challenging their identification and classification.

- *Hematolymphoid malignancies*: This category of tumors includes a range of malignancies affecting blood cells and lymphoid tissues, such as, but not limited to, leukemia, lymphoma, and multiple myeloma. Diagnosing specific subtypes within these types of malignancies can be formidable, a veritable labyrinth due to overlapping features and the need for very specialized ancillary testing techniques, some of which employ flow cytometric, cytogenetic, and molecular testing or combination of methods to elucidate the nature of the malignancy.

- *Rare or uncommon cancers*: Diagnostic Pathologists may encounter rare or uncommon Cancers with limited published reference data in the medical literature and diagnostic criteria available. In such cases, it can be challenging to determine a malignant tumor's exact nature and origin to guide appropriate treatment decisions.

It is important to note that advancements in diagnostic ancillary techniques, as enumerated, have significantly improved the accuracy of Cancer diagnoses. For instance, advances in molecular techniques, such as Next-Generation Sequencing (NGS) and gene expression profiling or "*footprinting.*" are becoming increasingly valuable in diagnosing undifferentiated tumors by identifying specific genetic alterations associated with the different tumor types. The integration of molecular analyses with diagnostic immunohistochemistry and other ancillary techniques enhances the accuracy of the diagnosis and aids in personalized treatment planning for patients with undifferentiated Cancers. A synergistic situation where one (1) plus one (1) equals three (1), or "The whole is greater than the sum of the parts," (or is it "the totality is not, as it were, a mere heap, but the whole is something *besides* the parts" (Aristotle; 1908 translation by W. D. Ross: of Aristotle Metaphysics VIII, 1045a.8-10).

7.2.2 ROLE OF DIAGNOSTIC IMMUNOHISTOCHEMISTRY (IHC) IN THE PATHOLOGICAL DIAGNOSIS OF CANCER — GENERAL

Immunohistochemistry (IHC) plays a crucial role in the Diagnostic Pathology workup of undifferentiated Cancers, where traditional histological H & E examination alone may not provide sufficient information to determine the malignant neoplastic tumor's origin or classification.

The typical preparatory IHC steps from start to finalization include:

1. Beginning with the Paraffin-Embedded, Formalin-Fixed (PEFF) neoplastic tissue and deparaffinization of the tissue.

2. Rehydration.

3. Protein, antigen-epitope retrieval with heat or enzyme treatment in a pH-adjusted phosphate buffered solution.

4. Blocking-quenching step to eliminate endogenous peroxidase and non-specific protein binding.

5. Temperature-controlled, timed application of the initial primary antibody.

6. Application of the secondary antibody previously coupled to an enzyme, Horseradish Peroxidase (HRP) or equivalent.

7. Add the chromogenic solution to amplify and optimize the antigen-antibody reaction and add hydrogen peroxide (H2O2).

8. Localization-visualization of the antigen-epitope reaction.

9. Analysis-interpretation.

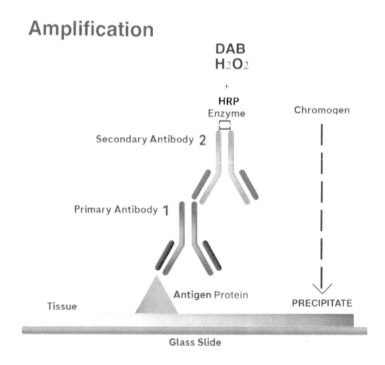

Amplification

DAB
H_2O_2
+
HRP
Enzyme
Chromogen

Secondary Antibody 2

Primary Antibody 1

Antigen Protein

Tissue

PRECIPITATE

Glass Slide

A typical diagnostic immunohistochemical panel utilizes a combination of specific antibodies to identify the expression of various proteins and antigens-epitopes in neoplastic tumor cells. In the primary immunohistochemical reaction, the protein antigen-epitope is revealed by way of an interaction with a primary antibody (primary Ab, rabbit, or mouse monoclonal), which in turn interacts with a secondary antibody (second Ab) conjugated to an enzyme that utilizes a chromogenic reaction that in turn amplifies the visualization of the target protein, antigen-epitope site of reaction. In this example, the chromogenic reaction described here uses the reagent 3, 3'- Diaminobenzidine (DAB) in the presence of Horseradish Peroxidase (HRP, a forty-four kilodalton protein enzyme). The activation occurs after a background reaction with Hydrogen Peroxide (H_2O_2). The oxidation of the substrate DAB produces an insoluble precipitate that is visible under the microscope, identifying (decorating) the protein or antigen-epitope target site of the reaction.

The antibody staining patterns assist the Diagnostic Pathologist in differentiating between diverse types of undifferentiated Cancers and ultimately arriving at an accurate diagnosis.

An illustrative image of an immunohistochemical staining reaction that compares:

- *Negative control* reaction

- *Cytoplasmic positive* pattern of reaction

- *Nuclear positive* pattern of reaction

- *Membranous positive* pattern of reaction localization

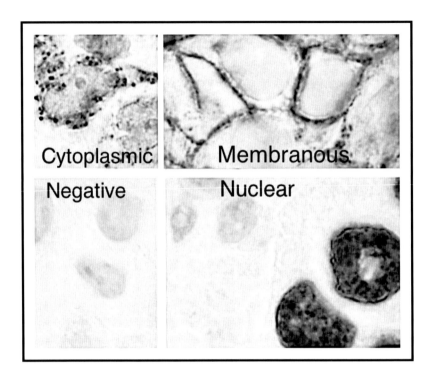

Cytoplasmic Membranous

Negative Nuclear

The following basic, traditional IHC information set forth is simplified to some extent and abbreviated, but this is illustrative of Problem Analysis and Decision-Making in Diagnostic Pathology. In this instance, it uses an extended immunohistochemical panel in the contextual setting of an undifferentiated malignant neoplasm suspected of being of squamous (epithelial) origin.

7.2.2.1 ROLE OF DIAGNOSTIC IMMUNOHISTOCHEMISTRY (IHC) IN THE PATHOLOGICAL DIAGNOSIS OF CANCER — UNDIFFERENTIATED MALIGNANT NEOPLASM SUSPECTED OF BEING OF SQUAMOUS (EPITHELIAL) ORIGIN

- *Cytokeratin (CK)* and related epithelial markers: CK is an intermediate filament protein in epithelial cells. The cytoplasmic expression pattern is detected by immunohistochemistry, which can help distinguish between epithelial and non-epithelial tumors.

- *Epithelial Membrane Antigen (EMA)*: A glycoprotein expressed on the cell membrane of epithelial cells. Its expression can further support an epithelial origin.

- *Pan-Cytokeratin (AE1/AE3)*: Positive in many epithelial tumors, a broad-spectrum cytokeratin intermediate filament marker useful for excluding melanocytic differentiation in tumors with an undifferentiated H & E histopathological appearance.

- *CK7*: Positive in many epithelial tumors, such as lung Adenocarcinoma, Breast carcinoma, and Ovarian carcinoma.

- *CK20*: Positive in Gastrointestinal epithelial tumors, such as Colo-Rectal carcinoma.

- *P63 and p40*: Monoclonal antibodies are both nuclear in their localization and can be utilized to diagnose Undifferentiated epithelial Cancer. They are relatively specific markers used to diagnose otherwise Undifferentiated Cancers, particularly in distinguishing between Squamous Cell Carcinoma (SCC) and other types of undifferentiated or de-differentiated tumors. Both p63 and p40 are homologous proteins and isoforms of the tumor suppressor protein p53 gene, both highly expressed in squamous epithelial cells. While p53 is broadly expressed in various cell types, the isoforms p63 and p40 are predominantly expressed in squamous epithelial cells, including the epithelia of the skin, the respiratory tract (e.g., lung), and other stratified squamous epithelia. P63 and p40 have demonstrated their utility in differentiating Squamous Cell Carcinoma (SCC) from different carcinoma subtypes, particularly in cases where traditional H & E histological examination did not provide definitive interpretation. In well-differentiated SCC, for example, p63 and p40 are usually diffusely and strongly positive in the nuclei of the tumor cells.

This robust, specific nuclear staining reflects the strong expression of these markers in squamous epithelial cells. In contrast, other types of carcinomas, such as Adenocarcinomas and Small Cell Carcinomas, typically show no staining or minimal expression of p63 and p40.

Example of the utility of p63 and p40 in Differential Diagnosis and cautionary notes: Undifferentiated Cancers can present a diagnostic challenge, as their H and E histological appearance may lack specific features to determine their origin. In such cases, immunohistochemistry (IHC) utilizing p63 and p40 can be instrumental in differentiating SCC from other tumor types. Adenocarcinomas are commonly positive for cytokeratin 7 (CK7) while negative for p63 and p40. Furthermore, Small Cell Carcinomas, positive for neuroendocrine markers, such as chromogranin and synaptophysin, are negative for both p63 and p40.

The pragmatic use of an algorithmic approach to the Pathological Cancer diagnosis of differentiated Lung Tumors is further elaborated upon in the cited reference: "Optimizing Tissue Use: A Stepwise Approach to Diagnosing Squamous Cell Lung Carcinoma (SCC) on Small Biopsies"— Lung Cancer sub-typing by stepwise algorithmic testing (Modified and updated, after Olazagasti, 2020):

Squamous Cell Ca

AdenoCa

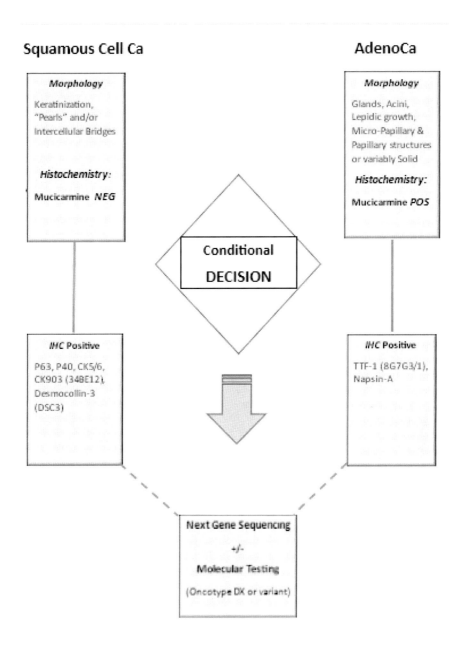

Morphology

Keratinization, "Pearls" and/or Intercellular Bridges

Histochemistry:

Mucicarmine *NEG*

Morphology

Glands, Acini, Lepidic growth, Micro-Papillary & Papillary structures or variably Solid

Histochemistry:

Mucicarmine *POS*

Conditional **DECISION**

IHC Positive

P63, P40, CK5/6, CK903 (34BE12), Desmocollin-3 (DSC3)

IHC Positive

TTF-1 (8G7G3/1), Napsin-A

Next Gene Sequencing

+/-

Molecular Testing

(Oncotype DX or variant)

7.2.2.2 ROLE OF DIAGNOSTIC IMMUNOHISTOCHEMISTRY (IHC) IN THE PATHOLOGICAL DIAGNOSIS OF CANCER—UNDIFFERENTIATED MALIGNANT NEOPLASM SUSPECTED OF BEING MELANOMA

- *S100 Protein*: A broad spectrum marker for neural crest-derived tumors, showing positive staining in Melanoma and other neuroendocrine tumors. It is evenly distributed in the cytoplasm and also found in the nucleoplasm.

- *HMB-45 (Human Melanoma Black-45)*: A monoclonal cytoplasmic antibody that targets the pre-melanosome complex (glycoprotein gp100), an antigen expressed explicitly in melanocytic cells, including melanocytes and neoplastic Melanoma cells. This protein is relatively specific for melanocytic differentiation, although not a sensitive marker. Of note, in benign nevi, it is concentrated in the nuclear compartment, whereas in malignant lesions, it is predominantly cytoplasmic in location.

- *Melan-A (MART-1 (Melanoma Antigen Recognized by T cells)*: Another melanocytic marker commonly used in diagnosing Melanoma. Melan-A (MART-1) is a transmembrane protein antigen specifically found on melanocytes and Melanoma tumor cells.

- *Tyrosinase*: A key enzyme that catalyzes Dihydroxyphenylalanine (DOPA) in the melanin synthesis pathway and is expressed by cells of melanocytic lineage and differentiation.

- *SOX10 (SRY-Box Transcription Factor 10)*: A neural crest lineage transcription factor heterogeneously expressed in melanocytes, Schwann cells, myoepithelial cells, and oligodendroglia. It is increasingly recognized as a sensitive and specific marker for melanocytic differentiation, especially in difficult-to-diagnose cases.

- *p16 (INK4a)*: A tumor suppressor protein that plays a role in cell cycle regulation. This is a cyclin-dependent kinase inhibitor. P16 (INK4a) expression is commonly observed in Melanoma and can be used as a supportive, not primary, marker for melanocytic differentiation. P16 (INK4a), moreover, has a predictive (negative tumor staining) and prognostic value for Melanoma evolution. A positive cytoplasmic immunohistochemical staining pattern with concurrent negative nuclear expression for this protein might serve as a negative predictor of lymph node status.

- *Vimentin:* An intermediate filament protein expressed in mesenchymal cells. It is positive in Melanoma cells, including those found in metastases, but is negative in most epithelial tumors, helping to exclude certain tumor types.

The Clinical Utility of Melanoma IHC Markers follows an evaluation and usage that analogously parallels Critical Thinking[2], Problem Analysis, and Decision-Making discussed elsewhere in this Book. In summary, the Pathological Diagnosis of Melanoma usually relies on a comprehensive immunohistochemical panel analysis. Specifically, a positive staining pattern for HMB-45 and additional markers like S100, Melan-A (MART-1), Tyrosinase, SOX10, and p16 (INK4a) provide compelling evidence of melanocytic differentiation. Negative staining for pan-cytokeratin and EMA helps exclude non-melanocytic tumors. Additionally, assessing the Ki-67 proliferation index marker aids in predicting the tumor's aggressiveness and may help guide treatment decisions. This expanded multiplex panel approach is analytical and diagnostic in its objective. The stepwise diagnostic approach allows the Diagnostic Pathologist to differentiate Melanoma from other types of malignancies and facilitates appropriate treatment planning and patient Management.

7.2.2.3 ROLE OF DIAGNOSTIC IMMUNOHISTOCHEMISTRY (IHC) IN THE PATHOLOGICAL DIAGNOSIS OF CANCER — ADDITIONAL IMMUNOHISTOCHEMISTRY (IHC) MARKERS FOR CHARACTERIZATION OF OTHER TUMORS

- *Desmin and Myogenin (MyoD1)*: Desmin and Myogenin (MyoD1) are markers for muscle differentiation that can aid in identifying tumors, specifically with muscle differentiation, such as rhabdomyosarcoma. Desmin is a cytoplasmic intermediate filament broadly present in cells with myogenic differentiation (rhabdomyosarcoma, rhabdomyoma, leiomyosarcoma, leiomyoma, benign smooth muscle and rhabdomyoblastic elements in other tumors), as well as vascular lining endothelial cells. On the other hand, Myogenin (MyoD1) encodes for a myogenic transcriptional regulatory protein expressed in early skeletal muscle development and regeneration. The latter is a sensitive marker for rhabdomyosarcoma but lacks specificity. Both these myogenic markers are found in rhabdomyosarcoma but may also be present in tumors with undifferentiated features and those exhibiting rhabdomyoblastic malignant characteristics.

- *CD45 (Leukocyte Common Antigen)*: This transmembrane protein marker for intrinsic tyrosine phosphatase activity is involved in B and T lymphocyte cell antigen receptor-mediated activation. Isoforms do exist. Its utility is that it represents a ubiquitous pan-leukocyte cell surface pan-leukocyte marker used by Diagnostic Pathologists to exclude lymphoma or leukemia involvement in tissues.

- *CD31 and CD34:* Markers for endothelial cells that can help identify vascular tumors or vascular invasion by tumors. CD34, in particular, is a glycosylated transmembrane protein marker for vascular endothelial cells. Sensitivity is high, but CD34 is not a specific marker for neoplastic angiogenesis.

- *CD99 (Mic2)*: A cell surface glycoprotein expressed in two isoforms found in small round blue cell tumors, especially Ewing Sarcoma and Primitive Neuroectodermal Tumor (PNET).

- *TTF-1 (Thyroid Transcription Factor-1, or NKX2)*: A nuclear transcription factor expressed in lung adenocarcinomas, small cell carcinoma, including a variable number of extrapulmonary Small Cell Carcinomas, and some differentiated Thyroid Cancers.

- *Napsin-A (Nap-A)*: A functional aspartic proteinase, considered an alternative IHC marker for primary lung adenocarcinoma, being more sensitive than TTF-1 for primary lung adenocarcinoma (87% versus 64%; P < .001), and more specific versus all tumors, excluding kidney (P < .001). A combination of Nap-A and TTF-1 was used in the algorithmic classification of primary lung carcinoma published by Olazagasti. et al. (2020), specifically in the differentiating primary lung adenocarcinoma (Nap-A (+), TTF-1(+)) from primary lung squamous cell carcinoma (Nap-A (-), TTF-1(-)), and primary lung small cell carcinoma (Nap-A (-), TTF-1(+)). A more recent study by Weidemann A. et al. (2021), notwithstanding, urged caution with the interpretation of Napsin-A since Napsin-A expression was found to be expressed in at least sixteen (16) different tumor types. The study of the prevalence of IHC expression in declining order of frequency was adenocarcinoma of the lung (85.6%), clear cell adenocarcinoma of the ovary (71.7%), clear cell adenocarcinoma of the endometrium (42.8%), papillary renal cell carcinoma (40.2%), clear cell (tubulo) papillary renal cell carcinoma (16.7%), endometrial serous carcinoma (9.3%), papillary thyroid carcinoma (9.3%) and clear cell renal cell carcinoma

(8.2%). Interestingly, in the latter (clear cell renal cell carcinoma) and papillary renal cell carcinoma, reduced Napsin-A expression was linked to adverse clinicopathological features.

- *PAX-8*: This is one of nine members of the paired box gene (PAX) family of nuclear transcription factors that regulate organogenesis, particularly those derived from embryonic Wolffian and Mullerian origin. Expression is found in epithelial neoplasms of the Thyroid, Thymus, Ovary, Endometrium, Endocervix, Fallopian tube, and Kidney.

- *Ki-67 (MIB-1)*: A non-histone nuclear protein marker of cellular proliferation that can provide information on the tumor's growth fraction and aggressiveness. For example, a high Ki-67 labeling index is associated with a more aggressive phenotype in Melanoma.

7.2.2.4 ROLE OF DIAGNOSTIC IMMUNOHISTOCHEMISTRY (IHC) IN THE PATHOLOGICAL DIAGNOSIS OF CANCER—PITFALLS

While both p63 and p40 immunohistochemical markers are highly specific for squamous differentiation, they can occasionally be expressed in some non-squamous tumors, such as Urothelial carcinoma, the so-called "Basaloid" variants of other carcinomas, and certain (epithelioid) Sarcomas. Proper correlation with clinical and hematoxylin and eosin (H and E) histopathological features is essential to reach an accurate diagnosis. The just-described pitfalls are another reason for using an expanded immunohistochemical panel. The combination of p63 and p40 staining, along with other relevant differentiating immunohistochemical markers, can aid Diagnostic Pathologists in providing an accurate diagnosis, facilitating appropriate treatment decisions, and improving patient outcomes since treatment protocols are tied to establishing correct diagnosis and categorization of the cyto-histopathologic tumor type.

As with any diagnostic approach, careful interpretation and integration of IHC results with clinical, radiologic imaging, and morphological findings remain crucial for arriving at a definitive, accurate diagnosis.

It is essential to note that the specific, chosen IHC panel of antibodies in a diagnostic immunohistochemical panel provides a decision matrix for Problem Analysis and final Decision-Making for the Diagnostic Pathologist. The results may vary widely depending on the suspected tumor type, its degree of ontogenetic differentiation, the consequences of concurrent or prior treatment (radiation and chemotherapy or both), and the clinical setting. The Diagnostic Pathologist, among other things, carefully selects the appropriate immunohistochemical panel constituent antibodies based on the tumor's initial histopathological Hematoxylin and Eosin (H and E) stained slide features, the location of cancer, radiological-imaging findings, the patient's medical history, and clinical presentation. Emerging knowledge in the oncology field constantly brings discoveries and updated classification and prognostication schemes. Diagnostic Pathologists need to stay abreast of the latest research, tumor taxonomic classification guidelines, and molecular-genetic advancements to accurately interpret H & E histopathological slides and apply ancillary testing, including IHC testing that provides the most relevant information useful for the patient's diagnosis, treatment planning, and tumor prognostication. Diagnostic Pathologists employ quality control and quality assurance programs to address these challenges, such as those sponsored by the College of American Pathologists (CAP) and other societies and regulatory bodies, and participate in regular educational activities, especially tumor board conferences, and engage in multidisciplinary meetings in addition to deliberative discussions to enhance their diagnostic accuracy and consistent, reliable tumor classification. Collaborations between Diagnostic Pathologists, Oncologists, Radiologists, and Radiation Oncologists, as well as obtaining additional (second and even third) opinions from expert Diagnostic Pathologists, play a crucial role in ensuring accurate Cancer diagnoses and optimizing patient care. Thus, while the diagnosis of

Cancer for common tumor types may be proforma, evaluating the initial H & E histopathological slide may become challenging due to the appearance of de-differentiation in neoplasms, morphological variations, inter and intraobserver variability of interpretation, mimickers of malignancy, sampling Bias and variability of sampling, and ancillary techniques interpretation. All these processes and technical variables may conspire to make the task of Cancer diagnosis difficult, if not baffling, for the Diagnostic Pathologist. Aside from what has already been outlined, the difficulty of establishing a Cancer diagnosis can vary depending on other inherent operator factors, including the breadth and rigor of the Diagnostic Pathologists' training, experience, and especially fellowship training specialization (or equivalent additional postgraduate training). These mentioned factors go well beyond the typical, routine diagnosis of Cancer and its nosological typing and staging.

7.3 THE WI-FI NETWORK — EXAMPLE 1 (BUSINESS)

One example of a simple Business and everyday Life problem that can become too complex and difficult to understand fully is troubleshooting issues with a Wireless Fidelity (Wi-Fi) network. While Wi-Fi is a standard technology many people use, identifying and resolving the underlying cause(s) can be frustrating and confusing when connectivity problems arise. One then goes "down the proverbial rabbit hole."

When faced with Wi-Fi connectivity issues, it might be challenging to determine whether the problem lies with the internet service provider (ISP), the router, the server, or the connected devices.

Common factors can contribute to the Wi-Fi network complexity:

- *Interference:* Wi-Fi signals can be disrupted by various sources of interference, such as neighboring networks, electronic devices in proximity, or physical obstacles like thick masonry walls or even heavy furniture. Identifying and mitigating these sources or reasons for interference requires understanding wireless signal propagation and adjusting the physical environment.

- *Network configuration:* Wi-Fi routers have various settings and options that can affect network performance. These settings include network name (SSID), security protocols (for example, WEP, WPA, and WPA2), channel selection, and quality of service (QoS) settings. Understanding and correctly configuring these options can be daunting for someone without technical expertise. Knowing your data plan, as well as network bandwidth capacity, is fundamental.

- *Software and firmware updates*: Outdated router firmware or device drivers can lead to compatibility issues and connectivity problems. Keeping all devices updated with the latest software patches, drivers, and firmware releases can be complex, especially when multiple devices are involved.

- *Network congestion:* In areas with dense populations or shared living spaces, multiple Wi-Fi networks can cause congestion, resulting in slower (sluggish) download/upload speeds, high latency, and intermittent, unreliable connections. Diagnosing and resolving network congestion requires analyzing Wi-Fi signals and potentially adjusting designated channel assignments.

- *Device-specific issues:* Different devices may exhibit unique connectivity issues. For example, smartphones, tablets, and laptops may have different Wi-Fi adapters, antenna configurations, or power-saving features affecting network performance. Troubleshooting device-specific problems may involve adjusting device settings or seeking device-specific external support.

- *Technical terminology:* The terminology (jargon) associated with Wi-Fi troubleshooting, such as Internet Protocol (IP) addresses, Domain Name System (DNS) servers, Media Access Control (MAC) addresses, subnet masks, and Dynamic Host Configuration Protocol (DHCP) settings, can be unfamiliar and overwhelming for individuals without a technical background.

To overcome the unperceived complexity of Wi-Fi troubleshooting, individuals can follow a methodical, systematic approach. This may involve rebooting the router and devices, checking network settings, conducting speed tests, analyzing signal strength, updating software, drivers, and firmware, and seeking assistance from the Internet Service Provider (ISP) or manufacturer support. Overall, Wi-Fi connectivity problems may initially seem uncomplicated but become a dark, deep morass after understanding its technical complexity. Breaking down the troubleshooting process into manageable steps and understanding the underlying concepts can help individuals resolve common Wi-Fi connectivity issues and improve their network performance.

7.4 THE SUPPLY CHAIN AND LOGISTICS — EXAMPLE 2 (BUSINESS)

A Business problem example that may initially seem simple or mundane but may become too complex to understand is the challenge of optimizing the supply chain for a manufacturing company. Superficially, the goal is straightforward: to streamline the flow of materials, minimize costs, improve productivity, and maximize efficiency. However, once you dive into the details, various input factors can make understanding the supply chain operation and inventory Management incredibly disheartening, sometimes appearing frankly unsolvable:

- *Firstly,* the manufacturing process may involve multiple suppliers and shippers, each with lead times, pricing structures, and quality standards. Coordinating and managing these aspects can be challenging, mainly when unexpected disruptions occur, such as natural disasters, labor strikes, boycotts, union actions, or changes in federal regulations.

- *Secondly*, demand forecasting plays a crucial role in supply chain optimization. Just-in-time inventory would be ideal, but objectively, its achievement may be difficult to attain. Accurately predicting customer demand is essential to avoid stockouts or excess (wasted) inventory. However, demand is influenced by numerous factors, including market trends, seasonality, economic conditions, and even geopolitical events. Incorporating all these factors into a dependable forecasting model is a confounding task.

- *Thirdly*, transportation logistics adds another layer of complexity. Determining the most efficient routes, considering factors like distance, traffic, routes, fuel costs, and delivery time windows, requires advanced optimization algorithms. Additionally, choosing the appropriate mode of transportation (e.g., mail, truck, rail, air, or sea) for assorted products and regions of the country further complicates the logistics Decision-Making process.

7.4.1 THE SUPPLY CHAIN AND LOGISTICS — SPECIAL CONSIDERATION, THE BULLWHIP EFFECT — FACTORS CONTRIBUTING TO THE BULLWHIP EFFECT

One of the more challenging subset problems in supply chain optimization is the so-called "*Bullwhip Effect.*" This effect refers to the phenomenon where small fluctuations in consumer demand lead to amplified, unpredictable fluctuations in placed orders upstream in the supply chain. The aberration of the demand relationship, as it moves upstream to the supplier or vendor, can result in inefficiencies, increased intrinsic costs, distortions, and disruptions throughout the supply chain.

7.4.1.1 THE SUPPLY CHAIN AND LOGISTICS — SPECIAL CONSIDERATION, THE BULLWHIP EFFECT — CONTRIBUTING FACTORS

- *Demand forecast inaccuracy:* As demand forecasts are passed up through the supply chain, they become less accurate due to random fluctuations and uncertainties. Suppliers respond by overreacting to these inaccuracies, leading to excessive production or inventory buildup. Excess inventory becomes the equivalent of revenue loss. Not only are assets frozen, but the value of extra merchandise loses value the longer it is held, as the demand for that good or product diminishes. "Shelf space" is theoretically and actually decreased for newer products with higher marginal profit.

- *Order batching:* Businesses and distributors often place orders in batches to take advantage of "economies of scale" or reduce overall ordering costs. This can magnify demand fluctuations, especially when these batches are not synchronized with actual demand.

- *Price fluctuations and promotions:* Temporary price reductions and promotions can lead to spikes in consumer demand, causing exaggerated orders to be sent up the supply chain. Suppliers may overproduce to meet these artificially inflated projected demands.

- *Lead time variability:* Variability in lead times can lead to distorted demand information. Longer lead times might prompt buyers to place exaggerated larger orders in anticipation of longer delivery times.

- *Lack of coordination:* When distinct stages of the supply chain operate independently without sharing real-time information, each stage makes decisions based on incomplete, non-visible data, exacerbating demand distortion.

7.4.1.2 THE SUPPLY CHAIN AND LOGISTICS — SPECIAL CONSIDERATION, THE BULLWHIP EFFECT — SOLUTIONS

- *Demand forecast improvement:* Efforts should enhance demand forecasting accuracy through data analysis, Statistical modeling, and incorporating external factors that influence demand.

- *Information sharing:* Improved communication and information sharing among supply chain partners can help reduce uncertainties and lead to more accurate demand signals.

- *Reduced order batching:* Smaller, more frequent orders can help smooth out demand fluctuations and reduce the impact of the Bullwhip Effect.

- *Responsive supply chain:* Developing a flexible and agile supply chain that can quickly adapt to changes in demand can mitigate the adverse effects of demand volatility.

- *Collaborative planning*: Collaborative planning, forecasting, and replenishment (CPFR) initiatives enable supply chain partners to work together on demand forecasting and inventory planning. Modern evolving technologies such as GPS tracking, peer-to-peer (P2P) databases, Blockchain, Machine Learning, Artificial Intelligence (AI), and the Internet of Things (IoT) can provide that real-time transparency tool.

Addressing the Bullwhip Effect ultimately requires a combination of computer, logistics technology, data analytics, process redesign, and collaborative efforts across the supply chain. Overcoming this challenge can improve efficiency, cost savings, and a more responsive and customer-centric supply chain. Supply chain optimization often involves balancing conflicting objectives. For instance, reducing inventory levels can help cut costs, but it may increase the risk of stockouts. Similarly, optimizing production for cost efficiency may result in longer lead times, negatively impacting customer satisfaction and market competitiveness. Moreover, integrating data from various sources, such as Enterprise Resource Planning (ERP) systems, supplier databases, Customer Relationship Management (CRM) tools, and external market data, all require robust data Management expertise and experience, not to mention computer analytic capabilities. Ensuring data accuracy, consistency, tracking, and cybersecurity throughout the supply chain adds other layers of complexity. Evaluating and implementing these technologies and Management systems effectively while considering their impact on existing processes and systems requires careful consideration and industry and sector expertise. Indeed, although optimizing the supply chain appears simple and uncomplicated, at first glance, the multitude of interconnected factors, ranging from supplier Management to demand forecasting, transportation logistics, conflicting objectives and demands, data integration, and technological advancements, all contribute to its manifest complexity. Successfully tackling these challenges requires a comprehensive understanding of the Business, industry, and sector expertise and sophisticated analytical and problem-solving skills.

CHAPTER 8

"NO MATTER HOW STRAIGHTFORWARD A PROBLEM INITIALLY SEEMS, NO DEFINITE SOLUTION WILL BE REACHED AFTER IT IS DISCOVERED TO BE TRULY COMPLEX"

8.1 INDECISION AND FAILURE TO REACH A CONCLUSION (BUSINESS)

In Business, what happens when there is Indecision? Indecisiveness impacts Business Decision-Making, with paralysis of action being the extreme consequence of inaction. However, the more common characteristic behavior is lengthy, prolonged front-end hesitation to reach a decision, especially the reluctance to make mission-critical choices. The reasons for inaction and indecisiveness, as well as fallout consequences, need to be examined by Organizations and Enterprises. If one cannot ameliorate the negative impact of a wrong, incorrect decision choice on a Business, then mitigation strategies come into play.

Indecisiveness is a paralyzed cognitive status that declares itself by a prolonged inability to select an appropriate course of action, primarily manifest when several competing viable alternatives or options are available. In the context of Business, the ensuing repercussions of indecisiveness are impactful and broad. Many adverse downstream effects are generated, particularly affecting operational efficiency, logistics, and resources allocated that are diverted. Short, as well as long-term strategic planning will become stifled. Organizational and Enterprise performance and efficiency are hampered and constrained in this scenario.

A myriad of factors contributes to indecisiveness in Business, both internal and external. The former (internal) factors include conflicting goals among stakeholders and shareholders, lack of confidence, fear of the unknown, fear of failure and untoward consequences of pursuing a wrong decision, information overload, and wondering if all the necessary input information has been factored into an expected, ultimate decision. The external factors, on the other hand, revolve around the cost of borrowing (debt burden and bond rates), market volatility, regulatory uncertainty, and rules, especially government intrusion, competition, and rapid technological advancements, not to mention disruptive technologies, or their threat, on the horizon. The interplay of these factors often leads to decision paralysis, hindering effective Management. The consequences of indecisiveness are felt throughout an Organization and Enterprise. Deferred Decision-Making can result in missed opportunities for purposeful action, market share loss, erosion of competitive edge, and growth stagnation. Lost opportunities mean unrealized profits and losses. The non-adaptable decision-maker without a vision will engender diminished staff loyalty, low morale, and heightened employee stress levels. The indecisiveness will become noticeable and undermine the Corporate and Enterprise reputation, stakeholders, and shareholder trust.

So, how does one deal with this perplexing situation? A turn-around *mitigation strategy* must be enacted as a multifaceted approach to this multidimensional problem. A Leadership that communicates and addresses this responsibly and forthrightly can foster a collaborative, decision-centric culture that places value on the decision and its timely execution. Problem Analysis employing, for instance, the Delphi technique, SWOT, Cost-Benefit analysis, Pareto analysis, and other data analytical methodologies, including Statistical analysis, can be implemented to reach the next step, decisive Decision-Making. The latter process must be data-driven and objective. The framework for Decision-Making then becomes structured. Simulation of various scenarios for planning can be used before arriving at a final solution. Predictive modeling with Bayesian analysis, Machine Learning (ML), and Artificial Intelligence (AI) can empower informed decisions. Mitigating any Psychological barriers contributing to indecisiveness needs to be addressed upfront and expeditiously to move forward. The pervasive nature of indecisiveness is a challenge that underscores the need for a proactive *mitigation strategy* measure to enhance the spectrum of Decision-Making. A decision-centric culture that incorporates informed action, leverages Decision-Making frameworks and embraces technological advancements can assist in navigating the complex landscape of Business with efficacy. As the Business landscape continually evolves, addressing indecisiveness has become a strategic Business imperative and a cornerstone of sustainability, viability, and future success.

8.2 INDECISION AND FAILURE TO REACH A CONCLUSION (MEDICINE) — OPINIONS, OPINIONS, AND MORE OPINIONS!

When a conclusive diagnosis cannot be reached, it can be frustrating for the patient and the healthcare providers involved. In such cases, further investigations and consultations may be necessary to gather additional information and consider alternative diagnostic and care plan possibilities. There *are a few potential outcomes or steps that may be taken:*

- *Further testing*: The healthcare team may recommend additional diagnostic tests, radiologic-imaging studies, laboratory analyses, or both to gather more information about the patient's condition. This can help rule out other likely disease causes or provide additional insights into an underlying problem or disorder.

- *Second opinion*: If a conclusive diagnosis cannot be reached, seeking a second opinion from another experienced healthcare provider or specialist may be beneficial. They may offer a fresh perspective or have access to different diagnostic tools or expertise that could aid in reaching a definitive diagnosis.

- *Third opinion* (?): Less commonly pursued, this is an option that some health care practitioners choose when facing an extraordinarily complex or challenging medical condition. A third opinion involves consulting with a different healthcare professional or an Uber specialist after obtaining two prior medical opinions, often outside the originating referral healthcare system. So, what occurs when seeking a third opinion?—A fresh perspective results.

A third opinion can provide a new perspective on the diagnosis, treatment options, or Management care plan. The healthcare professional, a specialist in a field often complementary to the expertise of the previous consultants or merely one with even greater advanced training and experience or both, may have a different, novel approach, niche expertise, or extensive experience that can offer new(er) insights for the patient and physician. A third opinion can help "break the tie" or clarify the situation if there are conflicting previous opinions or uncertainty. The third opinion may confirm one of the earlier opinions, provide a consensus, or offer an alternative perspective. Diagnostic reassessment usually ensues. The third healthcare professional will review the diagnostic workup, including medical records, laboratory, and ancillary test results, and radiologic imaging studies. They may even request additional tests. They may also (re)interpret the existing, provided clinical information differently, potentially leading to a different diagnosis or better understanding of the patient's condition. Regarding treatment options, a third opinion can unveil additional Management treatment options or care plan recommendations. The healthcare professional may suggest alternative approaches, procedures, medications, or therapies that were not previously considered or available. The newest professed, third consultant's opinion may be quite impactful with differing prognostic and therapeutic implications or both. It is important to note that seeking multiple opinions can be time-consuming and costly. However, it can provide valuable clinical information and peace of mind for individuals facing complex or challenging medical decisions. Effective two-way communication between healthcare providers is crucial during this process to ensure that all opinions are considered and integrated into a comprehensive diagnostic, treatment, and Management care plan. Eventually, the decision to seek additional opinions rests with the patient and should be made in collaboration with their healthcare team. They can provide guidance, help facilitate time-sensitive referrals, and ensure that all necessary medical records information is available to the third healthcare professional for a thorough evaluation. In some instances, the healthcare team may, instead, opt to monitor the patient's condition over time through regular check-ups, observations, or repeat testing. This approach allows for ongoing assessment and re-evaluation to identify any evolving signs or symptoms and detect disease patterns or changes that may aid in diagnosis. Another pathway to be pursued is Clinical Trial participation. Depending on the situation, the patient may be eligible to participate in a Clinical Trial or research study focused on investigating difficult-to-diagnose conditions. This can provide access to advanced diagnostic techniques and expertise that may help reach a definitive diagnosis. Unfortunately, when the results are contradictory or unhelpful, symptom Management may be the only remaining course of action. If a diagnosis cannot be made, the focus may shift simply towards managing the patient's symptoms and improving their quality of Life, particularly in an end-of-Life circumstance. Symptom-based treatments and therapies may be prescribed to alleviate discomfort and pain and enhance overall well-being, even without a specific, definitive diagnosis. It is essential to maintain open communication with the healthcare team members, ask questions, and express any concerns during the diagnostic process. They will collaborate with the patient to explore different options and strive to reach a definitive diagnosis or provide appropriate palliative care based on the available information.

From a primary care perspective, at least one cited study by Gorman and Helfand (1995) utilizing multiple regression Statistics demonstrated that only two factors were significant predictors for the pursuit of new information employing consultation:

1. The physician's belief that a definitive answer existed.

2. The urgency of the patient's problem.

Interestingly, other factors, including the difficulty of finding the answer, potential malpractice (liability) concerns, possible help for or harm to the patient, and self-perceived knowledge of the problem, were not significant considerations in the 1995 case study model.

8.2.1 INDECISION AND FAILURE TO REACH A CONCLUSION (MEDICINE) — THE SPECIFIC CHALLENGES POSED BY PERSONALIZED MEDICINE

Separately, although related, consider the challenges posed by Personalized Medicine, which aims to tailor individual treatment strategies to each patient's unique characteristics. Several obstacles make this problem a tangled web:

- *Genetic and molecular variability*: Diseases often have a genetic and molecular basis that varies between individuals. Identifying the specific genetic mutations or molecular pathways involved in a patient's condition can be intricate, costly, and time-consuming.

- *Limited data: Limited clinical data may exist for a particular patient profile for rare diseases or conditions.* The scarcity of peer-reviewed published data can hinder the development of effective personalized Management treatment and care plans.

- *Multidimensional factors*: Personalized treatment involves considering not only genetics but also environmental factors, lifestyle choices, comorbidities, and patient preferences. Integrating all these factors into a coherent treatment care plan requires sophisticated, coordinated planning.

- *Data interpretation and integration:* Analyzing and integrating diverse data types, such as genetic information, medical history, laboratory test results, and radiological-imaging data, requires advanced computational tools and interpretive expertise.

- *Treatment complexity:* Developing a personalized treatment plan often involves a combination of therapies, including drug treatments, Clinical Trials, surgeries, and lifestyle modifications. Balancing these diverse elements while considering potential drug-drug interactions and side effects is complicated.

- *Ethical considerations:* Personalized Medicine raises ethical concerns around data privacy, disclosure (especially Health Insurance Portability and Accountability Act (HIPPA, 1996), Protected Health Information (PHI)), informed consent for treatment, and potential unequal access to cutting-edge therapies based on merely socio-economic factors.

- *Regulatory and insurance approval challenges:* Developing protocols and gaining regulatory (including U.S. Food and Drug Administration (FDA)) approval, Investigational Review Board (IRB) endorsement, or insurance approval or consent for personalized treatments can be quite challenging due to the need to demonstrate safety and efficacy for specific patient groups and age strata, especially with unproven therapy in some cases.

- *Longitudinal monitoring:* Personalized treatments require ongoing, continuous monitoring and adaptation based on how patients respond over time. This necessitates patient registration, uninterrupted data collection, and trending analysis. Small numbers (low N) make drawing conclusions from data daunting, if not inferential. Moreover, the "law of small numbers" states that individuals underestimate small samples' Variance (Variability). Stated differently, individuals overestimate the information that can be derived from a small sample study, mainly when based on anecdotal data.

Addressing these challenges requires collaboration among clinicians, geneticists, data scientists, and ethicists. Advances in genomics, Artificial Intelligence (AI), and data integration technologies are driving progress in the niche field of personalized Medicine. However, the complexity of individual variability and the need for a holistic, comprehensive approach to the patient make personalized treatment care planning a demanding problem in Medicine.

8.2.2 INDECISION AND FAILURE TO REACH A CONCLUSION (MEDICINE AND PATHOLOGY) — EXAMPLE (THE SPECIFIC CHALLENGES POSED BY EQUIVOCAL (INDETERMINATE) PROBLEMS)

Equivocal (Indeterminate) problems in Medicine and Pathology are situations or medical conditions that present challenges or complexities in diagnosis, treatment, or Management. These problems often require extensive analysis and careful consideration of multiple factors, sometimes involving situations that entwine themselves around uncertainty, ambiguity, and indecision.

Equivocal problems in Medicine and Pathology can and do arise due to various, assorted reasons, such as:

- *Rare or uncommon conditions*: When dealing with rare or uncommon diseases or conditions, healthcare professionals may encounter diagnostic dilemmas due to limited knowledge, lack of established clinical guidelines, or atypical presentations. These cases may require extensive investigation, consultation with specialists, or collaboration with tertiary medical centers and research institutions.

- *Multifactorial or complex disorders*: Certain medical conditions involve the interplay among multiple factors, such as genetic predisposition, environmental factors, and lifestyle choices. Examples include rare conditions, autoimmune diseases, mental health disorders, chronic fatigue syndrome/myalgic encephalopathy, pain syndromes, and drug addiction. Diagnosis and treatment of such conditions can be quite challenging due to the raveled interactions of these diverse factors. Compounding the difficulty, occasional patients may present with multiple medical comorbidities, perplexing medical histories, or complicated Management treatment regimens. Managing these exceptional cases requires coordination among multiple healthcare providers, effective communication, and a comprehensive understanding of each patient's unique circumstances. Addressing complex medical issues requires a multidisciplinary approach involving collaboration among healthcare professionals from different specialties, using advanced diagnostic tools, and integrating evidence-based Medicine with clinical expertise. These cases highlight the evolving nature of Medicine and the ongoing need for research, Clinical Trials, and the possible use of off-label medications, innovation, and individualized patient care. An integrative inpatient-outpatient Medical records system is a necessity.

- *Undifferentiated symptoms*: Patients may present with a constellation of symptoms that do not fit into a specific diagnostic category, thus making it difficult to identify an underlying etiologic cause. The healthcare provider may need to conduct thorough evaluations, order comprehensive tests, and consider various differential diagnostic etiological entities.

- *Treatment resistance*: Patients may sometimes not respond to standard treatment protocols or therapies, leading to treatment-recalcitrant conditions. This can occur in various medical specialties, especially in infectious diseases, oncology, and mental health-addiction disorders. Finding effective alternative treatment strategies for these patients can be a disconcerting experience, necessitating specialist expertise. There is additionally a need for a patient care navigator in such situations.

- *Ethical dilemmas*: Medical practice often involves ethical considerations and Decision-Making. A quandary may arise when there are conflicting values, patient autonomy and informed consent concerns, or difficult end-of-Life decisions. These situations can require even more careful deliberation, consultation with an ethics committee, or the involvement of additional individuals, such as family members, clergy, and end-of-Life or Hospice legal experts.

8.3 "RETHINKING IT THROUGH!"

If one cannot reach a conclusion, or if a problem is equivocal (indeterminate), maybe one should "ReThink it Through!"- Should we denominate this as a "new cognitive skill?" Throughout Life, one needs to learn but also to "unlearn" and "relearn." According to Adam Grant (1981-), an Organizational Psychologist at the Wharton School of Business at the University of Pennsylvania, intellectual curiosity, openness, and emotional

armor will allow one to accept "Uncomfortable Truths" after "Rethinking." …
"We'll favor the comfort of staying connected to what we already know rather than the discomfort of doubt" (*Think Again* by Adam Grant with Book Review by Bibliophile Parul).

Reaffirming Learning, "Unlearning," and "Relearning"—Anecdotally, a Medical school Professor stated (to paraphrase) … "Half of what you will learn will likely be disproved over the following four to six years of your postgraduate educational training." … "You just won't know which half!" How unsettling for a young trainee-student. Accept that you do not know, nor will you have all the answers, so get a second (or even third) opinion, if necessary, and always exercise humility.

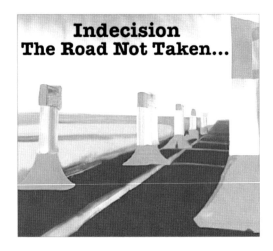

CHAPTER 9

"NOTHING SHOULD EVER BE SAID WHICH HAS NOT BEEN SAID BEFORE"

9.1 INTERPRETING THE APHORISM AND CIRCUMSTANCE

["NOTHING SHOULD EVER BE SAID WHICH HAS NOT BEEN SAID BEFORE"]

An Aphorism is a direct, concise, epigrammatic witticism that often conveys wisdom or Life's experience. It represents an observation about Life and a philosophical or worldview perspective that informs one regarding advice to be followed or lessons learned. Using metaphors and imaginative imagery allows for expressing recitable, to-the-point ideas.

How should we interpret this Aphorism?

- *Preservation of knowledge*: The Aphorism can reflect a cautious approach to communication, emphasizing the importance of relying on established knowledge and expertise and avoiding disseminating unverified or potentially false information. Notably, by adhering to previously expressed ideas, one ironically aims to minimize the risk of spreading inaccurate or unproven Arguments or Claims.

- *Respect for authority or tradition:* A perspective that stems from a belief in the Authority of established sources or traditions. It suggests that one should defer to the wisdom of those who have come before and refrain from introducing new, novel, or divergent ideas that might challenge existing beliefs, belief systems, and traditional norms.

- *Discouragement of creativity and innovation:* This interpretation suggests that creative thinking and innovation would be discouraged by limiting expression to what has already been previously stated. It suppresses the exploration of new ideas and perspectives, potentially hindering progress and limiting Intellectual curiosity and personal growth.

- *Avoidance of controversy and conformity:* By adhering to previously expressed or established ideas, individuals may seek to avoid controversy or the potential consequences of expressing different, unique, divergent, or unpopular opinions. This approach prioritizes Conformity and avoids challenging established norms or beliefs. Conformity is a Sociological-Psychological concept that refers to the tendency or predisposition of individuals to adjust their thoughts, attitudes, beliefs, and behaviors to match those of a particular group or societal norms. It involves how people align their actions and opinions with a given social reference group's dominant normative standards or expectations.

9.2 INTERPRETING THE APHORISM AND CIRCUMSTANCE — IS IT A "DOUBLE-NEGATIVE?"

A "Double-Negative" is a linguistic construct that occurs when two negative elements are used in a single sentence or expression, resulting in a "negation of the negation" and potentially altering the intended meaning. In some languages and contexts, "Double-Negatives" are considered grammatically incorrect or improper usage, while in other situations, they are used for emphasis, rhetorical effect, or to convey specific meanings.

Examples of "Double-Negatives:"

1. *In Everyday Life*

2. *In Business*

3. *In Medicine*

1. In Everyday Life:

"I don't have no time."—This sentence uses the "Double-Negative" ("don't have no time"), which means "I don't have any time." It emphasizes the speaker's lack of available time.

"I can't get no satisfaction."—This famous line from The Rolling Stones' song "Satisfaction" (1965) uses the "Double-Negative" ("can't get no") to express the idea that the songwriter is unable to achieve any satisfaction.

2. In Business:

"We cannot disregard the importance of not ignoring customer feedback."— This sentence employs the "Double-Negative" ("cannot disregard") and ("not ignoring") to emphasize the significance of paying attention to customer feedback.

"Our strategy is not ineffective."—This example uses the "Double-Negative" ("not ineffective") to convey that the strategy is, in fact, effective, although the speaker chooses not to use the straightforward positive phrase – "Our strategy is effective."

3. In Medicine:

"The patient is not unwilling to try the new treatment."—This sentence uses the "Double-Negative" ("not unwilling") to convey that the patient is open or receptive to trying the new treatment. The following statement ("The test results are not inconclusive.") as another example, uses the "Double-Negative" ("not inconclusive"), which implies that the test results are conclusive, meaning they provide a clear and definite outcome.

It is important to note that in formal or standard grammar, "Double-Negatives" are often considered incorrect usage of the English language because they can create confusion or ambiguity. However, in particular dialects or informal modes of speech, "Double-Negatives" may be deemed acceptable and used for emphasis or stylistic reasons. The header phrase (Aphorism) at the beginning of this Chapter ("Nothing should ever be said which has not been said before") refers to a perspective or belief that places a diminished value on originality and discourages the expression of novel ideas or statements that have not been previously articulated or discussed by others. The context might suggest that one should only communicate ideas, thoughts, or information that are classic, "tried and true," or previously well-established, written, or spoken. Alternatively, the antithesis of this conclusion is that the phrase could have other, more subtle interpretations and implications.

9.3 INTERPRETING THE APHORISM AND CIRCUMSTANCE — IS IT INSTEAD A CONUNDRUM?

A conundrum is a complex or puzzling problem that is difficult to solve or understand due to its contradictory or confusing nature. It is a situation or question that presents a dilemma, often with no apparent or straightforward solution. Conundrums are characterized by their elaborateness, paradoxical elements, or the existence of multiple conflicting elements:

Everyday use synonyms for Conundrum: *Enigma, Mystery, Riddle, Brainteaser, Mystification, Poser, Problem, Puzzlement, Puzzle, Secret, Why, Knot …*

Several key overarching aspects define a Conundrum:

- *Complexity*: Conundrums are typically abstruse and involve various entangled parts, making them challenging to unravel or comprehend fully. They often require deep, thoughtful analysis and consideration viewed from multiple perspectives.

- *Contradiction*: Conundrums often contain contradictory elements or present conflicting viewpoints, which contribute to difficulty finding a resolution. The contradictory nature of the conundrum creates a sense of puzzlement, unsolvability, or confusion.

- *Dilemma*: Conundrums present a dilemma, a situation where one must choose between two or more equally undesirable, challenging, or contradictory options. They pose a problematic step in the Decision-Making process with no apparent nor obvious optimal outcome.

- *Ambiguity*: Conundrums may have ambiguous or uncertain elements, making it hard to determine the precise nature of the problem or its potential solution. The lack of clarity compounds the complexity and frustration associated with the meaning of conundrums.

- *Intellectual challenge*: Conundrums are inscrutable intellectual or philosophical puzzles that require critical analysis, problem-solving skills, and, often, a creative approach. They stimulate the mind and often involve deep reflection, critical analysis, and the exploration of alternative perspectives.

- *Lack of obvious solution*: A conundrum is characterized by the absence of a readily apparent or straightforward solution. It may be unexplainable and defy conventional wisdom or resist traditional problem-solving methods. Conundrums often require thinking creatively or considering unconventional, ingenious approaches to analyze and resolve a situation or problem.

- *Thought-provoking*: Conundrums spark contemplation and reflection. They engage individuals in deep Critical Thinking[2], challenging preconceived notions and encouraging the exploration of different competing possibilities. Conundrums can, notwithstanding, lead to profound insights, personal intellectual growth, and expanded subject understanding.

Conundrums can arise in various contexts, including philosophical debates, ethical dilemmas, scientific inquiries, and complex social or political issues. They test our reasoning, problem-solving, and capacity to grapple with uncertainty. Conundrums are not easily resolved, and even when solutions are proposed, they may give rise to further debate angst. Conundrums captivate and invigorate our intellect by presenting complex, arcane problems with contradictory elements, a puzzle of sorts, defying easy resolution, and stimulating intellectual curiosity, Critical Thinking[2] skills, further deliberation, and discussion.

9.4 CONFORMITY AND OBEDIENCE

Conformity and its fundamental principles:

- *Social influence*: Conformity is driven by social influence, which includes the impact of peers, societal norms, and cultural values. Individuals may conform to socially fit in, gain acceptance, or avoid social rejection or expulsion.

- *Normative conformity*: Normative Conformity is driven by the desire to gain social approval and avoid social disapproval or punishment. People conform to societal norms to maintain a positive social identity and avoid social sanctions.

- *Informational conformity*: Informational Conformity occurs when individuals look to others for guidance or information in ambiguous or uncertain situations. They conform because they believe others possess more accurate knowledge or understanding of the situation.

- *Peer group pressure*: This plays a significant role in Conformity. Individuals may feel compelled to conform due to the fear of isolation, ridicule, or social rejection. The desire to maintain harmony within a group can lead individuals to go along with the majority opinion or behavior, even if they are knowingly wrong.

- *Obedience*: Obedience is a form of Conformity that involves following the orders or commands of an Authority figure.

9.4.1 OBEDIENCE AND CONFORMITY —
THE ASCH CONFORMITY EXPERIMENTS

Of note, the early *Asch Conformity Experiments* in the 1950s conducted by Solomon Asch (1907-1996), a Gestalt Psychologist and pioneer in Social Psychology, demonstrated the power of social influence and Conformity. Participants were asked to judge the length of lines, and Confederates deliberately gave incorrect answers. The majority of participants conformed to the erroneous judgments of the group, even when they knew they were wrong.

9.4.2 OBEDIENCE AND CONFORMITY —
THE MILGRAM OBEDIENCE EXPERIMENTS

Later, the *Milgram experiment on Obedience* to Authority in the 1960s, conducted by Yale Psychologist Stanley Milgram (1933-1984), demonstrated that individuals are often willing to obey Authority figures, even if it means inflicting harm on others. The latter merits a detailed review.

The Milgram Experiment:
This experiment, and those that followed, confirmed *the danger of Authority Bias*. Subjects were told that they were experiment participants studying the effect of punishment on memory. One participant in the study was identified as a "learner." The "teacher" was given a list of "paired associates." The "teacher" was, in this setting, informed that they should shock the "learner" when the "learner" gave an incorrect response. In this experiment, the "learner" was wired to what was represented as a "shock generating

machine" with thirty switches labeled, progressively "Slight Shock" to Danger (severe) Shock." The "teachers" were beforehand given a shock of forty-five volts to convince them that the shocks "delivered" were real. The "learners" response was scripted and recorded to playback. At one hundred and fifty volts, the "learner" was heard asking that the experiment stop … And so, the experiment began.

The "teacher" participants claimed they administered the shocks for three main reasons:

1. The Authority figure seemed trustworthy.

2. The cause was "good" (scientific research).

3. They believed that if anything "bad" happened, the researcher would take "full responsibility."

There is an innate tendency to trust and believe Authority figures and follow their orders, even cause harm, and up-end their ethical-moral compass, despite any belief that they are inherently wrong and that there is no concrete penalty for disagreeing with them. After the experiment, the participants were debriefed. All the actual participants went to at least three hundred volts of "pain inflicted" (punishment), and 65 percent continued until the whole four hundred and fifty volts (severe shock). Two-thirds (65 percent) to 90 percent delivered unreasonable levels of electric shock when told, "The experiment requires you to continue!" Victim behavior, such as screams, biting of lips, stuttering, sweating, and statements made regarding having a "heart condition" or the observed condition of silence, did not dissuade or change the decision to administer the shock. Stanley Milgram concluded that, under the right circumstances, "*ordinary individuals will obey unjust orders.*" Disobedience, when it occurred, was expected when the experimenter or a "normal" person left the room, when peers refused to obey, or when two experimenters made conflicting demands. Obedience was rank-ordered highest when commands were given by an Authority figure rather than another volunteer. Ultimately, individuals obey either out of apprehension, fear, or a desire to appear cooperative, to conform—even when acting against their own better judgment or intrinsic motivation and desires. When variations of the experiment were carried out to explore yet further factors affecting obedience and Conformity, Milgram found that obedience rates decreased when the "learner" was in the same room (in proximity) as the experimenters. Application of "lessons learned" to real Life does exist. The Milgram experiment emphasizes the importance of questioning Authority, the role of ethical Decision-Making, and encouraging Critical Thinking[2] in societal contexts. Parenthetically, the experimental study design and setup were described to forty psychiatrists. NONE predicted that a study participant would go beyond the tenth level, or one hundred and fifty volts!

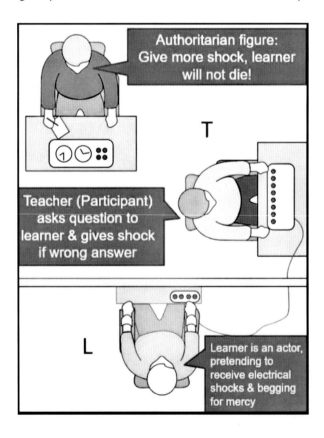

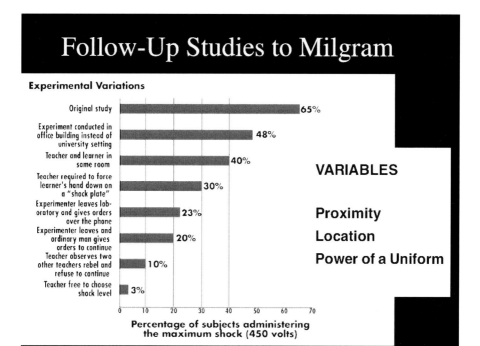

Follow-Up Studies to Milgram

Experimental Variations

- Original study — 65%
- Experiment conducted in office building instead of university setting — 48%
- Teacher and learner in same room — 40%
- Teacher required to force learner's hand down on a "shock plate" — 30%
- Experimenter leaves laboratory and gives orders over the phone — 23%
- Experimenter leaves and ordinary man gives orders to continue — 20%
- Teacher observes two other teachers rebel and refuse to continue — 10%
- Teacher free to choose shock level — 3%

Percentage of subjects administering the maximum shock (450 volts)

VARIABLES

Proximity

Location

Power of a Uniform

Conformity varies across cultures due to differences in cultural norms, values, and expectations. Some cultures emphasize individualism, autonomy, and independence, while others prioritize collectivism and group harmony, leading to various levels of Conformity. While Conformity is a prevalent social phenomenon, not everyone conforms. Individuals may resist Conformity and maintain their beliefs, values, or actions, often driven by personal conviction, independence, autonomy, or a desire for authenticity. Understanding Conformity is crucial for Sociologists and Psychologists as it helps explain how societal norms are established, maintained, and changed. It sheds light on group dynamics, social influence, and the power of social pressure in shaping and molding individual behavior within a society.

It is important to note that creativity, progress, and the evolution of knowledge often rely on introducing innovative ideas and perspectives. While there is value in building upon existing knowledge, there is also a need for innovation and fresh insights to advance any field of study, spark meaningful discussions, and drive societal progress. Conformity would obviously be at odds with the latter. Undoubtedly, it would limit the exploration of innovative, new(er) ideas and the potential for Intellectual curiosity, discourse, and innovation. It acknowledges the norm, the accepted, the customary, and the traditional.

"Nihil Amplius Dicere Habeo" (Latin for "I Have Nothing More To Say")
and
"Res Ipsa Loquitur" (Latin for "The Thing Speaks For Itself")

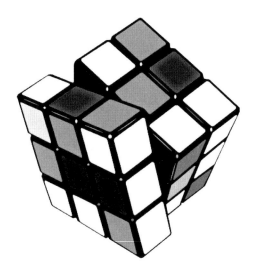

CHAPTER 10

"THERE IS NO LIMITATION TO HOW STUPID ONE CAN BECOME"

10.1 Are Intelligence and Ignorance Inversely Correlated?

10.2 "Nine Types" Model of Intelligence (Multifactorial and Multifaceted Dimensions) and Newer Concepts

10.3 The Traditional Intelligence Quotient (IQ) Tests

10.3.1 A Non-Traditional Intelligence Quotient (IQ) Test – The Cognitive Reflection Test (CRT, 2005) – "The New Kid on the Block" –Only Three (3) Questions!

10.4 Is There a Requisite Level of Cognitive Intelligence that Translates to Effective Leadership?

10.5 Select Listing of the Top Ten (10) U.S. CEOs – Salary and Educational Background

10.1 ARE INTELLIGENCE AND IGNORANCE INVERSELY CORRELATED?

Intelligence and ignorance are not necessarily inversely correlated in a strict sense. Intelligence refers to the ability to understand, learn, reason, and apply knowledge effectively. Conversely, ignorance refers to a diminishment of Intelligence and a tendency to make poor decisions or exhibit foolish behavior. While Intelligence can often be associated with making wiser decisions and avoiding foolish mistakes, it is crucial to recognize that Intelligence is a complex, multifactorial, and multifaceted concept. Intelligence globally encompasses various cognitive abilities, such as problem-solving, analytical thinking, creativity, and adaptability. Possessing these abilities, however, does not guarantee that an individual will always make intelligent choices or avoid idiocy. Ignorance, likewise, is not solely determined or defined by a lack of Intelligence. It can stem from a range of factors, including emotional or impulsive Decision-Making, a lack of knowledge or understanding in a specific domain, Cognitive Bias errors, or a simple failure to consider the long-term consequences of an action or series of temporal consecutive events.

It is worth noting that Intelligence and ignorance exist on a broad spectrum. Individuals can possess varying degrees of Intelligence and simultaneously exhibit varying levels of ineptitude in different situations. Someone can have high Intelligence but occasionally make injudicious or ignorant choices, just as someone with lower Intelligence can occasionally make wise decisions. Therefore, while there may be a general tendency for higher Intelligence to be associated with fewer instances of injudiciousness or ignorance, it is not a direct or absolute correlation. Intelligence and its polar opposite are nuanced and context-dependent concepts encompassing various cognitive, emotional, and behavioral aspects, an individual's analytical thinking skills, or lack thereof, and Decision-Making abilities.

Albert Einstein (1879-1955) made several commentaries about Intelligence and ignorance, brashly designating ignorance as stupidity throughout his Life with a comment that bears repeating here in a few notable *Quotes* attributed to him:

- "Only two things are infinite, the universe and human stupidity, and I'm not sure about the former"

- "The difference between genius and stupidity is that genius has its limits"

- "Insanity is doing the same thing over and over again and expecting different results"

- "The measure of Intelligence is the ability to change"

It is worth noting that while these Quotes have been attributed to Albert Einstein, their precise origins and context may be difficult to trace. However, they are commonly associated with his name and reflect his views on human behavior and Intelligence.

Albert Einstein, born in Ulm, Germany, on March 14, 1879, was one of the most renowned scientists in modern history. His genius is primarily attributed to his groundbreaking contributions to theoretical physics. In 1905, Einstein formulated the *Theory of Special Relativity*, which introduced the concept that the speed of light in a vacuum is a constant (c) and independent of the motion of all observers, even those moving with respect to one another. Therefore, it postulated that the laws of physics are the same for all observers in uniform (non-accelerating) motion. The Theory, furthermore, holds that there are relevant applicable laws of physics pertaining to all inertial reference frames, revealing the interplay between space and time, mass, and energy, and led to the famous equation:

$$E=mc^2$$

Postulating the equivalence of energy (E) and mass (m), with velocity squared (c^2) representing the speed of light (186,000 miles per second). By this relationship of Variables, there is immense energy related to matter in motion (velocity, defined as displacement in position divided by change in time). Shortly after that, Einstein again revolutionized our understanding of space-time and gravity with his Theory of General Relativity, published in 1915. This Theory proposed that gravity is not simply a force but rather a curvature of space-time caused by mass and energy. While the earlier (by one decade) Theory of Special Relativity argued that space and time are inextricably connected, it had not factored in nor acknowledged the existence of gravity. It provided a new framework for understanding the behavior of objects in the presence of massive celestial bodies and predicted phenomena such as heretofore unknown Gravitational Waves. Notably, Einstein's genius extended beyond his contributions to General Relativity. He made significant contributions to Quantum Mechanics, proposing the idea of the photon as a discrete particle of light, for which he was awarded the Nobel Prize in Physics in 1921. He also contributed to developing the Quantum Theory of Radiation (…that a radiation field causes an atom in an upper energy state to transition to a lower energy state at a rate proportional to the radiation density … termed "stimulated emission"). Remember that Einstein was also known for his exceptional breadth of intellectual creativity, deep philosophical insights, and innovative thinking. His ability to ask profound questions and challenge contemporaneously established beliefs led to groundbreaking scientific breakthroughs shaping modern physics. Moreover, Einstein delved into non-scientific areas in humanitarian and social causes as a vocal advocate for civil rights, pacifism, and nuclear disarmament. Einstein's ideas and contributions, especially in science, specifically physics and the humanities, continue to inspire scientists and philosophers worldwide today, making him an enduring symbol of what is genuinely genius, Intelligence and the essence of intellectual curiosity and Critical Thinking.

10.2 "NINE TYPES" MODEL OF INTELLIGENCE (MULTIFACTORIAL AND MULTIFACETED DIMENSIONS) AND NEWER CONCEPTS

There are numerous differing theories and models of Intelligence. Therefore, some newly recognized facets or components of Intelligence offer a novel perspective. You will realize that some of the novel models of Intelligence overlap with the above-described *"Nine Types Model"* of Intelligence:

Nine Types of INTELLIGENCE

Logical
Recognizing relationships, Patterns & Trends

Spatial
Visualing 3D & Manipulation

Linguistic
Verbal & Written

Musical
Tone, Pitch, Timber & Rhythm

Existential
Pensive, Contemplative, Life & Death issues

Intra-Personal
Introspection & Planning

Kinesthetic
Coordination & Object Manipulation

Naturalistic
Discernment of Nature & Survival Instinct

Interpersonal
Intuitive, Communication & Empathy

"Newer" conceptual framework of Intelligence:

- *Fluid intelligence*: Refers to the ability to solve unfamiliar problems, think abstractly, and adapt to new situations. It involves reasoning, pattern recognition, logical thinking, manipulating data, and working with novel information.

- *Crystallized intelligence*: Refers to acquired factual knowledge and skills accumulated over time through education and experience, leading to expertise in specific domains. It partly overlaps with Verbal Intelligence.

- *Verbal intelligence*: Includes language proficiency, vocabulary, and the ability to understand and use language effectively. It encompasses verbal comprehension, reading comprehension, verbal reasoning, and linguistic skills.

- *Mathematical and logical intelligence*: The ability to reason, analyze, and solve problems using mathematical operations, Logic, and abstract thinking. It includes numerical aptitude, quantitative reasoning, logical deduction, and mathematical problem-solving abilities.

- *Spatial intelligence*: Refers to the ability to perceive, visualize, and manipulate spatial relationships. It involves the ability to perform "mental rotation" (the ability to encode a representation of one object and rotate that representation to judge if it can match another presented view of an object), spatial reasoning, understanding maps and diagrams, and visualizing objects or scenes within one's mind.

- *Emotional intelligence (EI)*: This is the capacity to recognize, understand, manage, and express emotions effectively, both in oneself and in empathy with others. It includes emotional awareness, compassion, self-regulation, interpersonal skills, and social awareness.

- *Creative intelligence*: Involves generating novel and valuable ideas, thinking divergently, and approaching problems innovatively. It encompasses creativity, originality, imagination, and the ability to think beyond the conventional boundaries of imagination ("outside the box" thinking).

- *Practical intelligence* (also known as "street smarts" or "common sense"): Refers to the ability to apply knowledge and skills to real-Life, day-to-day situations effectively. It involves problem-solving in practical contexts, adapting to the demands of everyday Life, and understanding social dynamics.

It is important to note that these various facets of Intelligence are not mutually exclusive; some overlap with individuals excelling in some areas. In contrast, others have relative dimensional weaknesses in other aspects. These facets, taken in aggregate, contribute to an individual's overall comprehensive Intelligence and ability to navigate Life's exigencies and succeed.

Several standardized tests designed to measure Intelligence or intellectual ability are called Intelligence Quotient (IQ) tests. These tests assess an individual's cognitive skills and provide an objective numerical score.

10.3 THE TRADITIONAL INTELLIGENCE QUOTIENT (IQ) TESTS

There are several well-known IQ tests:

- *Stanford-Binet Intelligence Scale*: The Stanford-Binet test is one of the most widely used IQ tests. It assesses cognitive abilities across various domains, including verbal and non-verbal reasoning and abstract, visual, and quantitative reasoning. It provides an overall IQ score and specific scores in different cognitive areas.

- *Wechsler Adult Intelligence Scale (WAIS)*: The WAIS is designed for individuals aged sixteen and older. It measures a broad range of cognitive abilities, including verbal comprehension, perceptual reasoning, working memory, and processing speed. The test provides an overall IQ and individual scores for different cognitive domains.

- *Wechsler Intelligence Scale for Children (WISC)*: The WISC is specifically designed for children aged 6 to 16. It assesses cognitive domains similar to the WAIS but tailors the questions and tasks to be age-appropriate. It provides an overall IQ score and subtest scores.

- *Raven's Progressive Matrices*: Raven's Matrices is a non-verbal IQ test focusing on abstract reasoning and problem-solving skills. It uses visual patterns and matrices to assess an individual's ability to identify relationships, recognize and complete patterns, and make logical inferences.

- Cattell Culture Fair Intelligence Test: The Cattell Culture Fair test is a non-verbal test that aims to minimize the influence of cultural or language Biases. It assesses abstract reasoning abilities and problem-solving skills using diagrammatic and symbolic items.

It is important to note that trained, licensed psychology professionals administer and interpret these tests to ensure accurate, certifiable test results. The scores obtained from IQ tests are not absolute measures of Intelligence and should, notwithstanding, be interpreted cautiously. While they provide an estimate of an individual's cognitive abilities, they do not capture all aspects of Intelligence, such as creativity, Leadership, or practical skills. Intelligence extends well beyond what can be measured by any single test.

A pragmatic Layman's test for Intelligence:

Intelligence = (Number of times you can say "Why?" without annoying people) divided by (Number of times people answer your "Why?" questions)

This humorous, lighthearted equation highlights the curiosity and inquisitiveness often associated with Intelligence and the desire to understand and unravel the world around us.

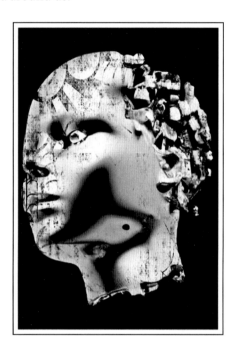

10.3.1 A NON-TRADITIONAL INTELLIGENCE QUOTIENT (IQ) TEST – THE COGNITIVE REFLECTION TEST (CRT, 2005) – "THE NEW KID ON THE BLOCK" –ONLY THREE (3) QUESTIONS!

Shane Frederick (1968-), Psychologist and Professor of Management at Yale School of Management and previously at the Massachusetts Institute of Technology (MIT), is the creator of the three-question Cognitive Reflection Test (CRT) in 2005. Developed while he attended Princeton University, it is aptly termed the World's "shortest" IQ Test. Yet, despite its brevity, over eighty percent of test takers fail to score 3 out of 3. Students at some of the world's top universities (including Yale and Harvard Universities) failed to get all three answers correct in the early published 2005 Frederick study (McCall, R. 2017). In fact, only seventeen percent achieved a perfect score. Deceptively "easy"—Not so! The test has been found to be "predictive" of the types of choices that feature prominently in tests of Decision-Making theories, like Expected Utility Theory and Prospect Theory. According to Frederick and others—"Individuals who score high on the CRT are less vulnerable to various Biases and show more deliberative patience in intertemporal choice tasks… affecting Cognitive Processing" – defined as the tendency to suppress an incorrect, intuitive answer and come to a more contemplative, correct answer. Frederick stated—"Reaching the correct answer often requires the suppression of an erroneous answer that springs 'impulsively' to mind."

The Cognitive Reflection Test (CRT, 2005) tests the ability to ignore your instinctive response (answer) and think slower and more rationally. In psychology, the test relates to how skillful you are at ignoring System I (Intuition) thinking in favor of System II (Analytical) thinking. To succeed in the CRT, you must reflect on your answer and question your initial, more spontaneous, intuitive response. Beyond achieving a 100 percent (%) correct CRT score, promptly and correctly answered questions were interpreted as an additional sign of a higher IQ.

The Quiz:

1. A bat and a ball cost $1.10 in total. The bat costs $1 more than the ball. How much does the ball cost?

2. If it takes five machines five minutes to make five widgets, how long would it take one hundred machines to make one hundred widgets?

3. In a lake, there is a patch of Lily pads. Every day, the patch doubles in size. If it takes forty-eight days for the patch to cover the entire lake, how long would it take for the patch to cover half of the lake?

The Answers:

1. Five cents – You likely guessed 10 cents. The answer is 5 cents. The $1.05 is exactly $1 more expensive than 5 cents. Interestingly, A Princeton University study found that people who responded 10 cents were "significantly" less patient (impatient) than those who got the correct answer.

2. *Five* minutes – You instinctively respond one hundred minutes. It takes exactly five minutes for one widget machine to make one widget. Therefore, it would take five minutes to make one hundred widgets from one hundred widget machines.

3. Forty-seven days – Many might have guessed twenty-four days. It seems intuitive to half the number of days because you are halving the size of the Lily pad patch. But, if the area of the lake covered in Lily pad doubles every day, then it would only take one day for it to go from half-covered to fully covered. Taking one day away from forty-eight days would leave you with the correct answer of forty-seven days.

10.4 IS THERE A REQUISITE LEVEL OF COGNITIVE INTELLIGENCE THAT TRANSLATES INTO EFFECTIVE LEADERSHIP?

Stated differently, is a threshold Intelligence level required for individuals to excel in Leadership roles?

Through a comprehensive analysis of cognitive abilities, Leadership competencies, and their interplay, one can elucidate and arrive at a nuanced level of Intelligence required in the context of general Leadership. Drawing from empirical evidence and theoretical frameworks, the cognitive dimensions underpinning successful Leadership and their implications for Organizational success are further discussed in the Epilogue.

The effective Leader represents someone who excels, in particular, at strategic Decision-Making. That individual possesses enviable, charismatic interpersonal skills and is an Organizational and Enterprise steward. Central to this role is the cognitive capacity of Leaders, which drives their ability to navigate complex challenges, problem-solving, and skills to guide Organizations and Enterprises toward sustained growth, development, operational improvement, and innovation.

The question was somewhat skirted, in part—to reiterate and re-frame the question …

Does a threshold Intelligence level required for effective Business Leadership exist, and what is its significance in contemporary Organizational and Enterprise contexts?

Cognitive Intelligence encompasses a range of mental faculties, including problem-solving, learning agility, analytical—Critical Thinking[2], and Decision-Making. These cognitive abilities underpin the capacity to analyze complex situations, anticipate trends (positive and negative), and make informed judgments, all of which are essential in today's dynamic, ever-changing Business landscape. Influential Leaders leverage their cognitive prowess and "brain power" to synthesize information, devise innovative strategies, and promote a culture of adaptability in the workforce. Notwithstanding, Leadership competencies extend far beyond cognitive prowess to encompass Emotional Intelligence (EI), interpersonal skills, vision, and analytical skills—Critical Thinking[2]. While cognitive Intelligence forms a foundational base, it interacts synergistically with the Leader, enabling Leaders to connect with their teams, navigate and manage Change and conflicts, and inspire collective participation. The interplay of cognitive Intelligence and Leadership shapes a Leader's ability to communicate a compelling vision and engender trust in those reporting to them and those stakeholders, shareholders, the Board of Directors, and the CEO to whom they report. A positive Organizational and Enterprise culture is a byproduct. Empirical studies have explored the notion of threshold Intelligence in the context of effective Business Leadership. While specific IQ thresholds remain debated, research suggests that a baseline cognitive aptitude is indeed necessary for effective Leadership. Cognitive abilities contribute to problem-solving acumen, adaptability to change, and capacity to manage ambiguity – attributes essential in Leadership roles. Moreover, Leadership excellence also hinges on integrating cognitive and interpersonal dimensions, transcending mere cognitive thresholds, universities attended, and degrees conferred. Notwithstanding, Cognitive Intelligence has implications for Organizational and Enterprise success. The same abilities are employed to select future Leaders and develop current, aspiring Leaders from the ranks. Organizations and Enterprises must consider cognitive assessments within their Leadership role identification and development programs. Mentoring processes are obligatory. This broader perspective highlights the symbiotic relationship between cognitive Intelligence and Leadership, indicating that an emphasis on what constitutes holistic Leadership competencies yields the expected, optimal results in order to lead. Balancing cognitive prowess with emotional acumen fosters ideal, adaptive, and inclusive Decision-Making skills. Employee engagement is virtually always a result, as is achieving sustainable Organizational and Enterprise outcomes. This paradigm for Leadership excellence transcends mere cognitive Intelligence thresholds. Accordingly, successful Leaders must leverage cognitive Intelligence and Leadership in synergy, empowering themselves to navigate difficult, complex, challenging scenarios, particularly on a global and international scale, inspire their teams, and drive Organizational and Enterprise success and profitability.

10.5 SELECT LISTING OF THE TOP TEN (10) U.S. CEOS – SALARY AND EDUCATIONAL BACKGROUND

Of note, the information provided – A select listing of the top 10 U.S. CEOs, Universities attended, and salaries (data last updated in 2021)—while relatively recent is not up to date, nor does it include information about stock-based compensation, and options, incentives, vested stock awards, payouts, and other benefits. Please verify the latest data from reliable sources for the most up-to-date information, especially by consulting Corporate Company reports and financial publications and searching official sources, some of which may include Investor.gov, Investopedia, Harvard Business Review (HBR), Bloomberg Business News (BBN), Korn Ferry (the global Organizational consulting firm), Wall Street Journal (WSJ), New York Times (NYT), U.S. Bureau of Labor Statistics (USBLS), and other sources. Data from SEC 10-K/A information, Corporate company annual proxy statements, and registry filings related to the sale of securities to the public are additionally invaluable.

Here are some selected examples of CEOs who were among the highest paid in Fiscal Year 2021, along with their universities attended, according to open-source information:

- *Elon Musk:*

   Company: Tesla, Inc.

   Salary: Elon Musk has famously taken a symbolic $1 salary in recent years, opting for compensation tied to the company's performance and stock price.

   University: University of Pennsylvania (attended briefly but left to pursue entrepreneurial ventures).

- ***Tim Cook***:

  Company: Apple Inc.

  Salary: Tim Cook's salary has varied over the years but has been in the range of several million dollars.

  University: Duke University (MBA from the Fuqua School of Business).

- ***Sundar Pichai***:

  Company: Alphabet Inc. (Google)

  Salary: Sundar Pichai's salary ranges from several million to tens of millions of dollars.

  University: Stanford University (MS in Material Sciences and Engineering) and the University of Pennsylvania (MBA from the Wharton School).

- ***Bob Iger*** *(until 2020)*:

  Company: The Walt Disney Company

  Salary: Bob Iger's compensation was tens of millions of dollars.

  University: Ithaca College (BA in Television and Radio) and Harvard Business School (MBA).

- ***Safra Catz***:

  Company: Oracle Corporation

  Salary: Safra Catz's salary has been in the range of several million dollars.

University: University of Pennsylvania (JD from the Law School) and Wharton School of Business (MBA).

- **Reed Hastings**:

  Company: Netflix, Inc.

  Salary: Reed Hastings' salary is several million dollars.

  University: Bowdoin College (BA in Mathematics) and Stanford University (MS in Computer Science).

- **Brian Roberts**:

  Company: Comcast Corporation

  Salary: Brian Roberts' compensation was tens of millions of dollars.

  University: University of Pennsylvania (BA in Political Science).

- **Larry Culp**:

  Company: General Electric (GE)

  Salary: Larry Culp's compensation was in the millions of dollars.

  University: Washington University in St. Louis (BS in Chemical Engineering) and Harvard Business School (MBA).

- **Leonard Schleifer**:

  Company: Regeneron Pharmaceuticals

  Salary: Leonard Schleifer's compensation was in the tens of millions of dollars.

  University: Cornell University (BA in Biology) and University of Virginia School of Medicine (MD, Ph.D.).

- ***Stephen Schwarzman***:

  Company: The Blackstone Group

  Salary: Stephen Schwarzman's compensation was in the tens of millions of dollars.

  University: Yale University (BA in Abnormal Psychology) and Harvard Business School (MBA)

EPILOGUE

[LEADERSHIP]

E.1 LEADERSHIP MANAGEMENT PROFILE AND LEADERSHIP PERSONA

A Management profile and Leadership persona can vary depending on the industry, sector, and specific job roles and responsibilities. Noteworthy, several defining characteristics and qualities often typify the above, especially attributes that are associated with effective Leadership:

- *Leadership skills*: Leaders are expected to provide direction, guidance, and motivation to their team members. Change Management forte is an asset. Effective and influential Leaders possess strong Leadership skills, including the ability to inspire and influence others, make timely executive decisions, delegate tasks, and resolve conflicts. Conducting interviews, planning, coordinating, communicating, conducting disciplinary reviews, coaching, and other administrative functions fall under this umbrella.

- *Communication abilities*: Communication is vital for Leaders to convey goals, objectives, expectations, and missions effectively and provide feedback to their team members. Leaders should be able to listen actively, articulate ideas clearly, and adapt their communication style to different individuals at different levels and to various contextual situations. Remember that "communication goes up and down as well as across" the Organization and Enterprise.

- *Strategic thinking*: Leaders need to have a strategic mindset, think ahead and critically, plan, and exhibit intellectual curiosity. They should be able to analyze demanding, complicated situations, identify problems, subsets of problems, and opportunities, and develop strategic plans to achieve Organizational and Enterprise goals and objectives.

- *Emotional Intelligence (EI):* A high level of Emotional Intelligence (EI) is crucial for Leaders to understand and manage their own emotions and those of their team members. This includes empathy, self-awareness, navigating interpersonal dynamics, and building positive, forward-looking mentoring relationships.

- *Decision-Making Skills*: Leaders frequently face Decision-Making situations that impact their team, Organization and Enterprise. They should be able to gather all relevant information, evaluate competing alternative solution choices, and make timely and informed decisions based on all the available data and their specific domain expertise. Taking ownership of mistakes and rudder course correction reflect responsibility and accountability. Deliberative *Decision-Making* can prompt you to anticipate and consider the potential consequences of action, secondary effects, interactions, and communications to evaluate the risks before making essential choices. Taking a serious, sanguine, purposeful, and calculated approach can help avoid hastily made or ill-informed decisions that may negatively impact a Business.

- *Time management and organization*: Effective Leaders are skilled at managing their time and resources efficiently. They are purposeful, prioritize tasks, set realistic, achievable deadlines, and ensure that projects and assignments are completed responsibly and promptly. as well as satisfactorily.

- *Adaptability and flexibility*: The Business landscape is constantly evolving, and Leaders need to be adaptable and open to change. They should be able to adjust their day-to-day (tactical) operations and processes, strategies, and approaches to problems, especially being open to opportunities, as necessary, to navigate shifting markets, changing economic conditions, and emerging trends.

- *Professional demeanor*: In Life, especially in Business and Management, a serious demeanor is often considered an important trait or characteristic. Demeanor varies qualitatively, depending on the demands of the industry or sector and specific role responsibility or job context. Maintaining a professional and laser-focused approach invariably yields positive outcomes. There are a few reasons why displaying a serious demeanor in Business is valued. *Firstly, demonstrating seriousness in your Business dealings and interactions helps build credibility and promotes trust. Secondly,* taking your work earnestly shows that you are committed to delivering high-quality products or services and responsibly assume your responsibilities. *Thirdly,* operating with a serious mindset promotes professionalism in your interactions. It involves being punctual, prepared, and respectful when dealing with clients, customers, vendors, employees, peer colleagues, upper Management, shareholders, and stakeholders.

  This professionalism and demeanor will enhance your reputation and contribute to short- and long-term success. It contradicts the notion – "Always be serious, unruffled, and sanguine in your demeanor." It refutes the adage—"Never laugh, no matter how funny the matter—since it likely was not meant to elicit that response." ... Being serious in Business and Management does not mean you cannot have a sense of humor or enjoy your work and camaraderie with your direct reports, peers, and boss(es). It emphasizes the importance of professionalism, dedication, and a focused mindset to achieve your Organizational and Enterprise goals and objectives.

- *Maintaining focus and being productive*: By approaching tasks with dedication, seriousness, and discipline, one can prioritize important activities, stay organized, and accomplish

Corporate and Enterprise goals and objectives more efficiently. This can lead to increased productivity and assist in achieving Business expectations.

- *Problem-solving:* When faced with challenges or obstacles, a Leadership Business – Management profile and personas mindset can help one approach the latter with determination and perseverance. It encourages one to analyze problems, seek creative solutions, and take the necessary actions to overcome anticipated and unanticipated difficulties. This can be crucial for sustaining and growing a Business against a rising tide of competition, strong Headwinds, and disruptive technologies. Leaders are often called upon to address challenges and solve complex problems. They should be analytical, creative, assertive, and resourceful in finding solutions to thorny issues that may arise within their team, Organization and Enterprise, or environment. Leaders are defined as being decisive in their Decision-Making.

- *Continuous learning:* Effective Leaders have a growth and development mindset and a commitment to lifelong Business learning. They actively seek new knowledge and maintain their competency, not to mention their skill set, stay updated on industry and sector trends, and invest in their personal growth and professional development to enhance their skills and expertise.

- *Reputation and brand image: Building a positive reputation and a strong marketing brand image adds to Reputation and Brand Image. When customers perceive your Business as legitimate and trustworthy, they are more likely to choose your company's products or services over those of competitors and recommend them.*

- *High ethical standards and integrity*: Strong Leaders uphold high ethical standards and act with integrity. They lead by example, are Values-driven, and demonstrate honesty, confidentiality, and fairness in interpersonal interactions.

It is important to note that these cited attributes or characteristics and qualities are often associated with effective Management and Leadership. A Leader's specific profile and persona can vary based on individual strengths, traits, characteristics, personality style within their Organization and Enterprise, culture, and the requirements of the job role and responsibilities.

E.2 HOW DOES A BUSINESS LEADER COMMAND PRESENCE IN A MEETING?

A commanding presence in a meeting is crucial for Business Leaders as it helps establish authority, influence others, and effectuate communication.

Listed are tips on how a Business Leader can have a commanding presence in a meeting:

- *Preparation*: Come to the meeting well-prepared. Familiarize yourself with the agenda, relevant information, data and references, counterarguments, and critical points to be discussed. Being prepared allows you to speak confidently and demonstrates your expertise and comprehension of the topic of discussion.

- *Body language*: Pay attention to your body language, as it conveys much about your presence. Maintain good posture, make eye contact, and use gestures purposefully to engage and connect with the meeting participants. Physical behavior and movements instead of articulated words can be used to express and convey information. One's body stance, posture, facial expressions, eye movements, gestures, use of touch, as well as the use of personal (eighteen inches to four feet) as opposed to social (four feet to twelve feet) spacing, become "telling" for the gathered group in a meeting. A Leader projects confidence and professionalism through their body language.

- *Active listening*: Demonstrate attentive and active listening during the meeting as an attendee or listener, focus on the speaker, nod your head to indicate understanding and acquiescence, ask relevant questions, or provide insightful comments when appropriate. Engaging in discussion shows one's participatory presence and interest in the topic.

- *Clear and concise communication*: Speak clearly and concisely to ensure your message is understood. Use a confident and assertive tone and timber of voice without being overly assertive or aggressive. Avoid rambling or using jargon or slang that may confuse others. Deliver your talking points with clarity, precision, and conviction.

- *Confidence and assertiveness*: Confidence is vital to a commanding presence. Believe in yourself, your abilities, and your expertise, and express opinions and ideas with conviction and certainty. Be confident in presenting your thoughts while respecting others' cultural, political, or other viewpoints while encouraging open, two-way dialogue.

- *Emotional Intelligence (E.I.):* Display Emotional Intelligence (E.I., vide supra section E.1) by effectively understanding and managing your emotions. Stay composed, even in challenging, interactive, and argumentative situations. Respond calmly and professionally to any disagreements or conflicts arising during or immediately after the meeting.

- *Being decisive*: Business Leaders often need to make decisions during meetings. Be decisive and demonstrate your ability to evaluate options, consider input from others, and make informed choices. Present your conclusions with confidence and explain the rationale and Logic behind them.

- *Empowering others*: Encourage participation and empower others to contribute to the meeting. Foster an inclusive environment where everyone feels comfortable sharing their ideas and opinions. Acknowledge and appreciate valuable contributions from team members. Value your team.

- *Delegation of tasks*: Leaders must recognize when someone else may be more capable or have more time and resources available to accomplish a particular delegated task. The Leader must know and be able to assess their team Leaders and members well enough to appraise their relative and absolute strengths and weaknesses. Delegation thus allows for determining potential future Leadership roles and evaluating the team's potential and functionality.

- *Time management and organization* (vide infra, Appendix section for additional tips): Respect the time allocated for the meeting and ensure discussions stay on track. Assign a timekeeper and recorder (notetaker) to measure the time taken to accomplish items on the agenda. Creating an agenda with time blocks assists in achieving the same, along with item prioritization. Keep the conversations focused and productive, redirecting tangents if necessary. Do not derail. Start and end on time, stating the plan for subsequent follow-up meetings. Demonstrating exceptional Time Management and Organization skills reflects your ability to lead and maintain control.

- *Follow-up and accountability*: After the meeting, follow up on actionable items, accountability, responsibilities, and decisions promptly. Take ownership of your duties and hold others accountable for theirs. Consistently delivering on commitments establishes your credibility and presence as a dependable and effective Leader. Remember, a commanding presence in a meeting is not about being domineering or overpowering the agenda but about establishing a strong and influential steering presence while fostering participant collaboration and productive discussions.

EFFECTIVE MEETING

Pre

- Define Purpose & Rationale
- Agenda sent 24 hours before
- Pick Necessary / Optional Attendees
- Set Venue, Date / Time
- Define Expectations ahead
- Prepare Materials, Attachments and References

During

- Arrive 10 minutes early
- Phones / Pagers Off
- Discuss Objectives
- TimeKeeper and Notetaker
- Open-Minded Discussion
- Avoid Group Think
- Stay on Topic
- Engage, Listen, Think
- Brevity
- Focus on Achievable Results
- Summarize Accomplishments
- Assignments given with Expectations and Timetable

Post

- Provide Minutes
- Action Plan for accomplishing Assignments
- Accountability
- Follow-up with Mail / eMail
- Schedule Future Meeting(s)

E.2.1 "READING THE ROOM"

"Reading the Room" or mastering the Japanese Art of kuuki wo yomu or learning to "Read the Air or atmosphere"—You drive the proposition of an Effective Meeting, its direction, and its agenda.

- First, never underestimate your audience or "talk down to them."

- Do not go off-topic ("off the rails")—a train wreck can ensue.

- "Reading" and "Leading" the room are obligatory if you are the speaker.

- Do not subordinate your Leadership in the meeting to non-agenda items, tangents, or politics.

The skill set required to have command and control of the meeting, according to Briody, P. (2023), encompasses:

- *Self-awareness*—Self-assessment, mindfulness, or "the ability to be aware of what we are aware of," also called metacognition. This is "reading" yourself and being reflexive of how the audience or attendees view and receive YOU—Is there a gap?

- *Situational awareness*—Giving attention to—"if You are the focus"—Do you have the audience's attention? Do nonverbal cues, body posture, and facial expressions reaffirm that you are engaging the other side of the room, or are you, instead, disconnected from your audience? Proactive pausing and checking intermittently is advisable with an online web-based meeting group via Zoom or another broadcasting method since visual cues may be inapparent or unseen by the speaker.

- *Strategic preparedness*—What is your message, and what are your talking points and takeaway discussion points? Have you delivered them appropriately and achieved what you set out to accomplish?

Gummary, M. (2022) has furthermore commented on how observing the audience for engagement and for having undivided attention is critical since "understanding precedes being understood," which he interestingly states utilizes all the five human Senses (Visual, Auditory, Kinesthetic, Olfactory, and Gustatory). He recommended using a Systems approach to "Reading the Room," namely, understanding the clear Purpose, Outcomes, Inputs, Outputs, and other Influencing Factors.

Always value your audience.

It is not enough to "tell," that is to say, "transmit" or recite information (content) if you are not engaging with the participants. Lastly, "knowing" does not equate with "Doing" ("Action"). Gummary has moreover provided indispensable Do's and Don'ts relative to "Reading the Room" and Interactions (modified):

DO	DON'T
Do engage the participants with questions	Don't answer all questions yourself
Do avoid offering solutions	Don't endlessly offer solutions
Do ask for group participation	Don't impose learning on the group ('Telling")
Do study the group interactions	Don't ignore group behavior
Do intervene when helpful	Don't lose control of the situation
Do ascertain participant understanding	Don't assume the group understands the subject
Do build upon ongoing relationships	Don't allow insensitivity in the interactions
Do act as a mentor and guide	Don't take participants on a "forced march"
Do avoid sarcasm	Don't satirize individuals

E.3 LEADERSHIP AND REQUISITE BUSINESS SKILLS – GENERAL

Business – Management Leadership is a multidimensional and complex skill set that has garnered significant Sociological and Psychological research attention. It encompasses the theories, practices, and qualities that contribute to effective Management Leadership within the Business context. Discussions on Business Leadership often focus on various aspects, including, but not limited to, Leadership characteristics, qualities, styles, traits, behaviors, and their collective impact on Organizational and Enterprise performance, adherence to mission, vision, and values. Employee engagement is requisite in the steps that follow.

Ultimately, the effective Leader will embrace Business Process Reengineering (BPR), which requires an iconoclastic Leader willing and able to effectuate change, (re)vitalizing a fresh perspective, reengineering, designing, and rebuilding to develop a process-centric Business model. Standardizing work, automating, and incorporating robotics, machine learning, and Artificial Intelligence (AI) algorithms will follow, along with a review of J charts (a phenomenon where an upward, strong response follows an initial paradoxical movement to change in the intended direction), workflow analysis, benchmarking, standardized and specific job descriptions, and Business process (re)mapping.

E.3.1 LEADERSHIP AND REQUISITE BUSINESS SKILLS — LEADERSHIP STYLES

Another widely studied area is Leadership styles. Researchers have identified several Leadership styles, including—transformational, charismatic, transactional, and laissez-faire Leadership:

- *Transformational leadership style*: Characterized by inspiration, intellectual stimulation, curiosity, consideration of individual talents, and idealized influence. This has been extensively studied and shown to positively impact employee motivation, satisfaction, and Organizational and Enterprise performance.

- Charismatic leadership style: Refers to a personal quality or charm that enables an individual to influence, inspire, and attract others. In the context of Business Leadership, charisma plays a significant role in shaping a Leader's influence and impact on their followers within the Organization and Enterprise. This last-mentioned style is often essential and widely envied. Charismatic Leadership is characterized by the Leader's exceptional charm, confidence, and persuasive abilities. Charismatic Leaders possess a compelling vision, persuasive communication skills, and the ability to inspire and motivate their followers. They typically display an elevated level of enthusiasm, energy, and passion, which captivates, energizes, and engages others. These Leaders are known for their ability to create a sense of excitement and purpose around their vision. They articulate a compelling future state, set lofty expectations, and inspire followers to work towards achieving shared goals. Their charisma and personal magnetism often lead to a solid emotional connection with their followers, increasing loyalty, commitment, productivity, and trust.

- *The Transactional leadership style*: Based on the theory that Leaders give their employees something they want in exchange for getting something they want. The presumption is that the employee is not initiative-taking and requires an incentive provided in a structured setting, in addition to instructions, delegated tasks, and action plan monitoring, to complete their tasks correctly and promptly within a specified time frame.

- *Laissez-faire leadership style*: One in which the Leaders have implicit trust and reliance on their employee staff. Guidance and micro-Management do not occur to any degree, nor is there any significant intrusive involvement by Leadership in operations. Employees are allowed to implement their ideas and creativity, utilize resources, and remain self-directed to meet Organizational and Enterprise goals and objectives.

E.3.2 LEADERSHIP AND REQUISITE BUSINESS SKILLS — LEADERSHIP TRAITS

One recently identified contemporaneous insight into Business Leadership is the Trait Theory, which emphasizes personal attributes and characteristics believed to be innate and serve to distinguish influential Leaders and Future Leaders. Sociological and Psychological studies have identified traits such as self-confidence, Leadership, integrity, and cognitive ability, all necessary for successful Business administration. However, it is essential to note that Trait Theory alone does not fully explain Leadership effectiveness, as situational factors and followers' perceptions also play a significant role.

Leaders possessing traits and behaviors contributing to their appeal encompass self-assuredness, exuding confidence, and demonstrating a strong belief in their abilities and vision. Their self-assuredness helps instill confidence in their followers and competitors. You can only be charismatic with excellent and effective communication skills, articulating a clear vision and inspiring others toward alignment. Leaders must be exceptionally persuasive speakers and adept at conveying compelling messages. Other indispensable traits embrace emotional expressiveness to a wide range of emotions, allowing Leaders to connect with their followers and team on an emotional level. An effective Leader can convey enthusiasm, passion, and empathy, which helps to create a sense of unity and shared purposefulness. It is personal magnetism that attracts and captivates others. The aura of confidence, positivity, and emotional appeal will draw employees and peers toward them to follow a particular Corporate and Enterprise message and mission.

> **"Ultimately,** *you cannot be an effective Leader if no one is willing to follow"*

E.4 TO SUCCEED AS A LEADER

One must project a vision. The charismatic Leader articulates a compelling and inspiring future state, in addition to the goals, objectives, values, and mission, embracing the Business and Enterprise culture. The transparent, unambiguous direction and Corporate and Enterprise vision resonate with employees, shareholders, and stakeholders. One note of caution—it is essential to recognize that while charismatic Leadership can have positive, beneficial effects, it also has actual or potential negative drawbacks. Charismatic Leaders must sustain their influential role with tangible achievements, especially during challenging, tumultuous times. Additionally, excessive reliance on charisma can overshadow other essential Leadership qualities, such as ethical Decision-Making, collaboration, and inclusive Leadership. In the end, however, charismatic Leadership is characterized by a Leader's charm, confidence, and ability to inspire and influence others. It can significantly impact followers' motivation, commitment, and performance, but it should be balanced with other Leadership traits, behaviors, and actual accomplishments for long-term effectiveness.

In recent years, Sociological and Psychological research has also focused on ethical and authentic Leadership, emphasizing the importance of the Leaders' moral values, integrity, and clarity. The concept of so-called authentic Leadership was introduced by Bill George (1942-), Professor of Management Practice and Ethics at Harvard Business School, in 2003.

Ethical Leaders are expected to make decisions based on ethical-moral principles, promote fairness and social responsibility, and serve as role models for ethical behavior. On the other hand, authentic Leaders are characterized by self-awareness, clarity, and congruence between their words and actions. Researchers have also examined the impact of Leadership on various Organizational and Enterprise outcomes, such as employee engagement, role or job satisfaction, commitment, and performance. Effective Leadership has been found to foster a positive work environment, enhance employee motivation and productivity, and contribute to Organizational and Enterprise success. Leaders are seen as essential Change agents who inspire, manage, and guide their teams through transitions, facilitate innovation and adaptability, and create a culture that supports innovative experimentation and continuous learning.

E.5 CHALLENGES AND TAKING CHARGE OF CHANGE MANAGEMENT – GENERAL

One of the most essential functions of an effective Leader is instituting and managing "Change," especially within the Organization and Enterprise. Change Management assumes even greater priority in these tumultuous times. The first step the Leader must take is to define Change.

So, just What is "Change?"

The *Historic* interpretation

> Heraclitus, the Greek philosopher, provided a definition: "Change is the only constant."

The *Modern* interpretation

> "The Times They Are A-Changin" (Bob Dylan, 1965)
> "Your Old Road is Rapidly Agin" (Lyric from the same song)

E.5.1 CHALLENGES AND TAKING CHARGE OF CHANGE MANAGEMENT – UPDATED DESCRIPTION OF WHAT IS "CHANGE?"

- *Change*, as a process, *is an iterative process* whose outcome may or may not lead to improvement.

- The *Change should be intimately entwined and meshed into the Corporate and Enterprise culture.*

- *"Buy-in" is critical,* and Change is *best effectuated when ideas well up from those who will be most affected* by the Change but do lead the Change.

- *Change is time-consuming and necessitates continuous oversight and tweaking.*

- *Change always happens,* regardless of circumstance, and is *ideally managed by the Organization and Enterprise.*

- *Change is invariably and ostensibly necessary.*

E.5.2 KOTTER'S EIGHT (8) STEPS TO ORGANIZATIONAL CHANGE AND MANAGEMENT (REVISED)

John P. Kotter (1947-), internationally known as a Leadership and Change Guru, emeritus at the Harvard Business School, and co-founder of Kotter International, eloquently described Eight (8) Steps to Organizational Change. Conditionally, he stated that each step was deemed necessary and that subsequent steps were to embody and require the previous effort for ultimate success. Change is defined as being inevitable and will become disruptive if not managed properly.

Steps to Organizational Change and Change Management (herein significantly revised and redacted):

ROADMAP

1. ***Establish Urgency:***

- Great opportunities may be identified using SWOT analysis. Those opportunities identified are preferable to potential or current, real crises.

- Do not underestimate the need to motivate the team and existing resistance to Change.

- Do not underestimate staff acceptance, acknowledgment, and prioritization of goals.

- Do not overestimate success, but do revel in the small, incremental strides on the way towards implementation of Change.

- Un-paralyze (senior) Management and ask for support from stakeholders, industry, and sector experts.

- Understand that patience is a virtue in the process.

An estimated 50:50 probability of success occurs in this first phase.

2. *Put Together the Change Management Team:*

- Review the Table of Organization (TO) and choose critical influencers, key contributors, and collaborators most likely to effectuate Change.

- The core of the team must include (senior) Management.

- Reinforce urgency, understand mission and purpose, and set a timetable.

- Monitor and establish guideposts along the journey.

3. *Understand the Reasons for Failure:*

- Lack of teamwork and coordination of efforts "at the top."

- Expecting the team to be led wholly by an executive.

- Failure to review the Table of Organization (TO), job descriptions, performance (current and past), and compensation systems that would assist the team in achieving alignment in goals and objectives. Also, not understanding the Organization and Enterprise values and impetus for the Change initiative.

- Identify those individuals resistant to Change and educate them on the benefits of Change.

- Remove obstacles and barriers (human or otherwise).

- Problems with bi-directional communication.

4. ***Inspire and Create a Clear, Succinct Vision that is Intrinsically Motivational:***

- The vision dictates the direction of the Organization and Enterprise.

- The vision, success, and untoward consequences of failure need to be (re)affirmed.

- "Buy-in" is critical.

- Encourage feedback to eliminate or lessen fear of the unknown, issues, and concerns.

- Answer concerns and anxieties, as well as address detractors.

- Communication must be immediate, credible, and trustworthy.

- Remember that "actions follow words." It has been often emphasized to "walk the talk," noting that "what you do is far more important and believable (credible) than what you say."

5. ***Empower Action***:

- Reward Change agents since these are your "faithful" emissaries.

- Recognize early adopters and reward those who help in achieving targets.

- Coach, mentor, train, and educate.

- Change must include Organizational and Enterprise processes, structures, policies, procedures, and reward systems.

6. ***Detour around "Roadblocks:"***

- Link "the means to an end" and celebrate individual and team accomplishments.

- Assist the team in finding common ground, then "aim high to hit the target."

- Help the staff and team members know and understand when and how to take action to move the process forward.

7. ***Identify Short-Term Wins but Focus on the Long Term***:

- The initial focus on "Low-hanging fruit" yields quick, early rewards.

- Make wins visible, unambiguous, and meaningful.

- Maintain momentum and continuously move forward, analyzing the reasons for the win and what needs continuous improvement.

- Sustain a need to achieve success.

- As needed, bring in new Change agents and Leadership for the Change coalition.

8. *Anchor and Institute Change—In the Business World, Empower Six Sigma-Lean, Which Identifies Kaizen* (改善 **in Kanji**), **Japanese for "Improvement."**

- Identify activities that continuously improve all functions.

- Use new situations, orientation of new hires, training, and circumstances to (re)launch successive waves of Change to eliminate waste significantly.

- Make Change permanent, pervasive, and a core of the Organization and Enterprise.

- It is not over until the Change has taken root; therefore, perpetuate the Change.

- Integrate Change into the skeletal structure of the Organization and Enterprise, operational processes, and systems.

E.6 STEPHEN COVEY AND "THE SEVEN HABITS OF HIGHLY EFFECTIVE PEOPLE" (REVISED)

Stephen Covey (1932-2012), in his Book, *"The Seven Habits of Highly Effective People"* (1989), presented readers with an overview of personal and interpersonal effectiveness," defining four (4) Quadrants," as well as providing Time Management advice. The former, The Covey Matrix, and variations are genuinely inspiring.

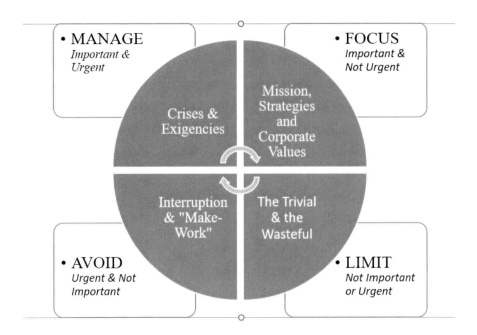

The "Seven Habits" can succinctly be summarized as embracing the following key attributes:

1. *Being Proactive*: Emphasizes taking rudder control of your actions, choices, and decisions rather than reacting to external circumstances and conditions. Self-awareness and commandeering situations, instead of passivity, come to mind. More recently, since 1989, Emotional Intelligence (EI) and mindfulness have been seen as a characteristic of a proactive, effective Leader.

2. *Beginning with the End in Mind*: Translation—Covey stresses setting clear goals and objectives and exhibiting purposefulness.

3. *Putting First Things First*: Effective Leaders prioritize tasks based on Corporate and Enterprise missions, goals, and objectives rather than the moment's urgency or day-to-day exigencies. Being Strategic trumps a tactical mindset in this regard.

4. *Thinking Win-Win*: The fourth habit promotes a mindset of seeking mutually beneficial, rewarding ("non-zero-sum") solutions in interpersonal interactions. Conflict resolution and negotiation skills take center stage.

5. *Seeking First to Understand, Then to Be Understood*: The original publication at the end of the 1980s emphasized the importance of empathetic communication ("taking another's perspective") and active, engaged listening in interpersonal interactions.

6. *Synergizing*: This habit relates to teamwork and encourages mutual collaboration between and among individuals, discussions with colleagues and peers, and the recognition of the value of exploring diverse perspectives.

7. *"Sharpening the Saw"* Lastly, Stephen Covey advocated energizing oneself and self-renewal with continuous improvement in four dimensions: a. physical, b. emotional, c. mental, and d. spiritual well-being ("staying at the top of your game").

Research on Business Leadership employs rigorous research methodologies, including quantifiable, Statistically measurable surveys, interviews, and case studies, to investigate Leadership theories and their practical implications. Academic journals, such as the Journal of Applied Psychology, Leadership Quarterly, the Academy of Management Journal, and others (References, select listed Journals), serve as important Business and Management literature conduits for disseminating research knowledge on Leadership. Studies have focused on a wide range of topics, theories, and empirical studies to understand the complexities of Leadership in the Business context, providing valuable insights for investigators and practitioners seeking to enhance Leadership effectiveness and Organizational and Enterprise performance.

ACKNOWLEDGMENT

To all those individuals who have touched my professional Business and Management Life, especially my teachers and mentors, during my early years at Case Western Reserve University, George S. Dively Weatherhead School of Management, in Cleveland, Ohio, and, later at the George Washington University, School of Business (GWSB), in Washington, D.C.

The source of inspiration for this non-fiction work was the headers (Aphorisms), terse witticisms about Management and Life, in general, that arose from daily discussions that occurred in the "Resident's Room" at the University of Rochester Medical Center during the early 1980s, while the Author pursued postgraduate specialty training in Pathology and Laboratory Medicine. An interest in Business and Management would lead the Author, over the years, to complement his education, initially at the Weatherhead School of Management, Professional Fellows Program, and Physician Executive Institute, both at Case Western Reserve University (CWRU) in Cleveland, Ohio (1993-1994, and 1999, respectively), that preceded obtaining a Master of Business Administration (MBA) degree at George Washington University, School of Business (GWSB), in Washington, D.C., conferred May 17, 2009.

APPENDIX

[TIME MANAGEMENT AND ORGANIZATION]

Critical Thinking[2] is ultimately distilled into the pot ale ("spent wash") of Problem Analysis and Decision-Making. Practically speaking, the efficacy of managing and organizing your time allows you to contribute to the success of the Problem Analysis and Decision-Making process. You can choose how to use the fourteen hundred and forty (1440) minutes in a day allotted to you. Efficiency allows you to reach your goals (you decide on the elements and prioritize):

- Set clear and realistic goals.

- "Do not re-invent the wheel."

- Do not procrastinate, and do not be derailed.

- Value the Day.

- Use a daily planner/calendar.

- Block time and batch the minor, more straightforward tasks to improve productivity.

- Avoid rigidity in your schedule and eschew "emergencies," especially someone else's exigencies.

- Delegate and outsource, if feasible.

- Say "NO" more often than "Yes" to your peers, particularly subordinates.

- Adopt a "Do NOT Disturb" mentality and persona.

- Focus, and stay alert.

- Plan the day and plan for tomorrow and the week ahead.

- Apportion your energy and expected level of enthusiasm accordingly.

- Use a To-Do list, check off, and celebrate the accomplishments.

- The Pareto (80:20) principle should guide your Life's plans, job tasks, and assignments – so choose the twenty percent of tasks wisely that will yield the estimated eighty percent of the expected results.

- The key questions are: "What is to be Done," "When," and "How."

- Broaden your "bandwidth" to do parallel processing of minor, more straightforward, and accomplishable tasks.

- Multitask uncomplicated tasks, to the extent possible, instead of doing "serial" (sequential) processing of tasks.

- Employ productivity software applications.

- Use voice recordings, notes, and reminders as an assistant.

- Maximize connectivity and communication, but not at the expense of "quiet," contemplative time.

- Turn off the phone, "ping" notifications, social media, and e-mail alerts.

- Avoid alarms and human as well as non-human distractions.

- Organize your dedicated workspace, desk, and Life, as well as avoid clutter in all, for that matter.

- Try headphones and earbuds to cancel out extraneous background sounds.

- Play "white" or "brown" (deeper bass, low frequency) noise in the background.

- Use proper daylight lighting (three to four thousand degrees Kelvin) and eliminate "blue light."

- Obtain "take-out" food for those "heavy-duty" days or when immersed in complex tasks and assignments.

- Stay motivated and positive in outlook

- "Refresh" in between completed tasks.

- Do not neglect your health and welfare.

- Get restorative (R.E.M). and slow wave (deep, non-Rapid Eye Movement)) sleep.

- The last task of the day should be achievable and re-energize the next day's anticipated activities.

- Do not neglect your diet and hydration status.

- Exercise

- Pray.

Remember that "Perfect is the enemy of good' (French writer, Voltaire (1770))

REFERENCES

1. Allen, D. *Getting Things Done: The Art of Stress-Free Productivity*. Penguin Books (revised edition), 2015.

2. Alshareeda, A., et al. Molecular Analysis of Tumors. J. Cancer. 11(13):3919-3931, 2020.

3. Antonakis, J., et al. The Nature of Leadership. Annual Review of Psychology. (65) 387-411, 2004.

4. Atanasiu, R. *Critical Thinking for Managers: Structured Decision-Making and Persuasion in Business*. Springer, Cham. 145-162, May 2021.

5. Bass, BM. and Riggio, RE. Transformational Leadership: Industrial, Military, and Educational Impact. Mahwah, NJ. Lawrence Erlbaum Associates, 2006.

6. Bennett, B. Logically Fallacious: The Ultimate Collection of Over 300 Logical Fallacies (Academic Edition), eBookIt.com, 2012.

7. Bennis, W. *On Becoming a Leader*. Basic Books, March 2009.

8. Bibliophileparul06 - Blog Post Review (Rhetorical Appeal and Ethos of Adam Grant's Book "Think Again"). September 4, 2022. https://bibliophileparul.com/2022/09/04/

rhetorical-appeal-of-think-again-by-adam-grant/
https://adamgrant.net/book/think-again/

9. Black, K. *Business Statistics: for Contemporary Decision-Making* (11th Edition). John Wiley and Sons, 2023.

10. Blanchard, K. and Johnson, D. *The One Minute Manager* (updated). Harper Collins, March 2016.

11. Briody, P. (Forbes Coaches Councils Member) Post. June 2023. https://www.forbes.com/sites/forbes-coachescouncil/2023/06/01/reading-and-leading-the-room/?sh=1991b1f46bf9

12. Browne, MN. and Keeley, SM. *Asking the Right Questions: A Guide to Critical Thinking* (10th Edition), Pearson, July 2011.

13. Canco, I., Kruja, D. and Iancu, T. AHP, A Reliable Method for Quality Decision-Making: A Case Study in Business (Special Issue: The Future of Facilities Management and Sustainable Development). Sustainability. 13 (24), 2021.

14. Cohen, DH. Logical Fallacies, Dialectical Transgressions, Rhetorical Sins, and Other Failures of Rationality in Argumentation (Chapter) In Van Eemermen, F. et al. Anyone Who Has a View: Theoretical Contributions to the Study of Argumentation (8):109-122, January 2003.

15. Cohen, J. *Statistical Power Analysis for the Behavioral Sciences*, 1969.

16. Coughlan, M., Cronin, P. and Ryan, F. Step-by-Step Guide to Critiquing Research (Part 1), Quantitative Research, June 2007. https://citeseerx.ist.psu.edu/document?repid=rep1&type=pdf&doi=26d5e9ac9adfe215a5c343b8bc920d4394da318d

17. Crusius, TW. and Channell, CE. *A Toulmin Model for Analyzing Arguments* (modified from *The Aims of Argument*). McGraw-Hill, 2003.

18. Deming, WE. *Out of the Crisis.* The MIT Press, October 2018 (first published 1982).

19. Downes, A. Stephen's Guide to the Logical Fallacies (electronic document), 1995. https://www.gospeloutreach.net/logical_fallacies.pdf

20. Drucker, PF. *Management - Tasks, Responsibilities, Practices.* Harper Collins (Second edition), 1993.

21. Dunning, D. and Kruger, J. Unskilled and Unaware of It: How Difficulties in Recognizing One's Own Incompetence Lead to Inflated Self-Assessments. Journal of Personality and Social Psychology. 77 (6):1121–1134, 1999.

22. Field, H. and Vanian, J. Tech layoffs ravage the teams that fight online misinformation and hate speech. MSNBC Tech News section, May 27, 2023. https://www.cnbc.com/2023/05/26/tech-companies-are-laying-off-their-ethics-and-safety-teams-.html

23. Frederick, S. Cognitive Reflection and Decision Making. Journal of Economic Perspectives, 19 (4):25-42, 2005.

24. Frey, D. and Schulz-Hardt, S. Confirmation Bias in Group Information Seeking and Its Implications for Decision-Making in Administration, Business, and Politics - Social Influence in Social Reality: Promoting Individual and Social Change. In: F. Butera and G. Mugny (Eds.). Hogrefe and Huber. 53–73, 2009.

25. Gardner, H. *Multiple Intelligences: The Theory in Practice*, 1993.

26. Gardner, H. Frequently Asked Questions - Multiple Intelligences and Related Educational Topics, 2013.

https://howardgardner01.files.wordpress.com/2012/06/faq_march2013.pdf

27. Gawande, A. *The Checklist Manifesto: How to Get Things Right.* Picador USA, January 2011.

28. George, B. *Authentic Leadership: Rediscovering the Secrets to Creating Lasting Value,* 2003.

29. George, B. and Clayton, Z. *True North* - (Emerging Leader Edition). John Wiley and Sons, Inc., August 2022.

30. Goleman, Daniel and Goleman, Danijel. *Emotional Intelligence: Why It Can Matter...* Bantam, September 1995.

31. Grant, AM. *Think Again: The Power of Knowing What You Don't Know.* Viking, N.Y.C. (Penguin Random House LLC Publisher), 2021.

32. Gorman, PN. and Helfand, M. Information seeking in Primary Care: How Physicians Choose Which Clinical Questions to Pursue and Which to Leave Unanswered. Medical Decision Making. 15 (2):113-119, 1995.

33. Gummary, M. Managing Director, NewLeaf International. "The Art of Reading the Room," or more importantly, "Reading the Situation" - Core Skills for a Change Agent. July 2022. https://www.linkedin.com/pulse/art-reading-room-more-importantly-situation-core-skills-gummery

34. Haber, J. *Critical Thinking.* MIT Press (Essential Knowledge Series), 2020.

35. Hammer, M. and Champ, JA. *Re-engineering the Corporation: A Manifesto for Business Revolution,* Harper Collins. 1993.

36. Hawkes, JS. and Marsh, WH. *Discovering Statistics.* Hawkes Learning Publisher (2nd. Edition), 2017.

37. Horstman, M., Braun, K. and Sentes, S. *The Effective Manager* (2nd Edition, completely revised and updated Edition), Wiley. May 2023.

38. Journal of the American Medical Association (J.A.M.A.) - Examining the Relationship Between Physical Activity and Cardiovascular Health in 500 Older Adults (>65 years old) Using Multiple Linear Regression Analysis (B value of 0.32 and a Coefficient of Determination (R^2) of 0.40) - Case Study Example for Educational Purposes (n.d.).

39. Karachi, J. Using Toulmin's Model of Argumentation. Journal of Teaching Writing. 81-91, 1987.
https://journals.iupui.edu/index.php/teachingwriting/article/download/821/810/0
https://www.atlantis-press.com/article/125953447.pdf

40. Kim, G., Behr, K., and Spafford, G. *The Phoenix Project* (Series, two books). IT Revolution Press, February 2018.

41. Kotter, JP. *Leading Change*. Boston: Harvard Business School Review Press, 1996.

42. Kotter, JP. *Accelerate: Building Strategic Agility for a Faster-Moving World*. Harvard Business School Review Press, 2014.

43. Lencioni, P. *The Five Dysfunctions of a Team - A Leadership Fable* (20th Anniversary Edition). Jossey- Bass, April 2002.

44. Lencioni, P. *The Advantage. Why Organizational Health Trumps Everything Else in Business*. Jossey-Bass, Wiley, March 2012

45. LeStage, G. How Have Kotter's Eight Steps for Change Changed? Forbes Leadership Strategy, March 2015.
https://www.forbes.com/sites/johnkotter/2015/03/05/how-have-kotters-eight-steps-for-change-changed/#6725f3a33c7b

46. Levitt, Theodore: *Marketing Myopia*. Harvard Business Review, 1960.

47. Levy, A. The Big 6 Media Companies. The Motley Fool. November 8, 2023.

48. Lievens, F., et al. Killing the Cat? A Review of Curiosity at Work. Academy of Management Annals. 16 (1):179-216, January 2022.

49. Loe, TW., Ferrell, L. and Mansfield, PA. Review of Empirical Studies Assessing Ethical Decision-Making in Business. Journal of Business Ethics, 25:185-204, 2000.

50. Magretta, J. *What Management is*. Simon and Schuster, 2012.

51. Mascia, J. "Should Suicides be Considered 'Gun Violence?" Ask the Trace (The "Fault Line" in the Nation's Conversation About Guns). December 13, 2021.
https://www.thetrace.org/2021/12/
gun-violence-suicide-rate-data-shooting-deaths/

52. McCall, R. [CRT] The World's Shortest IQ Test Is Just Three Questions Long, But Almost No One Can Get Them All Right. October 2017.
https://www.iflscience.com/prove-your-smarts-with-the-worlds-shortest-iq-test-44163
https://www.researchgate.net/figure/
Cognitive-Reflection-Test_tbl1_4905229

53. McFarland, A. 5 Best Deepfake Detector Tools & Techniques. October 2023.
https://tinyurl.com/5n73v82a

54. Milgram, S. Behavioral Study of Obedience. The Journal of Abnormal and Social Psychology. 67 (4):371–378, 1963.

55. Montgomery, DC., Woodall, WJ. and Johnson, CM. Statistical Methods for Quality Improvement: A Review and Managerial

Guide. In: Quality and Reliability Engineering International. 21 (4):343-366, 2005.

56. Nalbandian, M. Pathfinder - Best of SNO - The Big Six's Big Media Game. May 2022.

57. Neubold, P., Carlson, WL. and Thorne, B. *Statistics for Business and Economics*. Pearson (9th Edition), 2012.

58. Newhard, J. *A Correspondence Theory of Truth*. Dissertation. Brown University (2002).

59. Nix, N., Zakrzewski, C. and Joseph Menn, J. Misinformation Research is Buckling Under GOP Legal Attacks (Article). The Washington Post, September 23, 2023. https://www.msn.com/en-us/news/politics/Misinformation-research-is-buckling-under-gop-legal-attacks/ar-AA1h8NS8

60. Northouse, PG. *Leadership: Theory and Practice*. Sage Publisher (8th Edition), 2018.

61. Novianti, MNR. Toulmin Model: A Strategy for Critical Thinking, In Analytical Reading. Advances in Social Science, Education, and Humanities Research Series, Number 532 (Proceedings of the International Conference on Educational Sciences and Teacher Profession), 2020.

62. O'Connor, R. How DALL-E2 Actually Works. AssemblyAI. September 2023.

63. https://www.assemblyai.com/blog/how-dall-e-2-actually-works/

64. Olazagasti, C., et al. Optimizing Tissue Use: A Stepwise Approach to Diagnosing Squamous Cell Lung Carcinoma (SCC) on Small Biopsies - Lung Cancer Sub-Typing by Stepwise

Algorithmic Testing (Figure 1), Clinical Pathology. January-December May 20, 2020.

65. OpenAI - Artificial Intelligence Natural Language Generated Images Dall-E2.
https://labs.openai.com/

66. Pearson, AE. Six Basics for General Managers. Harvard Business Review. 67 (4):94-101, July 1989.

67. Pew Research Center Analysis of Data (CDC, FBI, and other Aggregate Sources) – "Suicides Accounted for More Than Half of U.S. Gun Deaths In 2021." April 24, 2023.
http://www.pewresearch.org

68. Pompon, R. (former Director of F5 Labs) and Vinberg, S. Cyentia Institute: A Meta-Analysis Risk Insights Study 20/20 - (IRIS Xtreme Edition). July 21, 2021.
https://tinyurl.com/44j555uy

69. Porter, PE., et al. Harvard Business Reviews Ten Must Reads 2020: The Definitive Management Ideas of the Year from Harvard Business Review (Bonus Article on How CEOs Manage Time). October 2019.

70. Roman, K. and Raphaelson, J. *Writing that Works: How to Communicate Effectively in Business* - Collins Reference (3rd. Revised Edition). August 2000.

71. Samawi, H. and Mouzughi, Y. Applications of Statistical Quality Control Techniques in Healthcare. Journal of Applied Statistics. 43 (10):1804-1816, 2016.

72. Sharda, R., Delen, D. and Turban, E. *Business Intelligence and Analytics: Systems for Decision Support* (10th Edition), Pearson, December 2013.

73. Shunailov, I. et al. The Curse of Recursion: Training on Generated Data Makes Models Forget. arXiv:2305.17493 (cs), May 2023.
https://arxiv.org/pdf/2305.17493.pdf

74. Strawson, P.F. "Truth." Proceedings of the Aristotelian Society (reprinted 1871), 1950b.
http://plato.stanford.edu/cgi-bin/encyclopedia/archinfo.cgi?entry=strawson

75. Telefónica Communication Team. What is a Deepfake and How to Detect It? March 2023.
https://www.telefonica.com/en/communication-room/blog/what-is-a-deepfake-and-how-to-detect-it/

76. Templar, R. *The Rules of Management: The Definitive Guide to Management Success*. Pearson Prentice Hall, January 2004.

77. Tensmeyer, S. Truth and Logical Structure in Strawson's Early Work. Aporia. 22 (1):33-44, 2012.
https://aporia.byu.edu/pdfs/tensmeyertruth_and_logical_structure_in_strawsons_early_work.pdf

78. Toulmin, S. *The Uses of Argument*. Cambridge University Press (First Edition), January 1958.

79. Tunney, C. China Linked to Propaganda Campaign Targeting Trudeau, Poilievre, says Global Affairs. CBC-Politics section. October 23, 2023.
https://public-assets.graphika.com/reports/graphika-report-deepfake-it-till-you-make-qit.pdf
https://www.cbc.ca/news/politics/china-spamouflage-mps-1.7005066

80. Vandehei, A. and Allen, M. Behind the Curtain: What AI architects fear most (in 2024). Axios-Column/Behind the

Curtain-Technology. November 8, 2023.
https://www.axios.com/2023/11/08/
ai-fears-deepfake-misinformation

81. Weidemann, A., et al. Napsin A Expression in Human Tumors and Normal Tissues. Pathol. Oncol. Res., April 2021.

82. Welch, Jack and Suzy. *The Real-Life MBA* (Your No-BS Guide to Winning the Game, Building A Team, and Growing Your Career). Harper Business, 2015.

83. Zhuo, J. *The Making of a Manager - What to Do When Everyone Looks to You.* Portfolio, March 2019.

MAJOR QUOTES

A. *STATISTICS:*

"Lies, Damned Lies, and Statistics"

Quote attribution to British Prime Minister Benjamin Disraeli (1804-1881)

B. *INTELLIGENCE AND IGNORANCE:*

1. "Only two things are infinite, the universe and human stupidity, and I'm not sure about the former"

2. "The difference between genius and stupidity is that genius has its limits"

3. "Insanity is doing the same thing over and over again and expecting different results"

4. "The measure of Intelligence is the ability to change"

Quotes attribution to Albert Einstein (1879-1955)

C. *CHANGE AND CHANGE MANAGEMENT:*

    "Change is the only constant"

Quote attribution to Heraclitus, the Greek philosopher (c. 500 BC)

D. *ARGUMENTATION:*

    "Argument is the worst sort of conversation"

Quote attribution to satirist Jonathan Swift

E. *WISDOM:*

    1. **"Perfect is the enemy of good"**

Quote attribution to Voltaire, French writer (1770)

    2. **"The whole is greater than the *sum* of the parts"**

Misquote? The 1908 translation by W. D. Ross: of Aristotle Metaphysics VIII, 1045a.8-10:
["In the case of all things which have several parts and in which the totality is not, as it were, a mere heap, but the whole is something *besides* the parts, there is a cause; for even in bodies contact is the cause of unity in some cases and in others viscosity or some other such quality"]

    3. **"Don't let schooling interfere with your education"**

Quote attribution to American Writer and humorist Mark Twain

F. *MISCELLANEOUS:*

    1. **"Critical Thinking^2 Lies at the Interface of Problem Analysis and Decision-Making"**

2. **"Doors are Passageways—Find the Next and Open Them"**

3. **"The Ability to Problem Solve, and Course Correct, Makes for Forward Progress"**

Quotes attribution to the Author (2023)

G. *LATIN:*

1. **"Res Ipsa Loquitur"** (Latin: "The Thing Speaks for Itself")

Quote attribution British legal case Byrne v Boadle (2H. & C. 722, 159 Eng. Rep. 299 (Exch. 1863)

2. **"Nihil Amplius Dicere Habeo"** (Latin: "I Have Nothing More to Say")

Quote attribution Unknown

H. *LYRICS:*

1. **"The Times They Are A-Changin"** (Bob Dylan, 1965)

2. **"Your Old Road is Rapidly Agin"** (Lyric from the same song)

JOURNAL PUBLICATIONS IN MANAGEMENT (TEN SELECTED)

Journal of Applied Psychology (ISSN 00219010)

Leadership Quarterly (ISSN 10489843)

Academy of Management Journal (ISSN 00014273)

Academy of Management Review (ISSN 03637425)

Strategic Management Journal (ISSN 01432095)

Journal of Financial Economics (ISSN 0304405X)

Journal of Management (ISSN 01492063)

Organization Management (ISSN 27538567)

Organization Science (ISSN 15265455)

Journal of International Business Studies (ISSN 00472506)

ABOUT THE AUTHOR

Dr. Jerry J. Marty received his Medical degree (MD) in 1976 from Wayne State University School of Medicine, Detroit, Michigan. After that, he completed six postgraduate years of training at Montefiore Hospital and Medical Center/Albert Einstein College of Medicine (Post Graduate Year one), Strong Memorial Hospital/University of Rochester Medical Center, Rochester, New York (Post Graduate Years two to three, and Post Graduate Years five to six), and, completed an additional year in straight Internal Medicine at Saint Joseph's University Hospital -VA Medical Center/Creighton University School of Medicine, Omaha, Nebraska (Post Graduate Year four). A Visiting Fellowship in Clinical Cytology and Fine Needle Aspiration (FNA) was undertaken during the fall of 1989 under the world-renowned Dr. Torsten Lowhagen at the Karolinska Hospital and Institute, Stockholm, Sweden. The author is Board-certified in Anatomic, Clinical, and Cyto-Pathology with a sub-specialization in Fine Needle Aspiration (FNA) Cytology. He has authored several publications in peer-reviewed medical journals and two separate Book Chapters in his field of expertise, specifically in Cytopathology and Fine Needle Aspiration (FNA) Cytology. Among his earlier responsibilities, Dr. Marty had teaching positions at Case Western Reserve University in Cleveland, Ohio, and, later, at the Northeastern Ohio Universities College of Medicine and Pharmacy (now Northeast Ohio University College (NEOMED)), Rootstown, Ohio.

A Master of Business Administration (MBA) degree at George Washington University, School of Business (GWSB), Washington, D.C., was conferred on May 17, 2009.

Dr. Marty's most recent professional position until 2016 was as Chairman of Pathology and Medical Director of Laboratories at MedStar Franklin Square Medical Center (MFSMC), a three hundred seventy-eight (378) bed Joint Commission (JC) accredited hospital facility in Baltimore, Maryland.

He is based in the United States and, when not working, enjoys travel, photography, and Chess.

COVER AND DESIGN

The Author used an OpenAI - Artificial Intelligence (AI) Natural Language algorithm to Generate this book's unique Cover Art Image and several content images employing Dall-E2.

Dall-E2 uses several technologies, including an AI transformer, Natural Language Processing (NLP), Large Language Models (LLM), and Diffusion processing. Dall-E2 makes use of a deterministic Diffusion model integrating data from the Contrastive Language-Image Pre-training (CLIP) paradigm to generate images. It combines distinct and unrelated objects in semantically natural language with its output transformed via a text encoder interface. CLIP is trained on approximately 400 million labeled images and their associated captions, learning how much a given text snippet relates to an image, additionally combining concepts, attributes, and styles. Rather than trying to predict a caption-provided image, CLIP learns how related any given caption is to an image. This contrastive rather than predictive objective allows CLIP to learn the link between textual and visual representations of the same abstract object. The entirety of the Dall-E 2 model hinges on CLIP's ability to learn semantics from natural language. The text encoder is trained to map the text prompt to a representation space. Following this, a model called the *prior* maps the text encoding to a corresponding image, encoding that captures the semantic information of the prompt contained in the actual text encoding. Finally, an image decoder stochastically (involving a random, probabilistic variable) generates an image, which is a visual manifestation of this "disputed" random semantic information (O'Connor, R. AssemblyAI. September 2023).

PostScript: Dall-E2 has now evolved into its latest version, Dall-E3, whose availability via OpenAI's API and "Labs" platform was provided to customers in early November 2023.